Intoxication Nation

A Polemic

GUY GRAYBILL

an imprint of Sunbury Press, Inc.
Mechanicsburg, PA USA

an imprint of Sunbury Press, Inc.
Mechanicsburg, PA USA

ISBN: 978-1-62006-087-2 (Trade paperback)

Library of Congress Control Number: 2018953011

FIRST BROWN POSEY PRESS EDITION: November 2018

Product of the United States of America
0 1 1 2 3 5 8 13 21 34 55

Set in Bookman Old Style
Designed by Crystal Devine
Cover by Lawrence Knorr
Edited by Lawrence Knorr

Continue the Enlightenment!

DEDICATION

This book is dedicated to the memory of the thousands
upon thousands of fatal victims of senseless acts by their
inebriated fellow Americans who willingly abandoned
their own humanity to enter an inebriated state of being.
May reason, someday, prevail.

———

Words of appreciation are required here for the special
help of my late wife, Nancy (who developed the "ALERT"
graphic) and to the late Charles Dorwart, who granted me
much time to let me listen to him recall the life-long pain
wrought onto his mother, his siblings, and himself, by an
alcoholic father.

Contents

A Modest Preliminary Lexicon

Herewith, a small list of terms that the reader should know if he or she wishes to navigate through this sea of words.

BARM (One of several definitions) ~ The froth on top of fermenting malt liquors.

CHASER ~ A drink used to soften the impact of a stronger drink, such as drinking beer after having drunk whiskey. The chaser might even be (May Bacchus forgive us!) water.

DIPSOMANIA ~ Dipsomania is a 19th century (1843) name for the uncontrollable urge to consume liquor.

ETHANOL ~ This is another name for intoxicating liquor, the result of the blending of ethyl and alcohol. Ethyl alcohol is just one of the four types of alcohol. The other three (butyl alcohol, methyl alcohol, and propyl alcohol) are even more dangerous than ethanol, since all three, if consumed, may blind or kill the drinker.

FINGER ~ a slang term indicating the level of alcohol in a glass, or about ¾".

PROOF ~ A term, combined with a number, to suggest the strength of a distilled alcohol liquor, such as "80 proof."

RUM ~ A late 17th Century (1694) term used to identify several types of liquor based on products from sugar cane.

RUMHOUND ~ One of countless names used to designate a drunkard. The term can be interchanged with many other terms, such as alcoholic, Bacchanal, barfly, bibber, boozer, carouser, dipso, dipsomaniac, drunk, drunkard, guzzler, inebriate, lush, reveler, soaker, sot, souse, sponge, toper, tippler, and tosspot. For anyone who is dedicated to increasing his or her vocabulary, there are few words so rich in variations. Thus, we encounter the language of the lush, which has given our vocabulary one helluva boost; even allowing us to insult a lovely winged creature, by saying "Drunk as a hoot!" In fact, one internet site (www. powerthesaurus.org) offers its viewer 168 synonyms for the word *drunkard*, with a 'balance' of just 5 antonyms for the same word! Our wealth of such synonyms is saddening.

SHANDY ~ Vitiated beer; beer that has been 'watered down' with some juice or with another alcohol-weakening liquid.

[Note: Anywhere throughout this book, when dates or letters alone are given, the related source would be *The Daily Item*, a newspaper published in Sunbury, Pennsylvania.]

Foreword
[By a prominent teetotaler.]

Guy Graybill's *Intoxication Nation,* is a story of the history of alcohol use in the USA from suffrage, to temperance, to alcoholism. He has done extensive research and has shared stories taken from true experiences of people and events. The book brings to our attention how alcohol affected some of the leaders of our nation and their decision making. Guy uses easy to understand language to share medical explanations.

Intoxication Nation is a book I will share with my grandchildren before they go to college or into the workforce. There are many instances in the book of situations that may occur in their everyday lives. Guy states in his book that the person who drinks excessively has chosen to do that and because of their choices are responsible for the consequences of their actions. I agree that using the disease of alcoholism as an excuse to remove the consequences of one's behavior is not acceptable.

I've been a Board-Certified Family Physician for greater than 40 years. I also received training at the Betty Ford Center in California and Father Martin's Ashley Center in Baltimore, Maryland. I have been working in the field of alcohol addiction for the past 40 years as well.

In my experience, the disease of alcoholism is most often hereditary and for many is not a personal choice. But, getting treatment for this disease like any other is a choice. Dopamine secreted in the caudate nucleus is the "high" received. To get high is very pleasurable; but it leads to the addictive behavior. However, the high becomes ever more difficult to obtain and eventually the disease of alcoholism is manifested. The alcoholic is always chasing the first high and is never able to obtain it. Eventually, the alcoholic has to use heavily just to feel normal. A good determiner of whether a person has become addicted to alcohol was shared with me by Father Martin. He stated "when drinking causes problems, you have a drinking problem".

In his book, Guy shares the stories of alcoholics and how their disease has impacted their lives. It is important to remember that there is treatment for this brain disease that affects the whole family. Guy also shares stories of the comedians, Foster Brooks and Dean Martin. We all were amused but their families were not laughing. Look at the family members of alcoholics that you may know: They are not laughing. The best treatment for alcoholism is doing two things everyday: Not drinking and going to an Alcoholics Anonymous meeting. Twenty-three million people use the 12 Steps of AA. Those that continue to go to meetings regularly, do well. We all need the 12 Steps because life is difficult. Turning over our weaknesses and fears to a power greater than we are, along with doing a daily inventory of our lives, is a good way of living.

Reading, discussing and sharing the stories and knowledge shared by Guy Graybill in *Intoxication Nation,* can give all of us new insight into the history of alcohol in our country and how it has effected all of our lives. We can all learn from Guy's story.

John P. Pagana MD
Family Physician

Sobriety's Symbol: the inverted shot glass

Introduction

Regarding an innocent term: alcohol
When considering a title for this polemic, the author considered the similarity between the term for an international Arab terrorist organization—al Qaeda—and *alcohol,* the term for the many strong drinks that Americans consume in such staggering quantities, for this work, I considered taking the liberty to change the spelling of the damnable potion to *Al Qohol,* to remind readers of the deadliness of the liquid that kills thousands of Americans every single year . . . before 2001 and since! Readers may be surprised to find that the very word, *alcohol* is from the Arab, *al-coh'l.* How fortuitous! That makes the author's intended use of the slight corruption, *Al Qohol,* to be a reasonable intention.

However, the use of the variant, *Al Qohol,* has been abandoned, to be certain that we are not insulting innocent members of the Arab world, many of whom have been very highly regarded for their moral, cultural and academic leadership. The author proclaims profound admiration for members of every culture in the universe, just as he reviles all the jackasses—fanatic or faithless, Occidental or Oriental, drunken or sober—who abuse their fellow humans. Further, if this year is like other years, the world will witness—through bloodshot eyes—about *two million* alcohol-related deaths!

May the catalog of horrors begin . . .
In July 2012, Kirk Mahaffey and his young son, Mayson, were traveling across the Veterans Memorial Bridge at Sunbury, Pennsylvania. Suddenly, a terrorist, approaching from the other direction, swerved in front of the Mahaffey vehicle, striking it head on! The terrorist survived. According to his brother, the terrorist

driver had been "snorting the prescription painkiller . . . and drinking alcohol for several hours before the crash." Kirk and Mayson were killed.

A somewhat different terrorist attack occurred in Mount Carmel, Pennsylvania in early 2016, according to an account in *The Daily Item* (3/1/16), under the byline of Justin Strawser. According to the news report, Robert Thurner was in the kitchen of his home, feeding his 18-month-old son when he was attacked by a knife-wielding assailant. He was stabbed in the chest and slashed on the arm. Thurner was able to push his attacker out the back door. He then called the police. They arrived to find that Thurner's infant was physically unharmed, although Thurner was visibly upset and had a still-bleeding wound. The police found the assailant hiding in the backyard. The attacker had bloodshot eyes, a strong smell of alcohol and had to be helped with walking. The assailant, who was then imprisoned, had recently been released from rehab. She was Thurner's girlfriend and the mother of their son. She had just come back from a night of drinking when an angry verbal exchange led to her trying to win the argument with a black-handled steak knife. Court documents indicate that her boyfriend told police that "There are usually problems when she drinks."

Another terrorist attack was reported (*TDI*) on March 8th of 2016. The terrorist, *"after drinking at a bar Sunday evening . . ."* entered the home of the unnamed woman She was seated in her kitchen. The man grabbed her by her neck and put a loaded handgun to her head! She broke free; but he wrestled her to the floor, choking her and preventing her from calling police on her cell phone. She again broke free and was out of the house before he overtook her and threw her onto the porch. While trying to drag her back into the house, his handgun discharged, striking the door frame! The third time that she broke free, she ran to her vehicle and escaped. Police arrived and found the 45-year-old terrorist, who was also her boyfriend, inside the bedroom, threatening suicide. He was arrested and charged with attempted murder, etc.

Amazingly (or perhaps not amazingly, in our binging society), the very next day, March 9, the same newspaper carried another story of alcohol and terrifying behavior. This incident exploded just about 25 miles west of the one just cited above. In this event, the man, Donald Moyer, *"returned home heavily intoxicated"* to

Millard Shambach, an early DUI victim (From the author's archives).

punch his female companion in the face outside the house. She ran into the house, where five children were located. When he found that she had locked the door behind her, he threatened to use a propane tank to blow his way into the house. The woman and five children, without coats, ran from the house, into freezing weather to escape into a wooded area. When police arrived and took Mr. Moyer into custody, they found that he had a cut wrist, the result of his punching through a glass pane. Later investigators found that Moyer had also filled an oven with flammable materials that had never been ignited. Among the several charges against the man were "misdemeanor terroristic threats."

All four of the preceding incidents are doubly troubling. Not only were innocent Americans terrorized, injured or killed; but there was no public outcry or government retaliation against those who supported the terrorists.

Surely, people have been suffering the results of violence from alcohol-driven behavior since the earliest days of antiquity. The primary difference seems to be that today's violence comes with far greater frequency and with more deadly incidents. Obviously, the advent of motor vehicles has increased the likelihood of grave injuries and a greater mortality rate. Consider an early case, with a result like those that would be repeated so many thousands of times over.

The need to recalculate one's longevity

As the account was passed along through the family, April 19, 1935, was a day of 'coincidences' for Millard Shambach, a retired farmer of rural Pennsylvania. Millard's family had earlier been mentioned in the local weekly newspaper for its trait of longevity. On that day, Shambach walked from his home in the small village of Kissimmee (Snyder County) along the rural road to the farm of his son. There he helped his son with normal farm chores. In the early evening, after the dairy cows were milked, he started walking across the road from the barn to the house. He was carrying a pale of milk. As he neared the gate that would give him entrance to the son's lawn, something terrible happened.

Just by coincidence, and despite relatively few automobiles being in this rural area in 1935, a car happened to be approaching. And, just by coincidence, the car's driver was blinded by the late afternoon sun. By coincidence, the car struck Millard Shambach. Just by coincidence, the car with the sun-blinded driver had enough speed to drag Millard for about *100 feet* before stopping; coming to a halt with Millard's lifeless body sprawled beneath. Also, coincidentally, the driver of the killer vehicle was a 19-year-old young man whom Millard had recently condemned publicly.

Suddenly, the question of Shambach's longevity became as trivial as the pail of undelivered milk. Shambach was dead at the age of 79, killed by a young man whom the coroner was heard to instruct to go directly home and to drink a lot of strong coffee. If the introduction hadn't been made before, rural Snyder County, Pennsylvania had now (4/29/35) met the exciting world of the DUI.

Billions for booze; but mere cents for sobriety

We don't need to launch military assaults, but we are woefully remiss for not retaliating with a volley of stunning facts and statistics. Our American government should easily spend some tax money to disseminate truthful facts and news releases to startle and awaken America. Our U.S. government offices should remind us, daily, of the unending alcohol-related tragedies, to try to offset the multi-billion-dollar propaganda campaigns of the booze peddlers. Even more importantly, we should create the legislation needed to curb the flood of alcohol advertising. Opposition forces barely exist and the amount they spend on anti-alcohol education would barely match the cost of the oats needed to feed a stable full of Clydesdales! For example, it's no problem for a large brewing company to spend millions of dollars for a single high-powered propaganda ad to appeal to the Super Bowl viewers of both sexes and every age group. How damned pathetic!

Perspective?
In September 2001, Al Qaeda terrorist attacks, on several targets in the United States, resulted in 2,981 deaths. That series of attacks rightly triggered a call for a strong military effort to counter the Al Qaeda attacks and to provide increased protection for Americans and others who might be living or working in the United States. However . . .

In 2001, the same year that Al Qaeda launched its cowardly attack, many times that many Americans were killed by alcohol, with no public or government outcry and with no declaration of war!
During the years since the awful attacks of September 11, 2001, there were less than two dozen additional deaths from foreign terrorist activity within the United States, but . . . just during the years 2006 to 2010, the Center for Disease Control (CDC) tallies show (http://www.cdc.gov/alcohol/fact-sheets/alcohol-use. htm) that excessive alcohol use led to an average of 88,000 American deaths per year! Yes . . . eighty-eight *thousand!* Alcohol, not Al Qaeda, continues to kill huge numbers of American civilians as history's most successful terrorist in America. We still await a declaration of war! Instead, our leaders are silent. Not a word of condemnation from our protectors in Washington! Not a whisper!
British Prime Minister Arthur Neville Chamberlain's 1938 appeasement of Nazi tyrant, Adolf Hitler, has come down to us as one of History's glaring examples of spineless appeasement. Rightly so; but America's leadership surpasses Chamberlain for its spineless appeasement! Hitler's success was achieved by bombast and saber rattling; while the alcohol industry uses bullion and bribery. England later paid a huge price for their prime minister's appeasement. Surely, the price paid for our appeasement of the alcohol industry in America is costly beyond measure.

A few days after a recent new year opened (1-7-16), the *Centre Daily Times* of State College, Pennsylvania, carried an Associated Press piece that told of two teenaged boys, both 16 at the time, who were involved in an ATV wreck in February of 2015. The passenger, Briggs Buck, was killed. *Both he and the driver were heavily liquored*, with the driver having a blood-alcohol level of at least four times the legal limit! Buck's blood-alcohol level was pegged at more than eight times the legal limit! The liquor was provided by a 33-year-old Steven Rider, Jr., who was charged with various crimes, including involuntary manslaughter. He is the individual who allegedly gave the liquor to the boys on the day of the fatal crash. Alcohol, the terrorist, had struck again!

A Pennsylvania news report (6-19-14) tells of a 13-month-old girl from Erie, Pennsylvania being hospitalized. The waif's blood-alcohol reading was a whopping 0.289! The account said that the person who gave her that dangerous quantity of alcohol was her 26-year-old mother. Another innocent American thrust into harm's way by the terrorist, alcohol.

Since this polemic will have reason to reference the blood-alcohol levels of several individuals herein, we might look at what the author would peg as a likely deadly level, the legal level, and one other level. One opinion of what levels should be recognized:

Blood-alcohol levels
Approaching the lethal: .40
Legal: .08
Mature: .00

A news account (*TDI*, 2-3-16) tells of what appears to have been an alcohol-driven act of terror that occurred east of Pittsburgh, Pennsylvania. An unmarried couple had returned home "from several bars." While she was in bed, their dog had its head resting on her head and her boyfriend shot the dog in the head. Apparently, it was one of those alcohol-driven mistakes, since the woman told police that her boyfriend explained the dog's death by declaring, "I meant it for you."

If you travel on the west coast of these United States, don't worry about the San Andreas fault. Just try to avoid the planes piloted by the 60-year-old commercial pilot named David Arntson. Despite decades of piloting commercial planes with no alcohol problems, in January of 2016 Arntson was charged with flying two Alaska Airlines flights along the west coast, from San Diego to Oregon and from Oregon to Orange County, California. All that flight time was made while Arntson was under the influence of alcohol. His two blood alcohol concentration readings were listed as .134 and .142; both beyond acceptable limits. The flights occurred in June 2014, after which the airline removed him from his piloting role and after which he retired. He was to face arraignment on February 10, 2016. Even if the pilot is only slightly impaired, passengers may demand a more reassuring form of transportation if their pilot's level of inebriation is known before takeoff.

How should one react if a passenger in a huge, modern aircraft suddenly—during flight—tries to open the plane's exit door? Should a fellow passenger feel terrorized? Imagine that YOU are one of the passengers and you've just flown across the Atlantic from Heathrow Airport in England and you're now nearing Boston, Massachusetts. Suddenly, a passenger is trying to open the exit door! Would *you* feel terrorized? You should! This very incident took place in mid-November of 2015. The terrorist was not some foreign fanatic and was not carrying a weapon. The terrorist was an unruly woman who was drunk! Alcohol, in sotted citizens, constantly terrorizes Americans. We need to better inform the public of the severity and the *frequency* with which alcohol terrorizes innocent U.S. citizens! Someday . . . perhaps.

Tens of thousands of America's 21st-century terror killings have occurred in the home, in and close to barrooms, and on the highways. Meanwhile, too many people in critical positions

---

Sober Slogan #1

Our two alcohol problems:

A. Underage drinking

B. Overage drinking

---

in government, in entertainment, in law enforcement, and in the media, are *covert*—and *overt*—members of alcohol terrorist cells. So, the crisis deepens . . . the widespread killings continue. We must face the sorry truth. We attack terrorists in Libya; but not Lynchburg; in Syria, but not St. Louis; in Ghazni, but not Golden. When the pathetic results of alcoholic license are involved, America lacks politicians with the gonads to govern.

A tiny segment of the tragic tally (From the author's archives).

The killer equation

Again, by coincidence, a recent (downloaded 8/11/15) internet blurb (www.slate.com/articles, etc.) tells of the problem in just one other nation of the world: France. There, says the source, current statistics tell the rest of the deaf international community that "a full 13 percent" of France's male deaths can be blamed on "French drinking habits." Meanwhile, back at the American trough . . .

Bob Sankey, of Kreamer, Pennsylvania, is hardly alone when he laments the nation's priorities regarding individual safety. He observed (*The Daily Item*, 12-27-12), "Every day there are more people killed on our nation's highways by drunken drivers than there are by guns." Why must a voice like Bob Sankey's be as one in a wilderness, in the face of our mounting death tolls from alcohol?

Let's look at a handful of tragic cases, none of which aroused national indignation against the abuse of alcohol . . .

■ Natalie Holloway, a recent high school graduate, left her classmates behind in a Caribbean bar, climbed into a car with three strangers and disappeared into the Aruban night.

■ Imette St. Guillen, left a bar late at night. Hours later, her corpse was found nearby. She had been abducted, tortured, raped and murdered.

■ George Smith, on a honeymoon cruise with his wife, drowned himself in alcohol before disappearing forever.

■ Tracy Hottenstein was visiting Sea Isle City, New Jersey, during "Polar Bear Plunge" weekend in 2015. That event is known to include 'revelry' late into the night. Tracy left a bar near closing time. A fisherman discovered her body on a nearby beach. Although authorities withheld some details, it was announced that she died of hypothermia resulting from "exposure complicating acute alcohol intoxication."

■ Michelle Gardner-Quinn, split from her friends after a night of barhopping. She asked a stranger on the street if she might borrow his cellphone. She was found murdered.

What is the common denominator in all the above tragedies? Either directly or indirectly, all who died were victims of the terrorist, alcohol.

Few problems are so obviously universal as drunkenness. Intoxication appears throughout recorded history and throughout the modern world. Today, as the days and years tick away into the new millennium, drunkenness remains the curse that it has always been. Today's social and political leaders insist on ignoring the curse of alcohol. It's time for them to admit: Intoxication cannot be treated as some sort of great historic relic. We must move beyond that notion. Let us summarize the problem. *Alcohol's greatest American* enablers are *apathy* and *glamorization*. That must stop!

Because much of the disastrous story of America's drunkenness is forgotten or ignored, this book was written . . . and written as an unapologetic polemic.

Sober Slogan #2

The horsefly is brainier than the barfly.

However, *Intoxication Nation* is not written to condemn, nor to impale the exemplary drinkers; but to ask our public and our public officials to move to deglamorize and to do whatever is needed to *eliminate* the dangerous drunkards from our homes and highways.

Chapter One

Fatal Alcohol Syndrome

When liquor trumps logic

Christians should NOT be able to quote the Bible to justify drinking alcohol. The Muslims disdain for alcohol is well known, as is the disdain of the American Mormons. If those groups can be teetotalers, why can't the mainstream Judeo-Christian Americans avoid its use?

Intoxication should NEVER be allowed to excuse a crime. It takes a criminal level of arrogance to even *suggest* that drunkenness excuses criminal behavior. When will we mature enough as a society to admit that, morally speaking, no one has the right to get drunk!

This book will not include the tens of thousands of worthy pictures of ghastly and murderous vehicular accidents wrought by the excesses of alcohol. While such images are needed, from time to time, we prefer to let the reader imagine the worst one that he or she has ever seen. Multiply that most vivid image by many, many thousands and one can sense the horrors that befall this nation whenever alcohol is consumed, unchecked by reason. The omission of such pictures in this volume will also avoid the depletion of vast stands of pulpwood.

Rather than simply giving mankind the ability to use, God gave us the ability to create. Thus, we can create a fiddle and use it to give pleasure to others. We can also create a nuclear warhead and use it to destroy a segment of humanity! Of course, alcohol sits far along on the spectrum, toward the end where our God-given ability to create is used to destroy ourselves, along with huge numbers of helpless innocents.

We offer the following cases as having *allegedly* occurred as herewith written, just in case there are any remaining unresolved issues. They are based on news accounts and, to our knowledge, are accurate as presented.

Two semi-celebrities get into the news

Andrew Koppel's father was a television news anchor. Andrew, however, made the news (*TDI*, 6/2/10) because he was said to have spent a day bar hopping with another gentleman. They were reported to have been drinking for much of the day and having nothing to eat, meaning that whiskey was his basic diet for the day. Koppel finally retired to 'sleep it off'. When his companions found him later, seemingly unconscious, they called 9-1-1. He died while still in the apartment.

The previous day's news item (*TDI*, 6/1/10) told of Sarah Ferguson, once the wife of Britain's Prince Andrew. She offered someone 'access' to her former husband. Her asking price for such a splendid favor: $724,000. Ms. Ferguson apologized for her bad judgment and said that she had financial problems and that she had been drinking and was "in the gutter at that moment." Presumably, her description of her whereabouts at that moment was figuratively speaking.

The rapist's accomplice

Within less than a year's time, rural Somerset County, Pennsylvania twice made national news. The first incident was the tragedy of September 11, 2001, when several of a plane's heroic passengers died in their successful attempt to stop the plane's terror-

ist attack on a Washington, DC, target. The nation's attention again focused on the rural county in July of 2002. The collapse of a coal-mine wall released millions of gallons of water into the Quecreek Mine tunnel where a nine-man crew was working. After a tense seventy-seven hours, all nine members emerged safely! Those two notable incidents made a more recent, tiny, Somerset County news item go almost unnoticed in 2015. In that year, a news item (*TDI*, 11/4/15) related the ugly news about a man who had been hired to be the designated driver for a woman who wanted to be properly chauffeured on Hallowe'en Night. Before the drunken woman arrived home, according to police records, her driver had raped her multiple times. Seemingly, it took much more than repeated sexual assaults for the inebriated victim to regain sobriety. As has been demonstrated repeatedly: Alcohol is the frequent accomplice of the rapist.

Here's a thought . . .

A motel room must be recognized as, basically, a bedroom. So, if a woman wants to chat with a man she meets in a motel, why not insist that the meeting occur in the motel bar or the lobby? I would suggest that states enact laws that say this: If a woman accompanies a man to his motel bedroom, she should not act surprised or offended if intimate advances follow. I'd call that "The Kobe Law."

A really big winner

Californian, Thomas Turnour, had built himself a modest rap sheet. His criminal record included arrests and a couple of imprisonments for arson, drug importation and delivery, and burglary. However, things changed in 2001. Turnour won a Bear State lottery worth $10,000,000. His legal problems were eased with the winnings. In 2005, five people, all related and occupants of a Ford Taurus, were stopped at a traffic signal in Victorville, California. That's when Thomas Turnour, driving his late-model GMC pickup truck arrived on the scene. Turnour, in a drunken state, slammed into the back of the Taurus, pushing it into two other vehicles! Thomas Turnour promptly left the scene and was just as promptly apprehended by witnesses to the grisly crash. Three of the five Taurus occupants were left mangled and dead. This member of the newly rich, Thomas Turnour, now has another California award to celebrate: A seventeen-year prison term.

Stopping near the scene

According to an account in the Allentown (Pennsylvania) Morning Call newspaper of 10/1/15, (http://www.mcall.com), there was a hit/run case in neighboring Bethlehem, in which 29-year-old

Jerry Magditch and his girlfriend saw a pickup truck hurtling toward them. Magditch pushed his companion to safety, before being smacked by the truck. While he was lying on the street, bloodied and unconscious, the driver of the truck stopped the vehicle nearby. However, he didn't stop to check on the condition of Magditch. He stopped to pick up three companions. Then he sped away, driving in and out of traffic and hitting several construction cones. When police got the driver to stop, he quickly got into the back of the truck and vainly urged one of his passengers to get into the driver's seat! However, the 30-year-old driver of the truck was arrested. He was charged with driving on a license that was suspended *due to a prior DUI incident*; failure to stop at an accident scene and, naturally, a fresh drunken-driving violation. Meanwhile, Jerry Magditch, according to the same news report, was hospitalized with a spinal cord injury, brain damage and a fractured skull. At the time of the newspaper report, Magditch was also in an induced coma.

What mixes with alcohol?

One town in Maine has a name that matches an historic port in France: Calais. But, it was the Calais in Maine that got into the Associated Press news item in the summer of 2015 (July 6). In that town, Devon Staples was enjoying a summer evening of drinking and igniting fireworks. Staples set off a fireworks mortar tube. When it exploded, Staples was instantly killed! Where had he placed it? Atop his head. This tragedy marked the first fireworks fatality in Maine since fireworks were legalized in the state in early 2012. For those who tally such things, this can be added to the growing list: *alcohol* and *pyrotechnics* don't mix!

No reindeer needed

Lisa Ann Casteel was the forty-year-old woman (T.D.I., 6-21-08) who reached the legal plateau of alcohol blood level for driving. Once over the legal limit, she stretched her level a couple of times more. That is when she backed out of a driveway and struck a woman sitting in a chair in the driveway. Lisa Ann backed over the woman, but stopped and checked her victim. She told the witnesses that the woman was breathing; got back into the car and left the scene. The woman who had Lisa Ann's SUV back over her was rushed to the hospital and was, there, pronounced dead.

Lisa Ann, who had a blood-alcohol content of .243, had suddenly become a drunken, *motherless* hit-and-run driver.

Over the river and through the woods

(2-19-13, 2-22-13) Sorry events, by the tens of thousands, follow a common, if senseless, progression. They go from the bar to the brawl to the burial grounds. For example: A local, married couple, Jennifer and Joshua Snook, were patrons of a bar in Northumberland, Pennsylvania. Apparently, another man made some inappropriate remarks to Jennifer. This was followed by a confrontation between the two men. The other man more recently admitted that he had thrown a pitcher of beer at Joshua. The other man, from prison (on an unrelated charge) said that, at the time, Snook was 'wasted'. The Snooks left the bar, long after midnight, and drove across the Susquehanna River and another twenty-five miles or so to the rural home of the elderly couple that was watching their nine-year-old son. Joshua was also intent on getting a gun. Joshua Snook later told police that he wanted to use the weapon to scare his barroom antagonist, although he had told his father, in a telephone conversation, that he wanted a gun to kill the man in the bar. However, when Joshua arrived at the sitters' home, there was a bloody confrontation between Joshua and the sitters, who resisted Joshua's attempt to take one of their guns. The nine-year-old boy was present during this confrontation that left two shattered windows, and several blood-splattered rooms, a hallway, and a stairway. Police estimated that the chaos lasted at least one-half hour. The attack ended when Joshua Snook left the house with his nine-year-old son and a 9mm Ruger handgun. The sanguine scene that Joshua Snook left behind also included the body of the 71-year old woman, who had died from a slashed carotid artery and a severed jugular vein. Snook related that "She tried to pull (the knife) out of my hand. *If I was drinking, she knew it was trouble.* [!!] Her 72-year-old husband had non-fatal injuries. The two residents were the great-grandparents of the nine-year-old boy and the grandparents of their attacker! Joshua Snook is currently serving a 20 to 60-year sentence, while his wife, who confessed that "I was extremely intoxicated," was charged with conspiracy and is serving from five to fifteen years. A later (3/18/16) article appearing in the *Snyder County* (Pennsylvania) *Times* reported that Joshua Snook wanted to withdraw his "guilty" plea and the more recent article reminded readers that he had initially testified that his grandmother's death was accidental since it had been caused by his "reckless drinking addiction." Where have we heard that excuse before, and since, and endlessly! If one had the time, one might tally such incidents of 'accidental' mayhem; *every one of which would have gone uncommitted had it not been for the influence of the terrorist,* alcohol!

My students in the last district in which I taught, told of the eighth grader (Yes, the eighth grader!) whose single father took him along to the barroom so that he'd have a sober driver for the return home. How appealing: Booze leading to familial bonding.

A gathering of brewers, vintners, and distillers. From the author's archives.

All the horrors of the great American binge are fueled by the hunger for money and the thirst for liquor. The owners and the bartenders seem to keep their eyes on one object: Not the slowly wasting patron; but the quickly-filling cash register. Evidently, some owners show no concern for the sober drivers who are innocently nearing the bar where his sotted patrons are struggling to get their cars into gear and out onto the highways for a risky drive home. Does the bar owner have any concern for the burden he helps to put on the staff of the local E.R.? The pattern of behavior of the drunk suggests that he encounters few people who deny a 'last drink' or a few drinks *beyond* a last drink.

Sober Slogan #4

This driver can't get a DUI.

Can you?

The bar owner, the bartender and the thirsting patron work in seemingly innocent harmony in their effort to fill the bladder of the patron and the coffers of the pub owners, the brewers, and the distillers. Thousands of times each year, such collusion results in a collision!

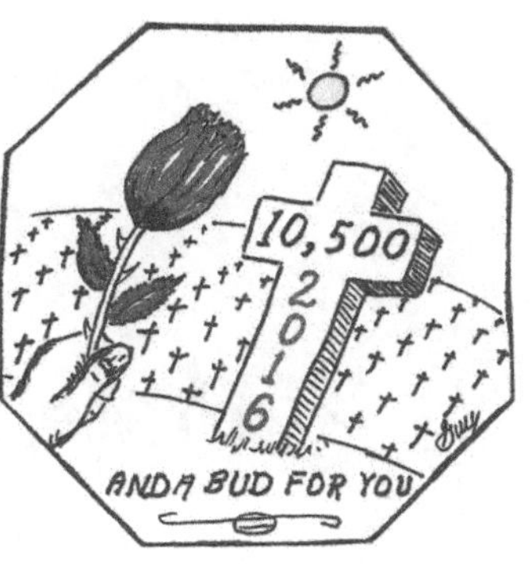

Since we cringe from trying to reduce the dangers of binging and driving, for example, we see these colossal numbers of fatalities each year. Drunkards and others who encounter them may all become victims of alcohol abuse. Then we see the equation forming: *The greater the alcohol supply, the smaller the blood supply.* Either innocent victims or the drunken driver, herself/himself, can become victims of their own bloody intemperance. Then, we again learn another sorry truism: "Martyr's get stoned to death by the crowd; drunkards stone themselves to death!"

Chapter Two

Frats, Vats, and Stats

T.B. Doremus left his hometown of Jericho Center, Vermont to attend Bucknell University, in Lewisburg, Pennsylvania. Strange things occur in central Pennsylvania. While partying at a house in Lewisburg late one night, in December 2012, he apparently lost consciousness. When he awoke, he was in an unfamiliar house a couple of miles from the institution of higher learning. He was also facing a stranger (the house's owner) and some Pennsylvania troopers. T. B. Doremus was also unable to explain why he had apparently taken a vacuum cleaner to smash his way into the stranger's house

and why his shoes and socks were missing. Police said that he was obviously intoxicated. Surely the police were mistaken since T.B. Doremus was under the legal drinking age.

Less than a week later, another student, Nathan Kendrick, of Athens, Pennsylvania, and a student at Susquehanna University, about 20 miles south of Bucknell University, had a similarly strange experience. Police theorized that he was intoxicated when he illegally entered a business place late at night. He eventually exited the establishment; leaving behind only his credit cards, his driver's license and his Susquehanna University student ID card.

Although better educated than some of his fellow Bucknell students, graduate student David Lee Wacker, of Parkton, Maryland, still couldn't navigate through sober society while drunk. As related in *The Daily Item* (4-4-13), it was nearly 3:00 A.M. when Wacker hammered on the door of a house in Lewisburg and demanded entry. Told to go away, Wacker eventually left, only to encounter some arriving local police. Caught after a brief chase through the neighborhood, Wacker couldn't say why he had been trying to enter that dwelling. The grad student, who had a blood/ alcohol level of .221, could tell the police, however, that he knew that he was in Pennsylvania; thus evincing a level of geographical proficiency that should gain him entry into a Ph.D. program.

To show the author's impartiality, it should be mentioned that besotted college students aren't the only ones who appear in strange houses at strange hours. *The Daily Item* (7-20-15) tells of Christopher Lee Jones, a 33-year old man from Watsontown, Pennsylvania, who was with his girlfriend in a bar where he drank several beers. Later, they argued in her car. Chris jumped from the car to find another bar. Soon, more fully inebriated, he found himself (3:25 A.M.) in an unknown house in Milton, Pennsylvania. The female occupant spotted the intruder, now shoeless. She screamed and her husband came running! The intruder was only chatting with the family dog. The husband shoved the intruder from the house and unto the porch. The husband then knocked Jones off the porch. He picked himself up and ran, with the husband in temporary pursuit. The police were discussing the incident with the homeowners when they spotted the shoeless and clueless boozer. Christopher Lee Jones was apprehended and charged with a fistful of crimes.

The preceding four incidents were similar in having drunken men appear in unfamiliar locations. Since they all occurred within a circle having a diameter of fewer than forty miles, one might suppose that this kind of alcohol-driven behavior has happened thousands of times in what seems to be developing into "Inebriation Nation."

The E.R. barometer

Colleges make college towns unique. Alcohol makes them colorful . . . and sometimes deadly.

A 2015 report by Carla Johnson of the Associated Press (*TDI*, 9-1-15) informs us that "Underage college students who have never tried alcohol before are most likely to have it for the first time in June." Her observations are based on a summary of the annual "National Survey on Drug Use and Health." Her report indicates that "many American teenagers start drinking in high school" although many don't. Once in college, her report indicates, about *1,200 underage students, per day*, will try alcohol for the first time. It becomes patently obvious that the students' self-restraint is an invaluable commodity when they enter the college environment and that it becomes even more important if they are going into the Greek community (the sororities and fraternities) or some other partying environment.

Local police offices and area hospital emergency rooms are excellent places to check for the activity levels of local colleges and universities. E.R. personnel can readily tell a visitor if college is in session or is not in session and if there are any particularly popular activities occurring on campus. It's sad; but certain: Emergency Room visits spike!

If someone wants to get into the espionage field, he or she is off to a good start when they learn how to get or create fake I.D. cards as college students who couldn't survive without underage drinking . . .

False protection

In August of 2008, the Associated Press reported that a group of American college presidents were advocating lowering the drinking age. This strategy, the learned leaders emphasized, would reduce the secrecy of drinking once students began their college careers since the excitement of sneaking their booze would no longer exist. This immediately suggests the following scenario: There would be a natural upsurge in surreptitious drinking by high school students, who would now be the ones to look at the exciting life of their campus neighbors and decide that they, of the high school crowd, are the victims of the unfeeling legislators who would deny them their natural right to the pleasures of intemperate boozing just because they sit on the opposite side of an artificial age barrier.

Say, wouldn't the opposite approach have the same effect? Why not *raise* the legal age for boozing to 28? Then it would be the 24 through 28-year olds who would fight the denial of their God-given right to liquor by secretly getting bombed. That approach, too, would get the problem off the campus; but with thousands less of the alcohol-related deaths.

The name of the college presidents' 'sobriety' program tells it all: The Amethyst Initiative. The amethyst is a jewel of beautiful purple hue, which turns yellow under heat. Used as a gemstone by the ancient Egyptians, the amethyst—in recent times—has been used for episcopal rings. Why is this gem an appropriate one to be associated with the 2008 college presidents' initiative? The ancients, most of whom were convinced that the earth was flat, were also convinced that the amethyst protected a drinker from the intoxicating effects of alcohol. The college presidents, who use the amethyst as the name for their cockeyed proposal to lower the drinking age, were using their brain power much as if they also believe in the flat nature of our celestial orb.

An ugly rumor

I've heard it as a rumor which I happen to believe, but I know of no way to validate it. I think that college officials sometimes intervene with hospital personnel to rescue drunken college students from their local E.R.s, to protect their students from police records and their own immaturity. If that is true it is one stat that will never be released. It would also help reinforce the phony "amethyst initiative."

Roomies

Just as children, mates, co-workers, fellow motorists, etc., are hapless victims of the actions of drunkards, so, too, the sober college student who is condemned to live in the same dorm room as a student who is majoring in *Advanced Socializing*. Consider the plight of the non-drinking or moderately imbibing college student who is condemned to room with a partier. She or he will quickly learn that the hours of dorm-room study are non-existent for the partier. He or she will learn that the partier provides special décor for their room: Items like stop signs, highway pylons, liquor advertising signs, etc. The sober student will soon learn that the partier may also need personal care from the hapless, serious student. One incident told of a student whose partying partner passed out in the dorm hall. The dorm leader and a policeman brought the sick partier to his room and told the sober scholar to watch that the other fellow didn't choke on his vomit or otherwise suffer some health crisis. The sober one spent hours on the alert, caring for a fellow student who belonged under medical care; not under the care of a drafted caretaker who had his studies to address. That same sober student also endured an incident when his partier-roommate was absent and the partier's drunken girlfriend arrived to wait for her boyfriend. While in the room, sitting on her boyfriend's bed, she announced that she had wet her pants. When the boozing lovers left, there was a large, wet ring on the boyfriend's bed!

Of course, the drunken theft of street signs and much more are only a small part of the senseless costs created by drunken college students. Those expenses are to be borne by the pathetic taxpayers. Meanwhile, the clutter from stolen souvenirs is but a small part of the disruption in his/her life to be endured by the sober roommate.

Young adults? Many college students are such; but not the campus partiers. They are light years away from adulthood and—despite the best efforts of the local E.R. personnel—many will never attain adulthood. Alcohol will kill thousands of them and perpetual immaturity will claim countless others.

Some may never realize that wisdom is easily diluted by alcohol.

A rolling stone gathers no facts

In a sense, the fraternities brought it on themselves. If fraternities didn't have endless examples of infantile, rowdy and, often, dangerous behavior, it would be harder for some errant publication (such as *Rolling Stone* magazine) to create a journalistic hoax, such as their fable about a shocking gang rape at a University of Virginia frat house. American readers are regularly being reminded: Sloppy journalism can be as bad, or worse, than no journalism. It appears that the editors of *Rolling Stone* were pretending to be doing some crusading and were, in reality, practicing the sleaziest sort of market scamming.

Let's disregard, if we may, the fabrications of a major periodical, and remember the *other problem*: There is an ongoing challenge confronting colleges and universities: Combatting sexual violence. It isn't anything imagined. There are cases to count; harrowing stories to hear; steps to be taken; new laws to apply. As so often occurs: it took a truly horrifying case to shake the consciences of the lawmakers.

Behind the dumpster

What a familiar opening to a pathetic story: There was a frat party . . .

One would think that every student on every college or university campus would know of the great potential that exists for calamity because of the heavy drinking among the lightweights who attend college fraternity parties. But, the stories continue to appear. This one occurred at such a party associated with California's Stanford University.

In January 2015 the victim, identified as Ms. Doe, was sexually attacked by a student named Brock Turner. He raped Ms. Doe behind a campus dumpster in an attack that was also violent in nature. He was violent and drunk. She was unconscious and drunk. The potential for her to have been even more brutally assaulted was averted when two Swedish fellows, graduate students at Stanford, came on the scene. They shouted at Turner. He fled, but they overtook him and held him until the police arrived.

Turner, the intoxicated rapist, was tried and found guilty of the attack. The callousness and severity of the attack suggests that the prosecutors' recommendation of *six years* in the state prison was a just response. Strangely, the judge, Aaron Persky—who also happened to be a Stanford University alumnus—thought the grisly crime required no more than *six months* in the county jail! Among other reasons for the light sentence, according to the judge, was the lack of a criminal record. One must inquire: Should the lack of a criminal record *ever* be used to decide the degree of punishment? Shouldn't the entire basis for a sentence be the *severity of the specific crime under consideration?*

It's worthy of note that Ms. Doe read a twelve-page statement to her attacker and the court. In that statement, she mentioned attending the party to spend the evening with her younger sister, who was attending. Ms. Doe, in her early twenties, admitted to being older than the other attendees. At one point she had written that "I knew no one at this party." Obviously, she did. She knew her sister, the one whom she appears to have abandoned to drink a surfeit of liquor that she, herself, admitted to being two shots of whiskey and two shots of vodka. Whatever booze it was that she drank, she was still drunkenly unconscious hours after being ravished!

To whatever degree their alcoholic consumption contributed to the ugly incident, both parties have some culpability. When will people admit how easily they may be victimized while being drunk? *Why do some individuals act as though society is responsible for their welfare while they go into a self-induced stupor? A* very ugly crime occurred behind a Stanford University dumpster. Both parties would be pursuing much happier lives if they had simply tossed their damned liquor into the dumpster.

Must alcohol always bring out the worst in people?

The parents of Jeanne Clery, of Bryn Mawr, Pennsylvania, sent their only daughter to college in what seemed to be a nice, safe school: Lehigh University in nearby Bethlehem. But, it was in the middle of the night, one Spring night in 1986, that a fellow student left a party, got into Jeanne Clery's residence hall (the doors of which had been propped open with pizza boxes for the convenience of late returnees), and broke into Jeanne's room. When she was awakened by his presence, the intruder attacked her. *People* magazine (2/17/90) says that Miss Clery "had been raped, sodomized, beaten, bitten, strangled with a metal coil and mutilated with a broken bottle . . ." *The report also said that her attacker "had been on an all-night drinking binge . . ."*

The positive result of Jeanne Clery's horrific murder was a federal law, now identified as the *Jeanne Clery Act*. It was enacted in 1988 and was amended in 1992, 1998, 2000, 2008 and 2013. That law is fully labeled as *"The Jeanne Clery Disclosure of Campus Security Policy and Campus Crime Statistics Act"* [20 USC § 1092 (f)]. The law requires colleges to keep and reveal statistics on a variety of major crimes that occur on campus and at non-campus locations with institutional ties. Crimes involved include murder, sex offenses, robbery, aggravated assault, some forms of burglary, motor vehicle theft and arson. Statistics are also required to be kept for three additional activities: the possession of illegal weapons, drug law violations, and *liquor law violations* [emphasis added]. The Jeanne Clery Act appears to have helped to reduce campus crimes, but it won't prevent the journalistic bullscat such as *Rolling Stone* fabricated.

Don't let your sons become Lord Jeffs

Amherst is a college in western Massachusetts, about 75 miles due west of Boston. It is among the oldest colleges in the nation and has been among the top-rated academic centers. Because of some historical influence, the students have been labeled as "Lord Jeffs." While the "Lord Jeff" reference is rather lame, it is at least better than being a "Hoya," the Georgetown University mascot name whose origin remains unclear to this day. Sadly, that western Massachusetts campus has recently (June of 2015) been shaken by a scandal. A female student reported to college authorities that, months earlier, she had been raped by a male student of the same institution. Without legal counsel being present, the college held a hearing and the presumed rapist was expelled. It was later established that the woman did have a sexual encounter that evening. It involved her roommate's intoxicated boyfriend. She also admitted her role as the initiator of the action. Later that same evening, when the accused had departed, she also invited another male friend to her room and had sex with him, too.

Despite these later revelations regarding the accuser's culpability, the college refused to reopen the case and the accused young man has remained off the lists of college enrollees. Although the college might be identified as Damnhurst, *the point is this:* There would likely have been no false accusations or expulsion from the college if alcohol had not been involved. It's also likely that many, many college rapes—particularly the *actual* cases—may never occur without the campus atmosphere and the related abuse of our national drink of sophistication . . . alcohol. There is now a book on the market that is entitled *The Campus Rape Frenzy: The Attack on Due Process at America's Universities.* The presence of such a book suggests that *this campus crime wave wouldn't exist without the presence of alcohol.*

Ponder this . . .

There is some interesting verbiage regarding drunken victims of campus assault. It goes something like this: A college or university must list a number of sexual crimes that are identified as "occurring where the victim is incapable of giving consent because of his or her temporary mental or physical incapacity." In other words, *when plastered!* Good grief!

The wounded animal in the wild becomes the logical prey of the beastly predator. It will be separated from its pack and turned into a pathetic and pitiable victim. There is one significant aspect of this timeless ritual: The prey did not *choose* to become wounded. *However, Ma'am, you were the one who chose to <u>incapacitate yourself</u> with alcohol.* Does logic prevail? If the woman is drunk and is raped, she is innocent because she was drunk. If a man is drunk and rapes, he is guilty because he was drunk. I'm grateful that I'm no judge. Perhaps, in the interest of fairness, any case involving two drunken litigants should be tried by a drunken judge and in a courthouse that is topped by an inebriate lass holding the scales of justice. This whole problem goes to the point raised through this treatise: All situations in life become fairer and simpler when sobriety prevails.

Time magazine, as recently as December 2014, offered the following (Issue of December 18) regarding the problem of sexual assault on campus: "At many schools, frats are the hub of campus social life—which means they're a center for the binge drinking . . ." that helps to fuel sexual assaults. The writer of that magazine piece also observed that regarding campus sexual assaults: "The kegs of cheap beer and barrels of sweet, high-proof punch that are a central draw of many frat parties can be a prime culprit."

The National Institute on Alcohol Abuse and Alcoholism, in a report downloaded 9/18/15, gave a number of items of troublesome data, including the following: "Roughly 20 percent of college students meet the criteria for an AUD" (an alcohol use disorder) while "97,000 students between the ages of 18 and 24 report experiencing alcohol-related sexual assault or date rape." These sorry developments all reinforce the above truism: Alcohol is the frequent accomplice of the rapist!

Coincidentally, Pennsylvania's Liquor Control Board ran an ad cautioning citizens about the possible connection "between date rape and alcohol." That was in 2011 (12-13), but they quickly pulled the ad because some people complained that it put too much responsibility for the rape on the victim.

Former vice president, Joe Biden was quoted on the internet site for *Global Citizen*, as viewed 5/7/18: "Guys, a woman who is dead drunk, cannot consent." Yes, Biden is, properly, putting blame on the male rapist. But, he is also condoning the act of getting dead drunk! How thoughtless!

The rape victim who was dead drunk should have been asked: Why didn't you run? Why didn't you shout for help? Why didn't you blow a loud whistle? Why didn't you spray the attacker with mace or pepper spray? Why didn't you counter-attack his testicles? It's just incredible that a young woman wouldn't have been told, by a teacher or counselor or, heaven forbid, a parent, that *the first defense against rape is sobriety*!

Lucidity traded for a zombie-like episode
Joe Biden might also have suggested that a woman who is dead drunk cannot vigorously object to sex, or to anything else! In fact,

she cannot make a single rational decision of the many decisions that everyone might need to face during any brief stretch of living. The former Veep might, at least, have suggested that—whether male or female, a dead drunk abandons a cluster of vivid moments of lucidity for a zombie-like episode where a myriad of ugly occurrences often bring terrible harm! Our ability to reason is a major positive trait that we humans use for self-protection. How can we so blindly disregard our college students' welfare by allowing them to temporarily destroy their critical, rational state of being? Of course, it isn't rape alone; it's any harmful act done to someone, woman or man, that they might, if sober, have resisted and/or avoided. Once again, let's stress: Society shouldn't be responsible for a person, male or female, young or old, who isn't concerned enough to remain sober and in some control of his/her own fate. By trying to shift all blame away from the victim, one is encouraging drunken behavior. A 2006 release from the Columbus, Ohio Division of Police, informs us: "Drugs and/or alcohol may compromise your ability . . . to make responsible decisions." Of course! So, once again, *bullscat!* A suggested solution: If you wish to avoid being easily robbed, kidnapped, raped, or whatever, while drunk; then, *damn it,* stay sober! Sobriety is such a small price to pay for one's very own well-being?

Same mistakes for three millennia plus
Never forget what it was that enabled the legendary Trojans to lose their beloved city and their lives. There were two things involved: That wooden equine beast and alcohol.

The Greeks had to have assumed that their enemy, the people of Troy, could be duped into believing that the decade-long Greek siege of their city had finally ended. They also had to assume that the Trojans would celebrate the war's end by getting drunk. Smart Greeks. Tragically foolish Trojans! For their trust and their drunkenness, most of the Trojans were slaughtered. Their city was destroyed, to become just another layer of rubble and ash on the ancient site. Was their slaughter the fault of the Trojans? It occurred while they were drunk. Reviewing the fate of the Trojans should make us realize a truth: *Drunkenness is an irresponsible behavior that has been making victims for more than 3,000 years!*

Jo-booze
A nationally-publicized sex-abuse scandal (finally culminating in an arrest in 2011 and in the firing of a handful of prominent

Beaver Stadium: The place that launched a thousand sips.

university leaders) shook the Penn State community. While the stench of that scandal was slowly clearing from "Happy Valley," a new stench was wafting in the malodorous aroma of a new beer which Penn State fans may have found to be refreshing. Pittsburgh's old Duquesne Brewing Company began marketing a beer that honored the late, great football coach, Joe Paterno, whose exceptional coaching career was thoroughly tarnished by the infamous scandal. The once-celebrated coach, known affectionately as "Jo-Pa," now had his name on a new brew, Duquesne Paterno Legacy beer. It sold nearly a million cans in its first week on the market. However, by 2-18-18 an internet site (*Beer Advocate*) offered this information: "This beer is retired; no longer brewed."

Penn State's alcohol studies program

The intoxicating atmosphere at the Pennsylvania State University ("Penn State") is not associated with the campus' natural setting in the picturesque Nittany Mountains but from the dozens of nearby purveyors of alcohol. As one of the larger schools in the nation, Penn State has its share of alcohol abuse problems, with fatal falls from open windows and nearby cliffs, as well as an annual cluster of alcohol-related arrests for drunkenness and property damage. Recognizing that nationality should not be a factor that limits activities, great hosts of non-Irish students join the celebration of St. Patrick's Day. As a sort of footnote to this paragraph, it must be stated that, for the sake of uniformity, the Irish spelling for whiskey is the one used throughout this polemic. Also, should the author refer to someone's whiskified state, he is using a legitimate term.

More *genuine* alcohol studies are needed

Do you know someone who needs a subject for a doctoral thesis? Herewith a cluster of suggested topics:

■ Investigate the incidence of U.S. killings that occur within, or in the vicinity of, bars as compared to those occurring elsewhere.

■ Of the gun-related killings in the U.S., in what percentage was the shooter found to be intoxicated.

■ What percentage of the profits from alcohol sales in the United States comes from the *illegal sale of liquor* to citizens who are underage or over intoxicated or both?

■ Why are such large numbers of college co-eds so enamored with partying and alcohol; knowing that boozing can never be synonymous with scholarship?

■ How many times is a serious college student paired with a college 'roomie' who is only a *partier*? That's the kind of sentence that should not be handed down to a hardened criminal; much less a serious, sober student.

Every college freshman should be so educated that he or she begins to acquire a loftier goal than one which defies scholarship and sobriety. Was John Belushi, in a popular movie, more influential than their parents or teachers or other mentors? "My advice to you: Start drinking heavily," was Belushi's counsel to a fellow student with a troubling problem. Only the truly witless among any student body can't recognize the phoniness of such an "animal house" mentality. Only the witless among the undergraduates are fool enough to decide that alcohol and anarchy form the perfect academic regimen. Sadly, at present, we are edging closer and closer to transforming America into a national "animal house"!

Before they leave the comfort of high school there is something every aspiring student should have learned: The acquisition of knowledge is no great feat. Praise is only warranted for those scholars who synthesize that knowledge into something beneficial to humanity.

Drinking responsibly simply means drinking within society's confining range; but we're never going to get this sotted land to drink responsibly when so many of the dispensers of alcohol and so many legislators and media members, and so many others, flagrantly disregard alcohol's mature and responsible use. Also blind to the irresponsible uses of alcohol are many, many, many parents.

Today, we have that large class of Americans who have no earned income, and who should be, on that basis alone, nonparticipants in the national binge. They are America's high school and college students, and their ranks spawn the most pathetic drunks. *Especially pathetic are the financiers of those teen-boozers, who also pose as parents.* Obviously, for this social group, "a parent's worst nightmare" is the challenge of having to refuse to pay for your child's liquor supply. So, this nation is left awash in a sea of alcohol, knowing that alcohol disrupts the lives of millions and ends the lives of thousands. Alcohol stalks the American landscape as the worst terrorist that we know, while we avert our eyes or bury our cowardly heads in the sand.

Is your college a national leader in sports? Why not make it the number one American school for scholarship and sobriety, two of our nation's healthiest sports?

One of the great characteristics of alcohol is that its prey often escapes its narcotic tentacles if that prey reaches a decent level of maturity before the onset of alcohol use. Statistics should be garnered to show when Americans first drank alcohol; when they became regular drinkers of alcohol and when they became alcoholic. The curse could then be better addressed and might suggest more effective strategies for reducing alcoholism in America. But, that's only if there are enough folks who seriously consider our national binge to be problematic.

A mixed drink for a hazing?
Penn State University, at State College, Pennsylvania, has had several rough years because of the major morals scandal that

hit the press in 2011, as related above. That scandal brought sanctions and fines to the school and its football program and besmirched the reputation of one of collegiate football's most successful coaches. Lawsuits followed. As that pathetic scandal was running its course, a different sort of scandal was on the verge of shaking the campus of Penn State.

Getting the facts can be another challenge

A Penn State electrical engineering student died (2005) when an electrical fire burned through the three-story brick house in which six students lived.

The student's body was found on the top floor. The county coroner refused to release the autopsy report until the local newspaper (*The Centre Daily Times*) filed for the information. The report, once reviewed, indicated that the dead student's blood-alcohol level was .271, more than three times the legal driving limit. Officials said that safety standards had to be strengthened. There was nothing in the newspaper account to suggest that the problem of alcohol on and off campus might be partly to blame. However, whoever created the article must have sensed some of the problem. The article had this headline:

Penn State student who died in fire was drunk, coroner says.

A haze that hasn't cleared!

Hazing is the humiliating abuse of an organization's prospective member. College fraternities are often such hazing organizations. It has been a curse on campuses for decades and has been outlawed in forty-four states. One of the states where hazing is illegal in Pennsylvania. However, in the early summer of 2015, a newspaper (*The Daily Item* of 6/9/15) reported that a different lawsuit was leveled against Penn State and one of its fraternities, plus other parties, by a Virginia student. The student claims, in the suit, that he got no response from university officials when he tried—for months—to report sexual assault, drug use, and hazing. He reported details of his own illegal hazing when he pledged with the Kappa Delta Rho fraternity at Penn State. His claim: He was burned with cigarettes and forced to drink a mixture of urine, vomit, hot sauce, and liquor. As this is being written (June 2015), it is known that the fraternity has been placed under a three-year suspension by Penn State; but that university officials are denying the claims made by the student.

However, several months earlier, in March of 2015, the president of the university, Eric Barron, issued the following, as part of a larger statement:

> "For decades, fraternities and sororities have played an important role at Penn State, providing leadership, community service, and support to their members and to the University. However, *incidents of sexual misconduct, hazing and alcohol abuse here and across the nation are all-too-common and demand immediate attention.* I am determined to conduct a focused examination of fraternity and sorority life in a manner that supports the best of Greek life while promising real and lasting change." (Quoted on the Philadelphia Magazine web site.)

When pondering the preceding quote, please bear in mind that this seemingly tough promise did absolutely nothing to prevent the senseless death of Timothy Piazza, or some other alcohol-related absurdities that rolled over the Penn State campus since that quote was uttered.

That action, promised by the university president in March of 2015, was caused, in part, by the Penn State fraternity (again, Kappa Delta Rho) that posted images of nude and unconscious women on the internet. President Barron also noted that the task force would also seek to learn the extent of the misconduct and alcohol abuse. Please read, again, that single italicized sentence in the middle of the above quote. The university president tells the nation that: "incidents of sexual misconduct, hazing and alcohol abuse here and across the nation are all-too-common and demand immediate action." Surely that shouldn't apply to all colleges, such as Penn State's neighbor to the east, Bucknell University. That school, recognized for scholarly excellence, was also recognized (2015) by the Princeton college ratings as being fourth in the nation for its party atmosphere.

Parental support

Bucknell was also the university that got front-page coverage in the local newspaper (*TDI*, 4/14/13) because it showed the support of one set of adoring parents in their child's college education.

The parents, from suburban Philadelphia, brought seven bottles of liquor to fuel a party in the room of their daughter.

The mother also informed the outside world, via Facebook, that she wished that she "was in college again!" The arrival of the residence hall manager brought a quick end to the party, but the memories thus created would include the supplying of drinks for a quartet of students and joining the students in consuming the alcohol and in the parents' garnering a quartet of misdemeanor counts.

Teaching the dynamics of favoritism
Slippery Rock is a small Pennsylvania university that a news account (*TDI*, 6/8/13) said had a professor who, allegedly, told a group of students that he had had more than a hundred sexual partners and suggested that some female student could become his favorite simply by performing a sex act on him! This led to the professor's being sacked from his job. What was the cause of his gross behavior? The paper reported that "He blamed his behavior on being intoxicated." Talk about clichés . . .

Treated as roadkill!
Putting a student in a frat party without his/her sobriety is like sending a soldier into combat without a helmet and weapon. This truth has been revealed countless times on American campuses and never more tragically than was shown in the Timothy Piazza case.

Timothy Piazza left Lebanon, New Jersey to become a student at Pennsylvania State University in State College. His goal was to gain the schooling needed to enter a career in which he could create prosthetic devices. Tragically, no prosthetic devices could help Timothy Piazza after he experienced the horrific results of an alcohol-fueled night of fraternity hazing.

Timothy Piazza was one of 14 pledges who were hoping to attain the glorious goal of fraternity brother in the Beta Theta Pi fraternity. On a February night in 2017, their antagonists— whose combined I.Q. apparently couldn't produce a single functioning brain—had their pledges consume dizzying amounts of beer, wine, and vodka. Timothy Piazza's estimated blood/alcohol level was pegged at *five times the legal driving limit!* Was it a wonder that Timothy fell down cellar steps . . . and that he fell several more times during the night, including another tumble down the cellar stairs?

When the regular members finally showed concern, they were too late to help! Bless them; they tried. The frat brothers poured alcohol on his near-lifeless body; one tried slapping him into consciousness, and someone covered him. The one remedy they avoided for hours: Summoning medical help. Frat members' callousness earned this condemnation from Timothy's father: "This was men who intended to force feed lethal amounts of alcohol into other young men . . . And what happened throughout the night was just careless disregard for human life. They basically treated our son as roadkill and a rag doll." (T.D.I., 5/16/17)

This event lends itself, much too easily, to the revision of the old English nursery rhyme, "Georgie Porgie."

BETA THETA
Beta, Theta, pudding, and Pi;
Breath befouled by rum and rye.
Haughty airs and time to kill;
Dad's *dinero* foots the bill!

> Far too drunk to weigh the cost . . .
> Fog profound; horizons lost.
> Beta, Theta, pudding, and Pi;
> Haze the lad, then let him die!

Am I the only person with this conviction? HAZING IS RIFE WITH SADISM. Do normal folk enjoy physically and emotionally abusing helpless schoolmates? Is it more than just coincidence, that when hazing laws are broken, laws against minors having liquor are also flouted?

Hank Nuwer is a journalism professor at Indiana's Franklin College. He maintains a well-researched internet site [www.hanknuwer.com] on which he observes: "At least one hazing death a year has occurred on a college campus every year from 1979 to 2017 . . ." Occasional deaths from hazing at American colleges have been occurring since the 19th century, with many of those deaths being associated with alcohol.

In desperation, one must ask: How could this happen in a law-abiding society? *Ah, but we forget what Prohibition taught us: Where alcohol is involved, laws are to be disregarded.* After all, Pennsylvania has a hazing law, [P.S.] § 5352; but it did nothing to protect young Timothy Piazza!

The palatial Beta Theta Pi fraternity house on the campus of Penn State, where members might find a haven from sobriety (Photo courtesy of Eric Graybill).

"Why?"

Why, in Heaven's name, do such tragedies occur? *State hazing laws shouldn't even need to exist!* Every college should have an administration that has formulated clear definitions of hazing and equally *distinct definitions of the prompt consequences* resulting from their violation! There is no excuse for an administration to be reactive in this regard. Do you want a clear case of awaiting the theft of the horse before locking the barn door? Here it is. In late June of 2017, the Penn State administration announced the establishment of an advisory panel to handle fraternity problems! Bullscat!

If a college administration *administered,* campus drinking would be immeasurably curbed and no student would be in danger from hazing.

Flirting with death

As though town authorities don't have enough problems, without having to deal with outside topers hitting the State College, Pennsylvania, area, they had a visiting student (University of Massachusetts) in town in September of 2016. How did town authorities know he was in "Happy Valley"? According to *The Daily Item* (9-29-16), The U. of Mass. student—a 19-year-old male—was found in one of the town's alleys, unconscious and nearly dead. Vodka was the culprit identified by police. Most alarming: his blood-alcohol level was a soaring 0.49 percent. Yes, you calculated it properly. That is six times the state's legal limit for drivers and, *for many drinkers, that blood-alcohol level identifies their last binge!* The obvious question: Who served him all that alcohol for so long after he reached the drunken level? Whoever did, should have been given free state housing for a very long time.

"Rally 'round the froth!"

As news events go in the 21st century, this one was minor; but it illustrated a couple of truths. In late June 2015, Katelynn Burge, a pitcher for Penn State's Altoona campus team was charged with assault for hitting the batter with a pitch during the team's batting practice! Her attorney then made a brilliant observation: It is assumed that one who steps into the batter's box is risking being hit.

On the other hand, the batter was the team member who was believed to have 'snitched' on their coach for violating the school's alcohol policy, although whether a violation occurred or a snitching act occurred was not yet established. Further, there is the allegation that after the batter was struck with the errant pitch, the pitcher informed her, "That was for . . . (the former coach)!"

What truths are suggested here? Frequently, alcohol abuse leads to furtive behavior and, again frequently, alcohol lovers flout the law when their boozing is threatened. Of course, secrecy and outlawry add to the ongoing agony of all who must deal with the imbibers.

Only here for the bier

Finally, in 2013, the leadership at Penn State announced a bold new plan for curbing the annual St. Patrick's Day binge-fest: Bribe the vendors! How novel. Each of 24 area dealers agreed to suspend alcohol sales for the day. In return, each got a check (emerald green?) for $5,000. That's a total bribe of $120,000! It's unfortunate that reasoning with the students, regarding sobriety, was never an option. Nothing dilutes reason better than alcohol. The local-vendor bribing program likely created additional hardship for those students who were then designated to make the booze runs to dealers beyond the Nittany Mountains! Such a dealer-bribing plan sounds as convincing as a morning-after pill for men . . .

The dichotomy

When colleges and universities are not pushing political indoctrination and pervasive intoxication, they are magnificent, contributing members of our communities. Frequently, they offer cultural and economic support that is exceptional. That's why it is important to maintain perspective, despite the negative aspects that one may find to be so annoying. Consider, for example, this singular activity to be found associated with Penn State University, located within the scenic Nittany Mountains at State College, Pennsylvania:

"Thon"

It is a truly laudable event . . .a beautiful act of charity. Several thousand Nittany Lions join in an annual fund-raising marathon dance known as the "Thon." The students plan the event and solicit the many donations that are collected. Then they conduct The weekend-long dance. The 2014 and 2015 events, combined, generated more than $13,000,000! These millions are used to aid young cancer patients. In fact, within the last four decades, the "Thon" has gathered more than one hundred million dollars! That is a sobering stat!

The sobering of Keene, New Hampshire

In June 2015—for the first time since the early 1990s, the town of Keene, New Hampshire failed to host a pumpkin festival. A news item (*The Daily Item*, 6-7-15) informed readers that the town withheld the necessary permit in 2015 because "last year's event turned violent, with alcohol-fueled parties nearby leading to injuries, property damage and more than 100 arrests." The news piece cited did not specifically mention college students as being involved in the mayhem, but the president of Keene State University made a public statement (October 2014) that lay most of the guilt on students; including some from Keene State along with students who journeyed from other colleges to join Keene's "alcohol-fueled" civic activity. The mayhem of Keene, New Hampshire automatically ignites thoughts of the Florida coast and the alcohol-generated behavior of 2015's very intemperate collegiate spring visitors.

We can conclude this chapter by mentioning just one more topic regarding colleges and the abuse of alcohol and by reminding readers that we've barely addressed the pervasive and pathetic phenomenon of nationwide campus intemperance. Again, let's spare the pulpwood forests!

Thanks for the mammaries!

How might one segue into the topic of Florida's shame; the behavior of visitors to that subtropical paradise and vacation mecca? This Pennsylvania news item (*TDI*, 9-10-15) might work. It tells of a 33-year-old woman who repeatedly exposed her 'augmented' breasts in public. She exposed her mammaries at a Northumberland (Pennsylvania) campground until complaints brought police, to whom she repeated her act. To one of her earlier critics, she had this cheeky reply, according to the newspaper account, "What, you don't like looking at $5,000?" The reporter's initial identification of this lass described her as "a drunken Hazelton woman" (0.149 breath test score), who now faces several charges.

The above incident reminds one of the tasteless films that were being sold a few years ago in which young women, *seemingly intoxicated* and on a public beach, would similarly display their 'bosoms' (as the British actor, Terry Thomas, once identified them in a film) for a cameraman. As I recall, one or two of those young women later admitted, *regretfully*, that they had been drunk at the time of the filming.

That "drunken Hazelton woman" seems to be tardy—as well as out of place—in her overly revealing effort for attention. She was too late for the 'boozers gone wild' craze and too far from the beaches of the Sunshine State, where scandal-loving college students mingle each Spring. One realizes that the college students' usual 'animal house' behavior was even wilder than usual in 2015 when we learn that one Florida mecca finally had 'had enough'!

A *Time* article of 2009 related the "Spring Break" story. Their report tells of a coach from Colgate University who took his swimming team to Florida in 1936. Other college groups followed. Over the passage of years, the Spring break phenomenon emerged, with more and more college students visiting Florida for their Spring break. By 1961, a movie was spawned by the Florida bacchanal, entitled "Where the Boys Are." Things have become busier and bolder over the more recent decades. Several Florida beaches have become involved and drinking and drunken behavior have become more popular, with an annual pilgrimage of hundreds of thousands of underprivileged college students finding the mysterious financial resources needed to fly south. Several Florida beaches have become the Meccas for alcoholic madness. Much of the drinking was among students, while some of the abuse came from non-students who drifted into the area to prey on the naïve and the drunken. Crime and arrests became commonplace. During the spring of 2015, however, things got even more out of hand. A film emerged that depicted a daylight gang rape, on the beach and among the milling revelers. That incident and the film it spawned, led to the arrest of several individuals. Local authorities said that that film was just one of several that had emerged. Although it was not the first such sordid film, officials seemed determined to make it the last such document. The talk in one city was in favor of raising the age of admission to clubs and of alcohol being prohibited on the beaches during the main time frame for revelry. If one is disturbed by such alcohol-driven behavior; be patient. Within a few years, those unbridled hell-raisers will be moving into the adult-level of our binging society. May we toast the future?

The behavior of college students has always been a challenge to administrators, as a glance at medieval college life has demonstrated. Drinking problems were common, as were many other forms of socially unacceptable behavior. Among the long list of transgressions of Europe's first college students (Durant, *The Age of Faith*, p. 928, from the multi-volume *The Story of Civilization*) we see that "some students earned excommunication by playing dice on the alters of Notre Dame." How tough would our college administrators have to become to minimize drunkenness within academia?

College administrators remain challenged by today's segment of a college student body (and *one must emphasize that such students are always but a 'segment'*) who violate today's mores and laws. Thus, we find a spokesman for the administration of one highly-regarded school (Bucknell University of Lewisburg, Pennsylvania) making the following admission (*The Daily Item*, 8-4-15): "that high-risk alcohol consumption is a problem, as it is on college campuses across the country."

It was a drunken Bucknell student who, while still below the legal drinking age, had consumed enough alcohol to fuel a late-night scene in the nearby hospital during which he bit and choked a security guard and kicked a nurse in the jaw. If credits were given for absurd behavior, his late-night seminar at Bucknell and the nearby hospital would have put him well on the path to a *cum laude* degree in intemperance.

Cause and effect?

Lawyers will probably argue the issue of cause and effect in the 2014 death of Marquise Braham. The 18-year-old freshman student at Penn State University's Altoona (Pennsylvania) campus jumped to his death from the roof of a Marriott Hotel while home for spring break. His family, in filing suits against the university and the fraternity (Phi Sigma Kappa) to which their son belonged, are claiming that Braham's hazing ordeal was a major factor in his suicide. "There are allegations of hazing, drug abuse, physical abuse and alcohol abuse," according to a statement by Ron Heller, the local police chief (cnn.com/2014/03/20). Heller's statement also noted that "if we link the young man's death to hazing, the individuals could be charged with criminal homicide in Pennsylvania." A New York Daily News account [downloaded 12/17/15] offers details of the extended hazing activities, *which include* Braham's being forced to fight other pledges; of having a gun held to his head; of being deprived of sleep for several days; of having to witness the hazing of future pledges and of being forced to drink "gross amounts of alcohol."

The website, *[http://pennlive.com/midstate/index.ssf/2014/03/altoona_fraternity_denies_hazi.html]*, mentions another fraternity that gets national attention. Sigma Alpha Epsilon has been connected to at least ten deaths in the past decade and, in recent years, has seen more than a dozen chapters of the SAE fraternity closed or suspended. Here, again, one must question the sources of their unlimited financial resources as well as the unwillingness and/or inability of colleges to properly regulate frat behavior *before* the onset of tragedy.

This topic's closing calamity

Lastly, while one can easily forget her name, her case is too recent and too tragic to be so readily forced from memory. Hannah Graham was the student at the University of Virginia who disappeared in September 2014, sometime after having attended her second party of the evening. She had been born in Reading, England in 1996; but never lived long enough to see her 19th birthday. Her ravished and horribly beaten body was found more than a month after her disappearance. Except for the eyes of her killer, the last time that Hannah Graham had been seen was at a restaurant where she was described as seeming to be drunk. How in the Hell could this have happened? Hannah Graham was below the legal drinking age.

The Hannah Graham murder led to many repercussions at the University of Virginia. Just one of those repercussions was the university administration's instituting some changes, such as some self-restricting behavior required of the fraternities, if they didn't want to lose their standing with the university. Although restrictions were meant to protect coeds at UVA, there were some expressions of indignation from both sexes regarding the administration's efforts to alter their behavior.

Two thoughts need to be expressed, regarding frats, vats, and stats. First, recent data from the *National Institutes of Health* suggests that underage boozing is a far greater problem than that which draws observers' attention to the college campuses. Secondly, fraternity and sorority members show a somewhat higher graduation rate than non-Greek college students. While both observations allow a fairer assessment of college life, neither one can obscure the fact that, generally, college students consume an inordinate amount of alcohol which leads to an inordinate amount of academic failure, crime and other types of tragedy.

Sober Slogan #6

Support your local E.R.:

Stay sober!

Sober Slogan #7

1500 college kids quit

drinking last year!

Chapter Three

The Great Temperance Tempest

From time's fermented mists
It has been, and remains, a lingering struggle. Some people are making themselves drunk, while other people are counseling against drunkenness.

Ancient injustice
The human story is replete with injustices. We continue to repeat ourselves as though each generation was the first to recognize the very concept of injustice. One of the most memorable Biblical stories tells of a grave injustice . . . and it involves alcohol.

Noah, according to the Biblical book of Genesis, was selected by God to save specimens of life from the great flood that God was about to create. Noah, the account informs us, executed this order to perfection. The deluge destroyed, but Noah's Ark preserved enough specimens to restore the world's population. Among the few human survivors were Noah, his wife, his three sons and his three daughters-in-law. Then, in the 9th book of Genesis, we are told that Noah got wine from the fruit of his own vineyards. Once drunk, Noah lay naked in his tent. One of his three sons, Ham, entered the tent, saw his drunken and naked father, and retreated from the tent. Hapless Ham then told his brothers of their father's shameless state. The brothers, Shem and Japheth, walked backward into the tent averting their eyes and draping a coverlet over the body of their drunken father. When Noah awakened and learned of the events that had transpired during his stupid stupor, he placed a curse on Ham. This was not just the plain, old, garden-variety curse; but a curse of servitude; a curse of slavery for Ham *and for all of Ham's descendants, forever!* What wrong had his daughter-in-law committed? What wrong had Ham's children and every descendant thereafter committed? What malice was involved in Ham's mistake, if it was, indeed, a mistake? *The real mistake was Noah's damned intemperance!*

Noah's behavior, here, is typical of one accustomed to trying to navigate through a sober world while in a drunken and irresponsible state. The drunkard . . . the sot . . . the toper . . . lacks respect for himself and for everyone else. Then, when his foolish drinking leads to something drastic, the drunkard blames others, including his very own, innocent son, and makes others the victims of his damnable flaw. Noah's drunkenness has led to tensions that have ravaged the Middle East for several millennia. We must constantly ask ourselves: How much less suffering . . . how much more dignity . . . would so many people have known, if Noah had simply remained sober?

Noah was not the only jackass who created immeasurable suffering because of his intemperance. Throughout the several millennia of its history, alcohol has been fingering fools. Thus, the Biblical Book of Proverbs (in the version attributed to King James' initiative) says, (20:1): "Wine is a mocker, strong drink is raging: and whosoever is deceived thereby is not wise." and (23:31-33) "Look not thou upon the wine when it is red, when it giveth his color in the cup, when it moveth itself aright. At the last it biteth like a serpent, and stingeth like an adder. Thine eyes shall behold strange women, and thine heart shall utter perverse things." King Lemuel passed along some impressive Proverbial advice that was given to him by his mother. The maternal advice which he passed along (31:4-5): "It is not for kings, O Lemuel, it is not for kings to drink wine, nor for princes strong drink: lest they drink, and forget the law, and pervert the judgment of any of the afflicted."

The two following verses (31:6-7) seem to permit the use of wine in extreme circumstances. These holy verses tell the reader, "Give strong drink unto him that is ready to perish, and wine unto those that be of heavy hearts. Let him drink, and forget his poverty, and remember his misery no more."

The Bible offers literally hundreds of references to drinking and to wine, although the word 'wine' can be read as simply grape juice or it can be read as grape juice in its fermented and intoxicating state.

Other Biblical accounts, found in the Old Testament and related to alcohol, tell of two daughters using wine to intoxicate and seduce their father (Lot) in order to become pregnant (Genesis 19); tell of a childless woman being instructed to avoid alcohol and unclean food while awaiting pregnancy and the birth of Samson, (Judges: 13); give a warning to those who want to become champion drinkers and drink mixers (Isaiah 5); identify the descendants of Ephraim (Jacob's grandson) as drunkards (Isaiah 28); advise simply that "Whoredom and wine and new wine take away the heart." (Hosea 4); have God cursing the Babylonians, whom God describes with several strongly negative terms, including 'drunkards' (Habakkuk 2); and have God placing a curse on a man who gets his neighbor drunk (again Habakkuk 2).

The New Testament of the Christian Bible is equally cautious about alcohol, beginning with the clear remonstrance of the first chapter of Luke, verse 15, "For he shall be great in the sight of the Lord, and shall drink neither wine nor strong drink . . ." Again, in Luke (21:34), "And take heed of yourselves, lest at any time your hearts may be overcharged with surfeiting, and drunkenness, and cares of this life, and so that day come upon you unawares." The fourteenth chapter of the Book of Romans advises, at verse 21, "It is good neither to eat flesh, nor to drink wine, nor anything whereby thy brother stumbleth, or is offended or is made weak." Lastly, in the tiny letter that Paul wrote to Titus (Titus, Chapter 1), he tells Titus that "For a bishop must be blameless, as a steward of God; not self-willed, not soon angry, not given to wine, no striker, not given to filthy lucre; but a lover of hospitality, a lover of good men, sober, just, holy, temperate . . ." Imagine this troubled universe, if Paul's advice had been universally heeded and if, therefore, we had a society of people who were sober, just, holy and temperate!

Europe's Medieval Period (c. 1000-1500 AD) found wine, cider, beer and ale to be the favored beverages. All had their distinctive potions and portions, but all were alcohol.

Origins known or hypothesized?

LeeAundra Keany tells us (*Discover* magazine, December 2011, p. 80) that "According to the *Drunken Monkey Hypothesis,* our zest for alcoholic beverages derives from our distant [simian] ancestors' impulse to seek the ripest, most energy-intensive fruits." Don't try to blame the apes! It might also be hypothesized that early humans were simply yielding to a natural sensuality. Certainly, when scorching heat caused thirst, relief of that thirst with a fermented liquid, or a juicy, pulpy fruit, would have been the most quenching sensation. In other words, it could be suggested that the search for a quenching sensation led to the use of naturally 'bubbly' quenchers. That's why we should thank the early scientist/clergyman, Dr. Joseph Priestley (1733-1804). He was the genius who among other accomplishments, discovered oxygen and invented *carbonated water.*

It was because of Dr. Priestley's discovery that we can totally avoid alcohol today and get that same *quenching* sensation from the vast variety of carbonated, non-alcoholic drinks that have been such a blessing to our society. In any case, a couple of questions linger. One, if we subscribe to the *Drunken Monkey Hypothesis,* why do one-third of adult Americans show no urge to use alcohol? Since the life expectancy was likely in the thirties when this so-called human urge developed, why aren't our teens and toddlers clamoring for booze? Does it not seem likely, as well, that if the folks who manufacture ethanol products didn't spend *billions* on promotion, many, many more people would not succumb to the lure of alcohol? It seems quite likely that we have a product to sell and find a drunken theory to spur sales.

Let's dwell on the 13th-century thirst of King John of England. John was the youngest son of Henry II. Having, initially, been given no slice of the realm, John became known as John Lackland. However, when his only surviving brother, Richard I, "The Lion Hearted" (1157-99), died childless, John quietly acceded to the throne of England. He proceeded to antagonize the pope and the English nobles as well as the rebels who resided in Sherwood Forest. Having been forced by the nobles to sign a statement of rights (the *Magna Carta*) in 1215, he was to become one permanently reviled ruler. That led to his being the only King John in England's long history of monarchy; a monarchy that saw—among others—eight Henrys, four Williams, a couple of Elizabeths and a sextet of Georges.

Try to imagine a sultry summer day in 1216. King John tried to slake his royal thirst by overindulging in ripe peaches and new cider. He was sickened and, within days, died. One could readily suggest that it was such a thirst, and his effort to find a sensual, satisfying relief in succulent peaches and draughts (swallows) of peach cider that led to the death of King John. Today, fortunately for those who don't succumb to the highly-glamorized lure of alcohol, carbonated drinks give a similarly satisfying experience to those who thirst; but *without* the dangerous intoxication factor.

One might also conclude: *If carbonated drinks had been discovered before alcohol, we'd not be cursed with today's damnable, sotted society.*

Richard Turner, a workingman of Preston, England, apparently gave us (1834) the word, *teetotal.* Turner, in a speech in which he was advocating the *total abstinence* from intoxicating drinks, coined the word that has come to mean just that. Although *teetotal* is a nearly-obsolete word, we teetotalers should push for the word's revival in the face of the 21st century's *national binge in America.* Perhaps, in its stead, we might begin emphasizing another pithy term: *nondrinker.*

Let us, early in this polemic, concede that wine is less potent than whiskey and beer. Let's also concede that, from an olfactory point of view, wine has a pleasant bouquet, while whiskey and beer compete for the title of most putrid alcoholic drink. Given its foul aroma, one can easily imagine an imported ale, from some Latin American nation, that is bottled under the label of *Orino Antiguo* ("Stale Piss").

Advice from a colonial sage: William Penn

How many people could have a king owe them a large sum of money? One who did was William Penn, a Quaker leader from England. Penn canceled the debt of King Charles II in exchange for a colonial grant of land in North America that eventually became the state of Pennsylvania. Two of Penn's quotes need to appear here. He wrote ("Some Fruits of Solitude") that "Strong Liquors are good at some Times and in small Proportions . . ." Another appropriate quote from the same source: "All Excess is ill: But *Drunkenness* is of the worst Sort."

Common sense from our mother country

As early as the 1770's, while Americans were more interested in freedom from George III of England, one Englishman, George Crabbe (1754-1832) was rhyming his yearning for freedom from drunkenness. One of his poems ("Inebriety," 1775) held the following lines:

Pennsylvania's founder, from the author's
archives.

Lo! the poor toper, whose untutored sense
Sees bliss in ale, and can with wine dispense;
Whose head proud fancy never taught to steer,
Beyond the muddy ecstasies of beer.

Let's add *George Crabbe* to any list of sobriety's heroes.

My guess is that some nameless Egyptian charioteer—over 5,000 years ago, was the world's first DUI! Further, not knowing an exact beginning for any temperance movement, I'd suppose that the temperance movement likely began when the world's first drunkard embarrassed, or hurt, or killed or abused another person.

Temperance's first American titan

There were several early Americans who were looking at the abuse of alcohol with a rather critical eye. I would suggest that the early hero of the temperance movement in America was Dr. Benjamin Rush (1745-1813). Rush was America's first temperance writer and a celebrated medical man who regularly advised against using intoxicating drinks.

An old sketch of colonial America's most
noted physician, Dr. Benjamin Rush.

Dr. Rush's rather fanciful temperance thermometer (shown below) was likely more cute than correct, but it used terms that were familiar to folks of the time and showed a strong bias against intemperance. According to the following illustration, the good doctor didn't consider beer to be a problem; but his chart suggested suicide, death or the gallows may be the fate of the truly intemperate. Dr. Rush, a Philadelphia-area native, brought luster to the city with his medical and his civic leadership. He was one of the signers of the Declaration of Independence and, during the deadly yellow-fever epidemic of 1793 he, alone, was considered to have treated the disease effectively, thus personally saving thousands of lives. Dr. Rush also advocated free public schools and opposed slavery. Before his death in 1813, he had also proposed the first dispensary in the country and wrote extensively on medical and political subjects, including a lengthy paper in support of two houses of Congress (a *Council of the States* and an *Assembly of the States*). His one writing had this sentiment: "Every man in a republic is public property. His time and talents, his youth, his manhood, his old age; nay more, his life, his all, belong to his country." (Quoted in *Harper's Encyclopaedia of United States*

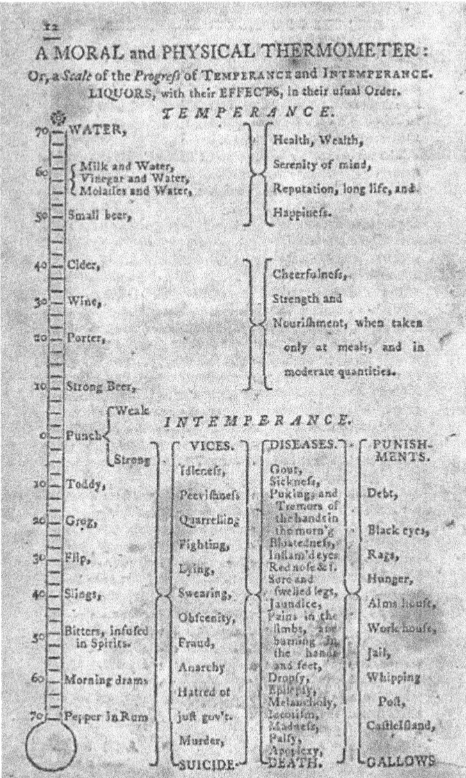

Dr. Benjamin Rush's creation of a temperance thermometer.

History, 1905, Volume 7, page 505) This individual was also the author of an 1874 writing, *"An Inquiry into the Effects of Ardent Spirits Upon the Human Body and Mind."* This is among the earliest temperance writings. Is it any wonder that John Adams said that Dr. Benjamin Rush was one of our top three founding fathers (along with Benjamin Franklin and George Washington)? This resume surely qualified Dr. Rush to be heard when he urged the nation toward temperance.

A temperance achiever named Cheever?

Before the death of Dr. Rush, a worthy successor was born in Hallowell, Maine. The Reverend Dr. George B. Cheever (1807-1890) was the son of a publisher/bookseller of Hallowell. The Cheevers were of Huguenot stock, having come to Salem, Massachusetts during the 17th century, by way of Canterbury, England. Dr.

Cheever was described as a 'controversialist' or one who skillfully gets embroiled in controversy. This would be a complimentary epithet for one who was tackling several of America's most pressing reforms.

After graduating from Bowdoin College and, later, from Andover Seminary, Cheever preached and wrote, becoming involved in controversies related to his favoring of the death penalty, his opposition to expanded church ritual, his support of Bible-reading in public schools, his opposition to certain secular activities on Sundays and his vehement opposition to slavery. From Cheever's pen flowed the stuff of many tracts, speeches, and twenty-three books. *Among his first controversies, and one which lasted throughout his lifetime, was his active work against intemperance.* His earliest, tempestuous writings included a fictional, but a thinly-veiled portrait of a local distillery owner, who was also a Bible-selling church deacon. That work, "*The True History of Deacon Giles' Distillery,*" was published in the *Salem Landmark.* It might be a forerunner of T.S. Arthur's later book-length story, *Ten Nights in A Bar-Room.* Whatever it was, Rev. Cheever's "*True History*" led to his being attacked by a distillery worker and to the offending printing press being destroyed by a mob. It also brought court action that cost Cheever a month's confinement and a fine of $1,000. That response was but a hint of the reaction one would witness if anyone should ever really try to outlaw alcohol.

Seeking utopia?

In 1870, Reverend W. B. Christopher and a couple of other gentlemen visited the Kansas frontier, searching for a site for a utopian temperance community. The founders anticipated a nucleus of 100 like-minded families. The town would be named Cheever, in honor of the above-mentioned Rev. Dr. George B. Cheever. Apparently, the temperance haven never developed, since there is no evidence of such a town having been established. There is, however, in Dickinson County, Kansas, the township of Cheever, as a wind-swept remnant of that idealistic endeavor. Rev. Dr. George B. Cheever was just one of the thousands of American men who put their manhood on the line to create a sober nation.

As the nation expanded westward, alcohol was a common companion of the pioneer men who were leading the expansion. As camps formed, saloons appeared. Boom towns were also booze towns. The thirsty cowboy or miner didn't wait for fancy surroundings to appear. He was quite willing to buy his booze in a tent or a shack. The prospectors came to mine the hills and the barkeeps came to mine the miners. A simple economic observation would be that the person who served the miners found more wealth than most of the miners ever found. All that an entrepreneur needed was a rude shelter, a supply of rotgut, an improvised bar and a spittoon. The spittoons, hardly easy targets for tobacco chewers when sober, must have been about the most disgustingly unsanitary objects in the entire west unless it would have been the open-trough urinals (see Chapter 8).

From the 1840s onward, saloons had a fast-growing presence in the American West. The old photographs of western (as well as eastern) barrooms show virtually no women being present. Aside from the prostitutes, 19th-century women rarely, rarely (did we mention *rarely*?) visited saloons. This aided the ongoing tradition: The manlier the drinker, the stronger his drink. Also, the alcohol was always served warm, until the 1880's, when the enterprising Adolphus Busch introduced refrigeration to the business.

Those old photographs also show saloon patrons playing a game called "Faro." "Faro" is a gamblers' game, with players betting on the anticipated appearance of certain cards. This was a favorite game on the frontier. Why is it no longer popular? Likely, it's because the odds favoring *the house* weren't long enough. It's far better to have the fool-proof slots of the present, where the take of the house is assured and the speed in which the house winnings are drawn from the patron is accelerated.

Saloons needed just a few dozen male clients to thrive. An actual example (Weiser, p. 6): Livingston, Montana, in 1883, had about 3,000 town folk (men, women, and children) and 33 saloons! Weiser (p. 11) also observes that "the saloon was an inevitable powder keg." How little some things change with time! As discussed elsewhere, even in the present day, many reported crimes occur within or near taverns.

The state of Maine, which was among the first to have a girls' school (in the town of Bath, in 1808), was also the very first to have the statewide prohibition of liquor (1846). It then passed a stiffer statute in 1851. Whether others envied the Pine Tree state its dryness or abhorred it, or feared its spread to other states, it got people's attention. An old diary entry from California (1853) shows that the dryness of the Down Easterners was being discussed a continent away. A laundress named Chastina Rix left this entry (month unknown), reproduced in Time/Life Books, *The Old West*, unnumbered volume, "The Women," p. 130.):

> "Friday 26. Ironing again. In all this week I have ironed sixty shirts, 35 starched ones and 25 plain besides hosts of other clothes & I have made twelve dollars by my labor. Went to a temperance discussion this evening at Mr. Brigg ['s] church. They are discussing the Maine law here. This requires considerable courage with their hundreds of rum selling places open in their faces. The rum seller was on the ground to defennd [sic.] his side."

Maine's spearheading of the dryness movement was followed by Kansas (1881) and North Dakota in 1889. The influence of those early 'dry' states led to hopeful speculation elsewhere.

Bless America

The American nation has always had robust boozing. For a specific alcohol-related incident, we might look at the one that occurred when General Andrew Jackson was inaugurated president in 1829. For the first time, the White House was opened to the public. Crowds swarmed into the hallowed building! The historian, Thomas A. Bailey (THE AMERICAN PAGEANT, page 256), described the scene thusly: "A milling crowd . . . surged in, wrecking the china and furniture, and threatening the 'people's champion' with cracked ribs. Jackson was hastily spirited through a side door, and the White House miraculously emptied itself when the word was passed that huge bowls of punch had been placed on the lawns." The punch was laced with whiskey.

As with hunting, trapping and many other Colonial activities, alcohol was a common part of early American life. Pathetic though it is, boozing was an integral part of our westward expansion.

How the West was pilfered

A pleasant turn-a-round has occurred in the study of how the United States gained full control of the American West during the latter half of the 19th century. Most now admit that the Native Americans were hustled and cheated by the American government; its agents and its military. Fairness was not going to interfere with our westward expansion, but alcohol would play a major role.

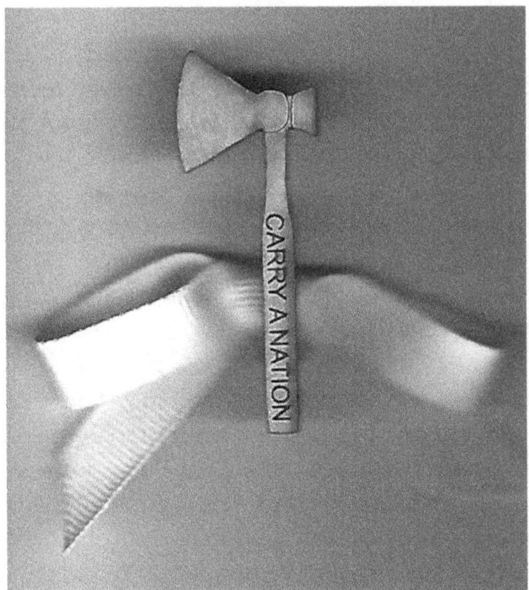

A symbol of opposition to the uncontrolled use of alcohol. See below.

In the year 2016, Peter Cozzens' book, *The Earth Is Weeping*, presented a very powerful accounting of America's 19th-century takeover of the Western lands still held by Native Americans. The account offered here is nothing more than a distillation of facts that suggests the unique role of alcohol in assisting the U.S. Army and the duplicitous government officials during our theft of Native American lives and land.

"While the men labored, Captain Kinney settled into a long drunk, leaving to the wolves the bodies of soldiers killed beyond the gates." (p. 35)

"All but the most righteous soldiers sooner or later succumbed to one or more of the three moral scourges of the military frontier: Drinking, whoring, and gambling." (p. 57)

"It came in early August, when a Dog Soldier war party, beaten in a skirmish with the Pawnees and liquored up on whiskey bought from ranchers on the Solomon River, ran into a posse, which opened fire on them." (87)

"There were sporadic Indian clashes during the autumn of 1869, but none rose to the level of open warfare, and a general peace appeared within reach. That is until an inebriated major in the Montana Territory violently upset the Grant administration's careful calculations." (115)

"Liquor was the agent of ruin. The Cheyennes and the Arapahos fell easy prey to Kansas bootleggers, who divested them of a fortune in buffalo robes and ponies in exchange for rotgut whiskey." (157)

"Neither commander was such as to inspire confidence. Baker was still a hopeless drunk. Colonel Stanley had compiled an estimable record during the Civil War, but the postwar years had been hard on the forty-three-year-old Ohioan, and he too turned to the bottle until, by the date of the expedition, he teetered on the brink of alcoholism. Prolonged stress, in particular, caused him to binge drink." (198)

"A reliable interpreter and licensed trader who lived on good terms with the Chiricahuas for two decades said they distrusted and feared Geronimo, especially when he was inebriated. Once while hopelessly drunk, he berated a nephew, 'for no reason at all,' so severely that the young man committed suicide." (380)

"That afternoon, [the Chihenne chief] Loco's captors chanced upon three freight wagons laden with nine hundred gallons of liquor. While they drank, Loco slipped his eldest wife and twenty-five other relatives out of camp . . ." (385)

"A showdown was inevitable. On the morning of May 15, 1885, Chihuahua, Mangas, Loco, Nana, Naiche, and Geronimo all staggered into Davis's tent. They had been on an all-night *tiswin* drunk. Chihuahua was still inebriated . . ." (396)

"Geronimo and Naiche returned to their stronghold and guzzled five gallons of Tribolet's rotgut whiskey. Naiche shot his wife in the knee when she flirted with a man; he then passed out, while drunken warriors fired a few harmless shots at the mule packers' camp." (404)

"Geronimo's divine protection ran out on a cold day in February 1909, when he rode into Lawton, Oklahoma, alone to sell some bows and arrows. With the proceeds, the old shaman bought whiskey, for which he had never lost his fondness, and began the return ride after dark deeply intoxicated. He was almost home when he fell off his horse beside a creek. A neighbor found him the next morning, lying partially submerged in the freezing water. Four days later, at age seventy-nine, the man whom no bullet could ever kill died in bed of pneumonia." (415)

The remaining quotes are plucked from Cozzen's account of General George Armstrong Custer's final engagement.

"Major Reno needed a bracer. As his men paused to water their horses in a shallow ford at the confluence of Trail Creek and the Little Bighorn at 3:00 p.m., he took a long draft from his whiskey flask. At that instant, a lieutenant splashed past him. "What are you trying to do?" snapped Reno. "Drown me before I am killed?" (253)

"Shock and liquor conspired to render [Major] Reno incoherent. First, he told the men to dismount. Then he ordered them to mount. And then he simply yelled, 'Any of you men who wish to make your escape, follow me,' and bolted.

"The major's panic infected the ranks." (257)

"Reno, it was clear, was of no use to anyone. According to many officers and men, after Benteen arrived, the intoxicated major returned to his principal worry—whiskey. "Look here," he allegedly boasted to the commanding officer of the pack train when it reached Reno Hill at 5:20 p.m. (about the time Custer died), I have got half a bottle yet." (266)

IN ANTICIPATION
How arduous the task,
And treacherous each shoal.
How daunting is the path;
But ahh, how grand the goal!

"Temperance" is, today, a nearly obsolete word. Still, it was likely a word familiar to almost all 19th-century Americans, whether they were opposed to the expansion of temperance across the land, or whether they were filled with joy and anticipation, hopeful that the temperance campaign was grinding, if slowly, toward a wondrous goal: *a sober nation.* "Temperance" is another term that was destined to face near-obsolescence with the collapse of 20th century Prohibition. The saga of America's temperance movement is a beautiful and inspiring one, from the moment it began until its tragic and failed conclusion.

The temperance movement, as a separate historical development, likely began in Europe where, in late 1600, the landgrave (prince) of the German state of Hesse started an *order of temperance.* In America, the movement developed in the early 19th century. Allentown, New Jersey (1805) is recorded as being the first location of an American temperance organization; but a few others sprouted within a decade or so. By mid-century, there were state societies as well as local ones. By 1833, twenty-two states were represented at the first national temperance convention in Philadelphia. In 1840, six individuals, all former drinkers, pledged *total abstinence.* By the first anniversary of their pledge, says a source (*Harper's Encyclopaedia of United States History*, 1905, pp. 39-40), they had a parade of one thousand former drunkards.

The temperance movement in the United States was bolstered by a parallel cause: The vote for women. As growing numbers of women rallied to the cause of suffrage for the American female, those same women often championed the cause of temperance. Obviously, those men who didn't want their liquor supply disrupted, also worked hard to keep women from voting. The champion of the women's dual crusade was Frances Willard. Ms. Willard had the skills needed to win women to two noble causes. Several women's organizations formed; but the most successful one was that which was headed by Ms. Willard, *The Women's Christian Temperance Union.* It became the most potent women's organization in the country. Frances Willard is recognized as a brilliant organizer who soon had a huge national organization, as well as state and local groups, making the W.C.T.U. a truly potent political force. Today, having been dealt the same killing blow as all things temperance-oriented, the W.C.T.U. barely exists. When the *Women's Christian Temperance Union* was at its peak, it had state and local chapters. Although the organization remains well-enough organized to remain viable and to hold regional conventions, its national membership has now dipped below the 1,000 mark.

While the W.C.T.U. was primarily a Protestant organization, there was a smaller; but equally dedicated, Roman Catholic counterpart: *The Catholic Total Abstinence Union. The Catholic Total Abstinence Union* was indebted to an Irish cleric and teetotaler, Father Theobald Mathew (1790-1856). Father Mathew was born in Ireland's County Tipperary and joined the Capuchin order. He worked for temperance in Ireland and won millions of Irish men and women to the cause. He also made a pair of visits to America. The result of the effort of Father Mathew was the formation of America's second largest women's temperance organization, the *Catholic Total Abstinence Union of America* (1782).

As an aside, let's look at the feminine quartet that Inez Haynes Irwin (*Angels and Amazons*, p. 91) identifies as "the four giants of the early suffrage movement" and see which ones, if any, were also speaking in favor of the temperance cause. As follows:

Elizabeth Cady Stanton ~ Ms. Irwin writes (p. 80), "Before her marriage she was absorbed in that temperance cause which in those days served as an introduction to general radicalism."

Lucretia Mott ~ (Irwin, p. 81) "And in her exalted, light-shot sermons, she was fighting a half a dozen social evils, including the low wages of the period, the monopolies, and the perpetual evil of indiscriminate drinking."

Lucy Stone ~ Ms. Irwin (pages 72,73) does not say anything specific about Lucy Stone and temperance, other than to say that she was embroiled in a procedural tussle at a Friends of Temperance assembly in New York City in 1853.

Susan B. Anthony ~ "She was agitating and speaking for temperance and against slavery." says Inez Haynes Irwin (p.90).

The result is impressive. Of the four historical figures for one cause, the vote for women, *each was, at one time or another, involved in temperance work!*

The Sons of Temperance

Sobriety-minded men also were uniting in several organizations. An early one was the Sons of Temperance. This organization was founded in New York City in 1842. One must question the reasoning behind this organization's strange rules and rituals. Membership in the Sons of Temperance organization was very restricted and was initially limited to males who, along with their pursuit of the total elimination of alcohol from society, had to deal with passwords, hand grips, signs and secret rituals. While such nonsense still fascinates some, it has no place in any organization whatever in a democratic society. Although they eventually admitted women, their numbers remained limited and they never had a chance to attain the size or influence of the more dynamic and democratic Anti-Saloon League.

The Anti-Saloon League

The Anti-Saloon League became the largest temperance group in the United States. Founded in 1893 by Reverend Howard H. Russell, it was very successful in achieving political victories. As with the W.C.T.U., and the Catholic Total Abstinence Union of America, the Anti-Saloon League was church oriented. It was headquartered in Westerville, Ohio, where it established the world's largest collection of anti-alcohol literature! It pushed for local dry laws and was part of the successful drive for the 18th Amendment that created Prohibition.

Another weapon in the war against alcohol was the *temperance pledge.* This pledge was promoted in churches. One, from a 19th century Bible, was colorful and clear (see page 60).

This impressive panoramic shot shows the Anti-Saloon League conventioneers in Columbus, Ohio and is dated at November 10-13, 1913. This image is found on the internet at Library of Congress images. A note informs: "No known restrictions of publication."

A scene from within the Westerville, Ohio temperance library, where a historic photograph shows an early curator and the fine collection of books related to the then-noble temperance struggle. Courtesy of the Westerville Public Library, just outside Columbus.

The propaganda war flourished in the late 19th century, with both sides pushing for the acceptance of their views. Among my grandmother's papers, I noticed a printed booklet that sold for ten cents a copy. It has my grandmother's maiden name handwritten on the back cover: Lizzie Medora Shambach. The title of the 4" x 6 ½" booklet: *Fenno's Dime Speaker, No. 5*. Its 29 selections include small essays and poems (including one *by* Joaquin Miller and one *about* Wendell Phillips). Naturally, the brief selection that caught my attention was the one entitled "A Solemn Warning."

This tale is credited to the memoir of "George N. Briggs, late ex-governor of Massachusetts." The memoir tells of "a certain town meeting in Pennsylvania," where the issue of local alcohol sales was being discussed. One woman took the floor and told of her husband and four sons, all of whom were drunkards and who are now buried in the graveyard. She also warns the gathering of the folly of thinking that moderate drinking of alcohol is healthy, so long as one avoids excessive drinking. Her pathetic example,

A 19th-century temperance pledge, from an old Bible. She or he who pledged was declaring: "We the undersigned solemnly promise by the help of God to abstain from the use of all intoxicating drinks as a beverage." This old Bible shows no evidence of signers.

of course, wins the day and the question of licensing a dealer gets a resounding and unanimous "No!" Thus, we read the expected conclusion of a story found in an 1895 booklet. If only it was that easy . . .

Among the earlier temperance cartoons, this one is a lithograph dating from 1846 and created by Nathaniel Currier. It carries the title "The Drunkard's Progress."

A fisher of men?

Irving Fisher was a Yale University professor of economics, who told of his own move toward temperance, in his 1926 book, *Prohibition at Its Worst*. Fisher recalled (page 1) advice received before his 1899 departure, for health reasons, to Colorado. The advice: Don't "let the Colorado doctors give me whisky; for at that time alcohol was still regarded by many physicians as a valuable medicine for many diseases." He indicates that his effort to avoid alcohol was borne of a belief that "total abstinence" rather than "temperance" is the truer ideal. That is why, Fisher asserts, "I soon became, for the sake of my own health, a teetotaler except for the occasional sips of wine at my friends' tables."

The American nation was fast turning into a two-camp country. The one camp was composed of the folks who wanted alcohol to remain readily available ~ the *wets*; and their opposite number, the *drys*. The drys would—by the late 1800's grow steadily in number, stirred in part by a woman who was newly arrived in Kansas with three weapons; her voice, her Bible, and her hatchet.

A late 19th-century booklet, filled with pithy morality and temperance advice.

Carrie Nation was one of the rare *lawbreakers* on the side of sobriety. The American struggle against alcohol was quite proper and—recognizing its hellish impact on today's mental and physical health of Americans—was a worthy crusade. However, while the teetotalers were trying to win the struggle by using all legal means to wage their battle, the booze lovers were eagerly employing any means—including the open violation of many laws—to more effectively wage their successful war on sobriety. As mentioned elsewhere, Carrie Nation (see below) was just about the only effective lawbreaker on the side that broke laws for the benefit of *sobriety.*

Making an observation on the men's clubs that seemed to be organized as a place to get alcohol, the legendary comedian, Will

Rogers (1879-1935) told of an old man from Oklahoma who explained, "I am neither an Elk nor an Eagle nor a Shriner. I'm just goin' to remain an ordinary drunkard." [O'Brien, p. 282]

Once again with the blinders

Do we realize how much more dynamic drunkenness has become in the past two centuries? Most of us comprehend the huge impact that technology has had on virtually every aspect of human society. Which of the following fields of human activity hasn't been overwhelmed by the forces of technology: education, medicine, transportation, agriculture and—especially—communication? Human activity as it involves the consumption of alcohol has seen great change: *Drunkenness was once far more personal and with little impact on others, as compared to the present. Public drunkenness was once, of itself, a criminal act; but as it became less criminalized, it was also becoming more dangerous to those interacting with the drunken individuals!*

Consider the scene in colonial times. An individual appears drunk in public: In accordance with contemporary law, the individual may receive a sentence of imprisonment. Today, an individual appears drunk in public and the impact could include drunken attacks on other individuals and on the highways, with far more innocent fellow-citizens being victimized. Yet, today, the stigma of alcoholic damage to fellow citizens barely rates a yawn. This includes considerable backsliding on the part of those citizens whose very professions are supposed to protect us from such illegal danger.

A growing number of 19th century Americans was determined to turn their young nation away from alcohol and drunkenness. Was it merely fanciful thinking? Not really. After all, there was the much-vaunted democratic process. Several states had voted themselves 'dry', if only temporarily. If the prohibitionists simply honed their message and expanded their numbers, enough states would be reached to pass a constitutional amendment. The reviled intoxicants would be outlawed and sobriety would saturate the nation, just as alcohol and drunkenness had saturated the land before. The opportunity to make such a sweeping change to our society was one of the blessed benefits of the democratic process.

The term, temperance, is an old term, synonymous with moderation. As it is applied to the temperate use of intoxicating drinks, the term dates—at least—to the 16th century. Medieval scholars, borrowing from the ancients, recognized four principal or cardinal virtues: courage, justice, prudence, and temperance. The term, *temperance*, seems to have lost its value in our own intemperate times. The revival and widespread use of the term should be welcomed in all fields; but, especially in the temperate use of alcohol.

America, in the latter half of the 19th century, would have been a great place to live if you wanted to be a crusader. You might join a crusade to get equal rights for Black-Americans or for women or for both, or to improve working conditions and pay rates for workers, or for civil service reforms, or for the prohibition of alcohol. All were worthy causes, but there were likely too many at one time to allow each the full measure of success.

Temperance societies begin to thrive

There was an old phrase, 'a tempest in a teapot'. However, thanks to the dedication of the tens of thousands of folks devoted to combating the negative aspects of alcohol, the 19th century saw such a tempest with the growth and activity of the prohibitionists. Their crusade involved their various temperance organizations, mentioned above plus another couple of score of similar organizations. Their bulging membership was becoming an impressive voting bloc. The 'wets' had reason for concern.

To the ballot box

What do the following names have in common?

St. John, Bidwell, Woolley, Swallow, Chafin, and Dodge?

Unfamiliar? Likely. But, they were all names of candidates for president of the United States. Those gents and a sprinkling of others were supported for the office of President of the United States by the National Prohibition Party.

The National Prohibition Party formed in 1869. They faced the obstacles faced by most third parties. They had such a limited menu ~ one main dish ~ that they could hardly hope to make much of a dent in either of the two major parties. Also, if their platform had any appeal and began to take votes from either the Democrats or the Republicans, whichever major party was most affected would begin offering the same programs to their loyal voters and leave the third party as hobbled as before. Still, the Prohibition Party was noticed in the early national elections. They got involved in the national presidential elections, beginning with the candidacy of James Black of Pennsylvania, who ran for president in 1872 and got just 5,608 votes of about 6,000,000 votes cast. The full table of vote tallies for the Prohibitionist Party candidates for president shows that the Prohibition Party ran candidates and participated in every presidential election from 1872 to the present (2016), This activity ensures them the distinction of being the most active third party in the nation's history; but the Prohibition Party never threatened the two major parties' efforts to have one of their members elected president. While the two major party candidates had national presidential vote totals in the millions, the Prohibition Party never tallied even 300,000 votes. Since the end of Prohibition, with the 1936 election and since, the Prohibition Party has struggled to get even 1,000 or more votes nationwide! Their heyday, as a political force, was during the two decades just prior to the adoption of the 18th Amendment and the start of Prohibition. In their day, they were an influential force, with some impact on the national mood that accepted Prohibition, at least on paper.

"Lemonade Lucy"

Although the Prohibition Party never got any of its candidates into national office, their members might take solace from the fact that no other third party, since 1860, has been able to get its candidate elected to the Oval Office. There was a period when the Prohibitionists might have felt as though they had elected one of their own. That would have been during the tenure of President Rutherford B. Hayes. Hayes, a lawyer, decorated Union general and three-term governor of Ohio, was married to Lucy Webb Hayes, a graduate of Wesleyan Female College. Both the President and Mrs. Hayes were *temperance advocates*. Lucy was a gracious hostess, but one who removed alcohol from the White House social functions. President Hayes wife and first lady would eventually acquire the nickname which she likely carried proudly, "Lemonade Lucy." To have a temperance advocate as president was difficult for many politicians of the time to accept. To have an authentic reformer, and non-politician, as president would, likewise, be difficult to accept. Rutherford B. Hayes was both! Luckily, for him, he had made a clear declaration early in his first term that he would not accept the nomination for a second term. Thus, he could retire gracefully and with solid accomplishments on his record. Sadly, he would not likely have been nominated for a second term by the politicians who didn't appreciate his reforms or his temperance. From the temperance worker's point-of-view, Lucy Hayes should be considered one of America's authentic heroines.

A dry report on wet America in 1898

One can gain another peek into the world of 19th century America by examining a dull government book issued in 1898. That book is the *Twelfth Annual Report of the Commissioner of Labor. 1897.* Its subtitle: *Economic Aspects of the Liquor Problem.*

While the book is loaded with state-related statistics and their alcohol laws, the national stats are worth reading. The *number of gallons produced* by those working in the alcohol industry at both ends of the period tallied reveal much:

	Distilleries	Breweries	Wineries
1880	91,000,000	13,000,000	23,000,000
1896	90,000,000	36,000,000	16,000,000

It appears that by 1896, the most growth was in the making of malt liquor; a beer or an ale.

Drunken employees

From ancient times to the present moment, employers have been plagued by employee drunkenness. Employers have had to face problems from substandard job performance to costly mistakes. Some employer efforts were identified in the 1896 U.S. Labor Commission report cited in the previous topic. Those efforts included: moral suasion [Today's rehabilitation efforts?], discharge, changing the payday, giving verbal warnings, having fewer paydays, forbidding liquor in the workplace, trying to influence the location of saloons, etc.

Obviously, if a list of efforts could grow until there were that many attempted solutions, the employers must have studied the problem. One example of an employer studying the problem was found in the coal handling business in Chicago (1896 U.S. Labor Commission report, p. 78). In that instance, the employer even checked locations *where the workers chose to cash their paychecks*. They tallied, by national groups, and converted the tallies into percentages, with the following results:

Percentage of paychecks cashed at:

	Grocery outlets	Saloons	Savings banks
Hungarians and Poles	23	77	0
Germans	30	70	0
English and Americans	30	61	9
Scotch and Irish	26	74	0
Swedes and Norwegians	91	9	0

Only the Scandinavian sobriety skewed the statistics away from a nearly unanimous exodus to the saloon, check in hand; but exiting with whatever cash escaped the bartender's grasp.

Putting the Burden Where It Belongs. An 1883 cartoon that suggests that alcohol costs should be borne by the dealers. *Harper's Weekly*, 1883 (From *The American Pageant*, 1956)

The Arthurian legend

Timothy Shay Arthur was a child of the Empire State. He was born in 1809 in the town of Newburgh, along the Hudson River north of New York City. He wrote more than 20 books; including *Orange Blossoms* (1871) a work that promoted marriage. However, his primary role in American History is based on the great success of his temperance novel, *Ten Nights in a Barroom and What I Saw There* (1854). Another of his temperance novels, *Three Years in A Man-Trap* (1872) argued that laws protect citizens from bad meat, so it would be logical to have laws protecting people from harmful drinks. He closes that lengthy novel with these lines:

Timothy Shay Arthur's 19th-century best-seller.

> "And so you have the story of a three years' effort to get rich and "live like a gentleman" by means of liquor-selling. It didn't pay in my case. It doesn't pay in any case. The loss is always more than the gain.

> "Many get rich, if you did not," I heard one say.

> To which I answer in the words of a Book I read oftener when a child than since: "What shall it profit a man if he gain the whole world and lose his own soul?"

> "Oh, that's cant [hypocritical]!" is returned with a sneer. "A liquor-seller turned preacher!"

> Is it? Well, have it so! But I leave you the thought, and it may be wise to give it consideration.

The Medicine Lodge battleax

The broadax was a deadly medieval weapon that came to carry the name, *battleax* or *battleax*. Somehow, in the United States, that name came to be applied to formidable and aggressive women.

Unfortunately, Carrie Nation, a staunch Prohibitionist, had several images for which that sobriquet might seem appropriate. However, as with written descriptions of the lady from Medicine Lodge, Kansas, varying images of Carrie Nation can be found and, more than likely, the ones we encounter are most often of the battleax variety. That is the same way that some media outlets want readers to view the mid-western crusader for sobriety. The picture one commonly sees of the woman shows an imperious demeanor on the face of a scowling woman who carries a Bible in one hand and a *hatchet* in the other. And this was the woman who would become a nationally-prominent leader of the anti-alcohol crusade in the last years of the 19th century!

Another T. S. Arthur book. Quoted on previous page.

Carrie Moore (November 25, 1846 – June 9, 1911) was a native of Kentucky. In many ways, she could remind one of a Wisconsin-born woman, Laura Ingalls Wilder (1867-1957). Both did some writing. Both moved from place to place in the middle part of the country and both were independent-minded women. They did, however, move in *very* different directions.

The Albert Wadsworth portrait of Carrie Nation. Courtesy of *The Medicine Lodge Stockade* of Medicne Lodge, Kansas. This portrait stands in stark contrast to the oft-published portrait that has Ms. Nation looking like a menacing warrior. *Surely, any drunkard is more dangerous to a fellow American than Carrie Nation ever was!* A liquor bottle in the hand is far more menacing than Carrie Nation's hatchet.

For the last couple of decades of her life, Carrie Nation was a crusader who carried her Bible and her hatchet and, usually leading a cluster of women followers, trashed taverns and other booze peddling establishment during the last years of her life, which ended shortly before Prohibition began.

Carrie, one of the 19th century's most prominent historical figures, was born Carrie A. Moore in Kentucky. While living in Missouri, she met and married Charles Gloyd, a young physician who had served in the Union Army during the Civil War. Although Carrie was his wife, his mistress was alcohol.

Gloyd didn't need to patronize saloons, of which their town of Holden, Missouri, had several. More often, he spent evenings imbibing in Holden's Masonic Lodge and within a week of their marriage, he came home in a drunken state. The drinking led to their marital breakup; so that, although pregnant, she returned to her parents' home to live. Within another half year, Charles Gloyd died. Authoress, Fran Grace, in a marvelously written and comprehensive biography of Carrie Nation, cites a source that tells readers (p. 48) that Gloyd died "reportedly from delirium tremens or from pneumonia compounded by excessive drinking." Carrie was widowed at the age of 22.

Sources suggest that Carrie's infamous hatchet-wielding and speechifying was caused by Charles' death from alcohol, but one can question that statement. Charles Gloyd died in 1869. Her first saloon-smashing incident didn't occur until December 1894, a quarter-century later. It would be just as easy to postulate that the saloon-smashing career began because she was an astute woman.

The Carrie Nation home in Medicine Lodge, Kansas. Photo by the author.

Carrie Nation, looking no more menacing than any other matronly lady of the 19th century. This image provided by the U.S. Library of Congress, Prints and Photographs Division.

Even President Theodore Roosevelt felt the sting of a Carrie Nation barb, having been identified by the Kansas crusader as a "maudlin drunk". (Grace, 243). Teddy's great-grandson, Tweed Roosevelt, has written this about his noted ancestor: "TR was a very light drinker although not a teetotaler he drank very little, once even going so far as to sue a newspaper for libel for calling him a drunk. He won." (Private email correspondence with the author, February 2018).

Carrie's second marriage was the one with the fortuitous name. In 1874 she married David Nation. They would stay married for about three decades before he obtained a divorce on the grounds of desertion. That marriage allowed her to change the spelling of her first name, retain her

original middle initial and become Carry A. Nation. That name blended nicely with her oft-repeated message that God was supporting her anti-alcohol crusade.

However, Carrie Nation has been one of America's most vilified women. Here are but a few descriptive words one might read:

"deranged" (Bailey, p. 560)

"a bulldog-faced woman" and "most outrageous" (Krass, p. 177, 178)

"bizarre figure," "fanatical aversions," "fanatic,"

"Touched with madness,"

"Half circus freak," and "mad old creature" (Irwin, pp. 205-6)

An early biographer of Ms. Nation seems to offer a fairer assessment of the lioness of Medicine Lodge. The following paragraph is quoted in Irwin's book (p. 206) and was written by Herbert Asbury as a passage in his biography of Carrie Nation (*Carrie Nation*, 1928). He wrote:

> "Her greatest contribution was not the wrecked barrooms her hatchet left, but the avalanche of publicity she turned out. It was aimed at the crime and corruption that originated in barrooms and there she hit a weak spot . . . Without Carry Nation . . . the anti-liquor agitation might conceivably have reached an entirely different conclusion . . . She gave direction and increased impetus to the movement."

Author, Philip Krass, also quotes one of her revealing messages, presumably as evidence of her mental instability: "We invite you to join us in the destruction of the machinery hell has set up here on earth to literally devour humanity." (p. 179)

Whether or not one thinks that Carrie Nation is a 'nut case' or whatever, it must be admitted that the abuse of liquor has devoured humanity by the hundreds of thousands, at least here in America!

Please ponder this observation: *We reside in a nation where millions of citizens are sometimes deranged.* One irrefutable fact: *Every drunkard is temporarily deranged?* Further, was Carrie

Nation dangerous while claiming support from God and brandishing her hatchet? She didn't attack people with her hatchet, but with her very effective civil disobedience. That puts her in company with a handful of history's most admirable heroes and heroines, such as Rosa Parks, Mohandas Gandhi, Emmeline Pankhurst, Henry David Thoreau, Dietrich Bonhoeffer, Martin Luther King, Jr., and Mother Jones (Mary Harris)! This author would rather have a dozen Carrie Nations in the neighborhood than a single drunkard! Make the comparison: a Midwestern crusader who used a hatchet to attack property or the drunken American driver who goes hurtling down our highways and byways in an out-of-control, 4,000-pound missile! Again, we ask, "Isn't every intoxicated individual in the world temporarily deranged?" Of course, they are. And for the safety of themselves and all others, they should be temporarily in an asylum. Instead, we foolishly put them into vehicles, into dormitories, onto our public beaches or into our homes. This mania shouldn't be happening!

Let's make another comparison: Carrie Nation and Jack Daniels. We have Carrie, who told of speaking with God, while fighting the curse of intemperance and we have Jack, in failing health at the age of sixty, who decided to join the local church and get baptized by dunking in Mulberry Creek. Thus, he spent his last days trying to book passage into Heaven after a lifetime of fueling the intemperance of many.

Temperance crusaders and other teetotalers are easily limned as weird in appearance and behavior, but they can never come close to matching the pathetic and threatening behavior of alcohol's acolytes.

A word of praise for another leading lady

While reviewing a bit of the life and work of Carrie Nation, we might mention another of the author's heroines. This one was mentioned a few lines earlier: Mary Harris, who has gone down in history as "Mother Jones." Mary Harris was known for her size. She was not Amazonian, as one might suppose a warrior in the coal fields of America might be. She was diminutive. Originally from Cork, Ireland, she became an outspoken leader of striking miners, known for successfully appealing to the wives as much as, or more than, to the miners themselves. She left a few assorted quotes, the most memorable of which was likely, "Pray for the dead and fight like hell for the living."

Because her principal role in history was as a firebrand among striking miners throughout the country, she belongs in other books. However, this tirade seems the truly appropriate venue for Mary Harris's shout [quoted from *Hearts of Fire*, p. 417] to an audience in Roosevelt, New Jersey. "Women, see that your husbands use no firearms or violence no matter what the provocation. Don't let your husbands scab. Help them stand firm and *above all keep them from the saloons.*" [Italics added] Those words should still be ringing across America.

Let's say a kind word for the exemplary drinkers

For that seeming minority of Americans who use but don't abuse alcohol, we should be grateful. However, their temperance is totally overshadowed by that segment of society that allows alcohol to temporarily turn them into the deadly menaces who terrorize our society! Why are the laws not crafted to virtually eliminate alcohol-related recidivism? What a pathetic spectacle: A society that sees the victims of alcohol abuse becoming sickened, injured or killed with increasing frequency; but lacks the will to address the crisis.

As we watch the growing tsunami of alcohol inundating our nation, we might observe that we could use a battalion of battleaxes like Carrie Nation to help awaken those responsible for addressing the nation's ongoing alcohol-related terror.

Right message; wrong audience

As the golden dandelion blooms and thrives on the untreated lawn, lovely and *unappreciated*, the American temperance crop bloomed and thrived, *unappreciated* throughout the late 19th and early 20th centuries. Those who supported the temperance movement were of two groups: those who wanted drinking to be moderate and those who wanted utter abstinence. There were temperance orators, temperance writers, temperance poets, temperance organizers, temperance singers, temperance playwrights, temperance legislators and so on.

A review of the temperance writings of 18th and 19th century America suggest that striking changes had settled on America by the late 20th century. No longer would alcohol be referred to by such doom-laden terms as 'bar of destruction', 'demon rum', etc. No more would women stay clear of bar-rooms and the products offered in them. No longer would books and pamphlets boldly

A temperance song from 1907. Note the hopeful lyrics.

condemn alcohol as one condemns a deadly enemy. Sadly, it was the winning of a great victory for the temperance crowd that was going to give a pass to the very purveyors of alcohol that the temperance supporters believed were finally brought under control. The entire Prohibition affair drips with bitter irony.

Let the closing words of this chapter be the closing words of T. S. Arthur's monumental book, *Ten Nights in A Bar-room*. That book ended with the following two paragraphs:

> "But good sense and reason prevailed. Somewhat modified, the resolutions passed, and the more ultra-inclined contented themselves with carrying out the second resolution, to destroy forthwith all the liquor to be found on the premises; which was immediately done. After which the people dispersed to their homes, each with a lighter heart, and better hopes for the future of their village.
>
> On the next day, as I entered the stage that was to bear me from Cedarville, I saw a man strike his sharp ax into the worn, faded, and leaning post that had, for so many years,

Sobering presentation from pages 30-31 of the 1912 book, "The Man That Rum Made."

borne aloft the "Sickle and Sheaf;" and just as the driver
gave word to his horses, the false emblem which had invited
so many to enter the way of destruction, fell crashing to the
earth."

As the First World War concluded, the forces of sobriety were
prevailing. The 'Great War' might have turned the tide. Of Americans who wanted to live in a 'dry' nation, the numbers had grown
to such a figure, that a constitutional amendment was within
reach.

Add to the anti-alcohol songs and books, the very maudlin
poetry that was circulating. A very fine example of such poetry
appeared in the Philadelphia *Press* of 1914. The poem's title was
"Bessie, the Drunkard's Lone Child."

> Out in the gloomy night, sadly I roam.
> I have no Mother, dear; no pleasant home;
> No one cares for me, no one would cry,
> Even if poor little Bessie should die.
>
> Barefoot and tired, I wandered all day,
> Asking for work, but I'm too small they say.
> On the damp ground, I must now lay my head.
> Father's a drunkard and mother is dead.
>
> CHORUS
> Mother, Oh, Mother, why did you leave me alone?
> With no one to love me, no friends no home.
> Dark is the night and the wind rages wild,
> God pity Bessie the drunkard's lone child!
>
> We were so happy till father drank rum,
> Then all our sorrow and trouble begun.
> Mother grew paler and wept every day,
> Baby and I were too hungry to play.
>
> Slowly they faded till one Summer's night
> Found their sweet faces all silent and white.
> Then with big tears slowly dropping I said
> "Father's a drunkard and Mother is dead."

> Oh, if the Salvation Army could find
> Poor wretched father, and talk very kind,
> If they could stop him from drinking, why then,
> Poor little Bess would be happy again
>
> Oh, it is too late, won't someone try?
> Poor little Bessie will soon starve and die
> All day long I've been begging for bread,
> Father's a drunkard and Mother is dead.

That anonymously-written rhyme seems almost silly in its sadness. However, when we compare the true account of Charles of Antes Fort (see Chapter Six), his life was as pathetic as was that of little Bessie, and Charles was a real child of a drunken father. Are there not countless 'little Bessie' characters living in 21st century America?

It was, however, the First World War that seemed to be the impetus for wider acceptance of legal limitations on alcohol. The war effort required the conservation of grain and that same war effort encouraged a crusader mentality. Both finally helped to push the states and the federal government into supporting the temperance drive and the wide push for prohibition.

The work of many individuals and three stalwart organizations had finally yielded success. The three largest pushers for the prohibition of alcohol had been, as mentioned earlier, the *Woman's Christian Temperance Union*, the *Catholic Total Abstinence Union*, and the men's organization, the *Anti-Saloon League*. The fourth pillar, of course, was that of the young *Prohibition Party*.

Article V of the Constitution authorizes such an amendment if approved by three-fourths of the states. That historic 18th Amendment, then, came into existence on January 16, 1919, with the state of Nebraska officially giving approval. The amendment and the initial enabling legislation (the Volstead Act of October 18, 1919) heralded what law said was to be a 'dry' or sober American nation.

That, America would quickly see, was the easy part.

The amendment writ with disappearing ink

One could imagine that a century of hope; a half-century of monumental effort had borne glorious fruit and that, now, the United States of America had become a sober and safer nation.

A message by the famed 19th-century cartoonist, Thomas Nast. Note the title.

The much-vaunted democratic process—given us at great personal effort and sacrifice by our founding sages--never looked worthier of our gratitude and praise.

Amendment XVIII

Section 1. After one year from the ratification of this article the manufacture, sale, or transportation of intoxicating liquors within, the importation thereof into, or the exportation thereof from the United States and all territory subject to the jurisdiction thereof for beverage purposes is hereby prohibited.

> Section 2. The Congress and the several States shall have concurrent power to enforce this article by appropriate legislation.
> Section 3. This article shall be inoperative unless it shall have been ratified as an amendment to the Constitution by the legislatures of the several States, as provided in the Constitution, within seven years from the date of the submission hereof to the States by the Congress.

Stripped of its enabling clauses, the 18th Amendment is quite brief. "[T]he manufacture, sale, or transportation of intoxicating liquors within, the importation thereof into, or the exportation thereof from the United States and all territory subject to the jurisdiction thereof for beverage purposes is hereby prohibited."

Sober Slogan #8

Stay alert

Alcohol

Lessens

Everyone's

Reaction

Time

According to one of our once-popular television series, the being who would teach us Earthling loons how to use logic was from the planet *Vulcan* (although he had an Earthling mother). One must question how a far-away planet got a name from Earth's mythology, or how the beings of that far planet, with their own complex system of evolution, could develop creatures so similar in height and other physical features to our very own? Of course, that silly world is still a half-millennium in our future. However, when we look at the way we embrace the intemperate use of alcohol, it appears that we do need some serious help in the application of logic.

That new amendment to the U.S. Constitution, despite all the 'thereofs', was clear. On January 16th of 1920, the United States was to become a 'dry' nation.

We can conclude this chapter, on the great struggle for sobriety, by reiterating: The temperance leaders of America, from William Penn to the early 20th century champions, were the titans of temperance. They were sobriety's heroes, everyone. The men and women listed here, and their countless companions in the struggle for a sober society were America's lions of logic; its pillars of reason.

Chapter Four

Prohibition

Not a single woman voted for the 18th Amendment
There is another astonishing fact to note regarding the adoption of the 18th Amendment, prohibiting the manufacture, sale and transporting of "intoxicating liquors." *It was passed before women were given the vote! That was an impressive development.* Note that the 18th Amendment was born on January 16th of *1919.* Women were finally, and very, very belatedly, given the right to vote with the ratification of the 19th Amendment, which did not occur until August 18th of *1920!*

Every American could celebrate. This was an entirely new world. This was the world created by the Grand Eighteenth! Now, one should be able to stroll the streets of a sober nation! Every American could imagine his or her relatives, neighbors and co-workers going through the day free of the tyranny of alcohol. One could drive the highways, confident that all the pursuing horse-drawn and horseless carriages were being operated by clear-headed drivers, just as all approaching vehicles were being driven by sober citizens. Spouses everywhere in the nation could sigh with the relief of one who once had to deal with a drunken mate for months or years. Every child could see only sober parents at the dinner table and know the comfort of being tucked into their beds only by lucid and loving parents. Thanks to the Grand Eighteenth, the yoke of alcoholic tyranny was finally cast off all Americans!

However, horror of horrors! It never happened! Those millions who had worked for decades to outlaw alcohol were about to be betrayed . . .

There was never a transition from a hard-drinking segment of the American population to a law-abiding and sober population. The drinkers of America went from a legally-liquored segment of American society to an illicit and utterly law-breaking segment of society . . . and those damned lawbreakers have never ceased to blame their criminal behavior, during the 14 years of Prohibition, on the law! Within nanoseconds of its legal birth, the Grand Eighteenth was being shredded and trampled and vociferously damned! Those who wanted to create, sell and consume alcohol, were determined to break the law. They were going to create hell on earth. Teetotalers and exemplary drinkers . . . run for cover!

For anyone who thought that the anti-Prohibition forces had been hypocritical outlaws before passage, there was to be a genuine *Olympus Mons* of crime and hypocrisy once the 18th Amendment became the law of the nation!

January 16, 1920, should have been a major turning point in American history. The 'turn' was never made!

Prohibition was a victim of infanticide, brutally wrapped in its own umbilical cord and strangled before it ever emerged from the womb!

There promptly occurred one of the nation's—and one of the world's—great tragedies. The American nation suddenly mutated into a nation of outlaws, a land of rogues. It happened overnight. In fact, before the ink was even dry on the enabling legislation (the Volstead Act of 1919), countless criminals were defying that act as well as the U.S. Constitution.

Sobriety never had a chance!!

It seems highly likely that many Americans did little more than set down their legal drinks *only to raise those same glasses or bottles* as illegal drinks mere seconds later! Within hours after Prohibition swept the nation, its laws were being violated. It took a mere two hours or so for *revenuers* to make their first known Prohibition-era raid, in Peoria, Illinois. The 'wets' drank to the

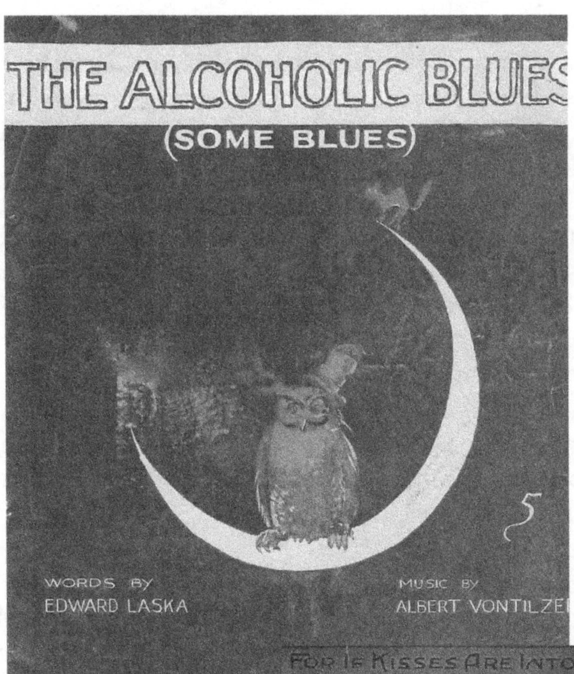

Two pieces of sheet music that were published in 1919, in an apparent effort to capitalize on America's move into a presumed-Prohibition mode. Sophie Tucker, one of America's early 'vamps' was the female vocalist on a song that told listeners that if alcohol was being prohibited, kissing could succeed in replacing it.

end of legal alcohol mere minutes before they drank to their own defiance of the new law. It soon became crystal clear: Thanks to its despicable weakness for alcohol, America had two professions with excellent job security: revenuer and bootlegger. The first was without resources and the second was without scruples!

The century-long labors of the temperance crowd were being 'mooned' by the bastards who instantly began to manufacture, sell and distribute the proscribed alcohol. *Democratically-established* sobriety was doomed from day one.

One can muse about whether a less inclusive law might have succeeded and it would be nice to think that such might have been the case. However, full prohibition had been created by the 18th and the opponents were, as stated, obligated to work to obey the new law while working to effect change. But, that's when the forces of anarchy burst onto the national stage.

Misnomer of misnomers

Prohibition! They named the entire era "Prohibition." Who in Hell named that hopeful era with a term that emphasized the lawful absence of alcohol, rather than some hopeful term for sobriety? This period in American history, that lasted from 1920 to 1933 should carry a purely positive moniker. We should identify those years as the "Temperance Era." "Ah," one might inject: "but there was a *wealth of intemperance* disrupting whatever temperance existed." Of course, that's true. But, effective "prohibition" surely was lacking during that so-named era!

All those who had struggled for decades to win a sober society were cheated! In little more than a decade, the tyrant, alcohol, had crushed our second great American Revolution. We've been under the yoke ever since . . .

Of course, the wealthier Americans, as usual, had the advantage. While waiting for the 18th Amendment to officially ban alcohol, the wealthy began storing great quantities of alcohol in their homes. Cider, a sweet fruit drink when fresh, was often allowed to ferment and become 'hard' and intoxicating. Oddly, cider making was never illegal, despite characteristics that matched several other forms of alcohol. Similarly, wealthy Americans could take small watercraft to reach destinations beyond the confining national limits, where floating saloons were fully stocked and ready to serve their parched patrons. Thirsty members of America's working class, with less money to expend on liquor, were still

A Prohibition Era 'recipe' booklet.

Succulent on the bush; seductive in the booze.

able to find local bootleggers and local speakeasies that would sell them the hard drinks that they craved. As revenue agents raided and smashed speakeasies and back-mountain distilling equipment ('stills'), new ones sprang up in other locations. The old tales of "cops and robbers" became the modern stories of "revenuers and moonshiners." The whole business of moonshining and bootlegging provides fodder for some exciting books or movies; but, never forget the agony behind the allure.

Democracy be damned!

The sore losers, who should have been sober throughout the 1920s, became incorrigible lawbreakers for more than a decade, while the decade of the 1920s spun out of control with so much illegal activity that the era became known as "The Roaring 20s!" A name that would have been far more appropriate would have been "The Lawless 20's." Rather than delineate the many aspects of the anti-Prohibition crime spree, one might simply suggest that interested individuals consult one of the books that dwelt on events of that pathetic period. The sun had barely set on the decade before Frederick Lewis Allen wrote a marvelous book, *Only Yesterday*, that captured the pace and significance of the time. Nearly a century had elapsed until Daniel Okrent wrote a much broader and lengthier work (*Last Call*) on the subject. The title struck this reader as being odd since the story seemed to indicate that a "last call" was never really recognized. There was virtually no lapse in the drinking of alcohol. The transition was nearly lacking in any stopping and starting activity among the dedicated American boozers.

The land of hockey and hooch

During the American Revolution and, again, during the War of 1812, American troops invaded Canada. In 1813 U.S. troops, during an invasion of our northern neighbor, left major buildings in the Canadian town of York (Toronto) in ashes. A century later, as Prohibition opened in the U.S., the Canadians were eager to retaliate for those century-old indignities. They helped U.S. citizens to break the law by rushing Canadian whiskey across the borders in huge quantities. Gallons and gallons of Canadian liquor helped the Americans usher in a Prohibition deluge. Add to that flood, the large shipments that were smuggled in through the nation's

Prescription liquor was another way to flout the law. Perhaps Daisy was an outlaw.

endless maritime coast. Also, add the huge quantities of moonshine liquor that was created within our homeland. No scarcity of liquor existed for even a single day of what one could reasonably recognize as anarchy's decade.

The 18th Amendment was quickly in trouble. Prohibition was despised by too many of the American populace. Far too many citizens found it easier to deny the law than to deny their thirst. Because of their thirst for alcohol, many thousands of citizens could be counted as converts to crime.

There was never anything rational about drunkenness; nor is there anything wrong with Prohibition. The thing that was wrong was this: After the democratic process theoretically rid the nation of the evils of drunkenness, huge numbers of citizens chose to flout the law, rather than to accept the democratically-established change. Those citizens thumbed their criminal noses at the law even to the point of condoning the violence generated by the lawless. It was President Herbert Hoover who gave us a memorable quote late in the "Twenties," when he stated, "Our country has deliberately undertaken a great social and economic experiment, noble in motive and far-reaching in purpose." Thus, we have one of the few positive legacies from the era, a two-word phrase, "noble experiment." It's difficult to imagine where the president got any notion that something noble was occurring at the time of his statement.

That same president, Herbert Hoover, was one of America's noblest historical figures. Herbert Hoover was a humanitarian. He led the drive to get aid to a hungering Europe following World War I. In fact, Herbert Hoover's humanitarian leadership is considered to have saved more human lives than the efforts of any other person in history.

Sadly, the decade-plus of Prohibition lawlessness saw the influence of many criminal elements that began to flourish and thrive, including Irish, Jewish and Italian mobsters. These thugs bought and sold liquor and politicians throughout the decade. Author Nicholas Gage ended one passage of his book on the Mafia with this thought (p. 85): "By 1925 the Mafia in the United States was reaching new and undreamed-of heights of wealth and power *because of Prohibition* and the organizing genius of Al Capone in Chicago and Charlie 'Lucky' Luciano in New York." What Gage identifies as 'organizing genius' might impress some people as simply being "utter ruthlessness." While the Italian Mafia has left America with a lingering, and undeserved, stereotype for Italians, it must be emphasized that—over the years—some of the individuals who were real crusaders against New York City mobster activity included the police lieutenant, Guiseppe (Joseph) Petrosino (1860-1909), Mayor Fiorello La Guardia (1882-1947) and Mayor Rudy Giuliani (b. 1944).

Don't condemn a law for the lawlessness that follows its passage. Condemn those who refused to obey that law while they adjusted to its presence or while they undertook its repeal. Such law-abiding approaches rarely occurred during the anarchic years of Prohibition.

It's a pathetic nation that allows money to replace morality. One must condemn the purveyors of alcohol; but one must also condemn—in terms equally harsh—the hordes of average citizens who kept the bootleggers and rumrunners scrambling to meet their wild demands! Lastly, one must condemn those federal agents who were so quickly corrupted. Prohibition perverted responsible citizenship. A less-than-robust economy also made the repeal arguments of the Prohibition opponents that much more convincing. Alcohol sales are good for the economy. There are obviously jobs with the brewers and vintners, the liquor transporters and the tavern owners. Then there are the ancillary jobs: A binging society also has more openings for traffic police, collision repair shops, defense attorneys and emergency medical professionals. Such is the economy that we are now experiencing . . . the 'we' being those of us who haven't yet become another statistical victim of the abuse of alcohol.

The overlooked key in this puzzle is the democratic process. Under the democratic system:

A. The merits of legislation are debated and both sides offer their best points as forcefully as possible.

B. Once the vote is taken or, in this case, the Amendment is adopted, the losing side must accept the change.

C. Those whose effort failed must begin to obey the new law while working through the democratic process to have the new law modified or reversed! This never occurred with Prohibition. Countless Americans who opposed the outlawing of alcohol were privately declaring: "You teetotalers let us have our way or we will simply disobey the law!" Once the 18th amendment became law, it was the right and the obligation of the losers to respect that law. It didn't happen! It never happened! If that had occurred, perhaps the nation would have found a modified approach that would have been tolerable to both sides. Instead, the losers grabbed the prohibitionists by the scruff of the neck and dragged them to the polls to force their vote for the 21st amendment. It was one of the sorriest displays of anti-democratic bullying in the nation's history! If but a few thousand Americans would have chosen to flout the Volstead Act, it would have been manageable. Historian, Thomas A. Bailey observed (*The American Pageant*, p. 791) that "many ardent wets believed that the way to bring about repeal was to violate the law on a large enough scale." It worked! When several million booze makers, procurers, haulers, and customers declared, "To hell with the democratic process! To hell with the law!" one of humankind's most hopeful pieces of legislation was scuttled! A brief, but brilliant, addition to the U.S. Constitution was trampled beneath the boots of the bootleggers and all others who defied a legitimate and wise law. Every American—those who urged temperance as well as those who embraced gangsterism—became the victims, including those as-yet-unborn generations. After all: *Every fetus should be born into a sober society.*

Federal efforts to have more people obey the 18th amendment were made, particularly with the Volstead Act of 1919, as mentioned above. States, too, tried to legislate obedience to the democratically-developed amendment. For example, Pennsylvania's governor, Gifford Pinchot (PIN show) called a special legislative session in 1926 to have the legislature create laws to support sobriety within the Keystone State.

Folks can reach their own conclusions about the American acts of aggression against a neighbor in our early days of nationhood, such as our failed invasion of our Canadian neighbor in 1775. It was that same neighbor, Canada, that retaliated a hundredfold, by producing huge quantities of alcohol for sale to the illegal U.S. market during Prohibition. Throughout the decade of the 1920s, and for four years beyond (1930, 1931, 1932 and 1933), the huge lawless segment of the American populace trampled proper laws that stood between them and their beloved narcotic, alcohol. The lawlessness that accompanied the 18th amendment was viewed as the automatic curse of creating something so perverted as to prohibit the manufacture, distribution, and sale of alcohol. All this lawlessness reached a climax on St. Valentine's Day in 1929. That was the day that some heavily armed henchmen, presumably working for the king of mobsters, Al Capone, pretended to be lawmen and walked into the S.M.C. Cartage Company on Clark Street in Chicago and gunned down seven men of the rival O'Banion group. The public expressed outrage. Obviously, such barbarism and anarchy needed to be addressed.

The Wickersham Report
President Hoover tried. In May of 1929, he appointed a study commission of eleven members, to be headed by a former U.S. attorney general, George W. Wickersham, to study the situation created by the 18th Amendment and its sorry aftermath. After about two years of study, the Wickersham report was released.

The author, primping for a 1920's-style shindig, 2017.

It offered a brave conclusion. Stay the course with Prohibition, but make some modifications. However, the nation had already demonstrated no willingness to accept modifications.

Franklin Delano Roosevelt and the death of Prohibition

This author (who belongs to neither major political party) greatly admires some of our nation's presidents of both parties. Among my favorites would be Thomas Jefferson, Grover Cleveland, Jimmy Carter (more for his integrity and goodness than for his political skills) and Harry Truman among those associated with the Democrat party. I consider the outstanding Republicans to have included Herbert Hoover, Gerald Ford, George Herbert Walker Bush, Abraham Lincoln, Theodore Roosevelt and Ronald Reagan. I also admire the record of the first George and I consider our very worst president to have been Teddy's cousin . . .

Franklin Delano Roosevelt was the man who once tried to thwart our delicate democracy by adding five more justices to the U.S. Supreme Court for him to gain a personal phalanx of like-minded jurists. He also interned Japanese-American citizens and Italian-American citizens; allowed the U.S. Army ("Operation

Keelhaul") to forcibly return about two million war prisoners and displaced persons to the clutches of their nation's murderous tyrant, Josef Stalin, where they were executed or put into slave labor camps. Franklin D. Roosevelt had, earlier, turned away Jewish refugees who had to go back to Europe and into Nazi concentration camps. Also on my list of FDR's ugly negatives was his unabashed and active support for scuttling Prohibition. If not his, then on whose doorstep do we place the responsibility for the ever-expanding tally of crimes and deaths that have been caused by alcohol since 1933? The tens of thousands of deaths that are the direct or indirect result of alcohol may not have occurred if the hustler of Hyde Park had championed sobriety.

Party politics had been very influential in the entire Prohibition circus. Republicans generally favored Prohibition. Democrats generally opposed it. The presidents during the entire Prohibition era were Republicans (Harding, Coolidge, and Hoover). For the 1932 election, the Democratic candidate, Franklin D. Roosevelt of New York, promised many economic and social reforms, including the repeal of Prohibition. He won the election over the sitting president, Hoover, by a landslide of about 23 million votes to 16 million votes! Sobriety's days were numbered. The repeal of the noble 18th amendment was rapid. The extreme brevity of the repeal process only added to its ignominious role. Basically, the new amendment declares:

Article XXI. Prohibition Repealed

18th Amendment repealed. The eighteenth article of amendment to the Constitution of the United States is hereby repealed.

An additional two small paragraphs offer details. December the 5th of 1933 was the day when America's thirsty could celebrate their return to a law-abiding posture. For them, it was just one more excuse to hit the booze!

Early Christmas for the lushes: December 5, 1933.
A century of effort at building a sober nation was about to be scuttled by a wide assortment of criminals, politicians and everyday boozers. The period from ratification to repeal was a mere 14 years. Remember, the period from ratification to flouting was

likely too brief to measure. Finally, after 14 years of raucous, chaotic life, 'control' of the manufacture and sale of alcohol was returned to the states.

A nation, made weary of pro-alcohol lawlessness, decided to drown the 18th Amendment in a legal vat of alcohol. Weighted with heavy kegs of 90-proof alky, the 18th amendment quickly sank into oblivion. The Volstead Act was also weighted and drowned in a lake of alky. The bunghole of the national keg was ripped open and the handle that would stem the flow was crushed. Alcohol, the timeless terrorist, returned to the control of our nation . . .

The ignoble experiment
From the time it had been submitted to the states, the 18th Constitutional Amendment had taken 394 days—somewhat more than a year—to get enough states' approval to become law. The 21st Amendment, the sole purpose of which was to toss out, or repeal, the 18th Amendment, took less than eight months to gain the required support to give it legitimacy. An idealistic 18th amendment, that had never been properly observed, became today's much-maligned document. The nation could return to legal binging, with all the ugliness that legal and illegal binging has always produced.

Pro-alcohol lawmakers, booze manufacturers, peddlers, and imbibers could now wreak vengeance on any teetotaler who dared to raise his or her voice. Those who abhorred alcohol's pernicious effects on America were silenced.

It should be clearly understood:
■ It was the absence of democracy that caused Prohibition to fail!

■ The repeal of the 18th Amendment was not the result of democracy, but was the triumph of anarchy!

As early as 1936, just three years after the 18th Amendment was ripped from the U. S. Constitution, a book's authors observed that "A national revulsion against the breakdown of law enforcement was what caused prohibition's repeal." [Harrison and Laine, p. 228]

That observation seems to be both succinct and precise.

To even suggest that the scuttling of Prohibition showed that "Democracy worked," is pure Bullscat! What a witless observation. The truth? Anarchy worked . . . to perfection!

A last gasp . . .
When Prohibition ended, a few sobriety lovers tried to keep the cause alive; but the great sobriety edifice that took a century or more to build, crumbled within a few years.

The anti-alcohol organizations with their many thousands of members began to see their membership dwindle. The wind had been brutally knocked from their sails. Their cause, a great and growing hope in 1915 was a riddled and deflated balloon by 1935.

A booklet that was among the last gasps of a dying cause: Prohibition

After Prohibition had been ruthlessly garroted, pro-sobriety writings were left looking like empty afterthoughts; which is what they were. The booklet, whose cover page appears above, was copyrighted in 1936. It presented a collection of short prose pieces and poetic observations that rang hollow three years after their cause had utterly collapsed. From its century of pages, three selections are offered: The first is the opening verse of a longer poem; but enough is presented here so that one can see that its style was borrowed, as revealed, from Rudyard Kipling's 19th-century lines.

FOR WE FORGOT
Apologies to Rudyard Kipling

God of our fathers, known of old
Have mercy on this age of crime,
Forgive our love of drink and gold,
Our deafness to thy voice from time.
Lord God of Hosts is with us not,
For we forgot—for we forgot.

[Untitled]

"One evening in October
When I was far from sober
And dragging home a load with manly pride,
My feet began to stutter,
So, I laid down in the gutter
And a pig came up and parked right by my side.
Then I warbled 'It's fair weather
When good fellows get together,'
Till a lady passing by was heard to say,
'You can tell a man who boozes
By the company he chooses.'
Then the pig got up and slowly walked away."

And, lastly . . .

OLD RYE'S SONG

I was made to be eaten,
   And not to be drank;
To be thrashed in a barn,
   Not soaked in a tank.
I come to be a blessing,
   When put through the mill
As a blight and a curse,
   When run through a still;
Make me up into loaves,
   And your children are fed;
But, if into drink,
   I'll starve them instead.
In bread I'm a servant,
   The eater shall rule;
In drink I am master,
   And drinker a fool.
So, remember the warning;
   My strength I'll employ,
If eaten, to strengthen;
   If drank, to destroy.

Another tragedy: The booze lovers still use Prohibition as a whipping boy to make today's national binge seem legitimate. Some of today's ads illustrate this disgusting practice. The folks who sell Bacardi's rum ran an ad, as recently as 2012 (*Time*, 2/13/12) that bragged about their flouting of the laws of Prohibition, claiming "When your story begins with the creation of the world's smoothest rum, it's not long before you're rubbing elbows with rebels and royalty, introducing rum to cola and *partying through Prohibition.*" [Emphasis added] Using the phrase, "partying through Prohibition," is merely sneering at the law-abiding temperance people. Bacardi's isn't the only producer of alcohol to express an exciting and 'rebellious' attitude in their advertising. A 2007 (11/28/07) Dewar's liquor ad also sneered at the temperance crowd with an ad showing a Prohibition ship sinking. Today, only a few of us seem to become upset when watching the law's flouters flaunt their flouting!

Once national prohibition was scuttled, how did the states respond to their new-found authority to control their own alcohol spigot? State after state quickly returned control to the localities, making control pretty much a personal thing. Unfortunately—as we've witnessed a million times over—countless individuals are unable to exert any control over their drinking patterns. With no authoritative check, the binge continues.

A saloon sign in old Trinidad, Colorado (illustration, Weiser, p. 91) announced that "No Minor or Habitual Drunkard" was to be served. Even the most gullible people cannot be reassured by such phony signs from our frontier past or our pathetic present. The alcohol merchants are *still* telling patrons to "drink responsibly." For the countless alcoholics, these bits of advice are empty rhetoric. It's easy to form the opinion that the alcohol merchants are the last people in the world who would want patrons to stop investing once their alcohol intakes reached 'responsible' levels. When alcohol makers and sellers tout "responsible" drinking, they understand the great army of abusers is "responsible" for the handsome profits involved in the dangerously irresponsible consumption of alcohol.

Sometime, perhaps, we'll see an ad that shows some leggy young blonds and the message: the Finnish swim team loves men who are mature and sober!

Last line spoken
The film, *The Untouchables* (1987), was an excellent film about the violence surrounding Prohibition and that era's conclusion. The last line spoken is by Eliot Ness (as portrayed by Kevin Costner).

Last home of famed Prohibition-enforcer, Eliot Ness, in scenic Coudersport, Pennsylvania.

Ness says: "I think I'll have a drink." Sadly, that expression might have had a basis in history, since Ness did drink alcohol in his post-Prohibition years, before his early death in 1957 in the small mountain town of Coudersport, Pennsylvania.

Logic drowned in liquor

The argument has been proffered (*Slate*, quoted in the opening page of "*Last Call.*") that Prohibition failed because it went against 'human nature'! Once again: Bullscat! For most humans, human nature involves the search for comfort and safety. That's why we no longer rely solely on nature to provide our food supply. That's why we're no longer content to yield to the heat and chill of our natural environment. That's why we no longer live in caves. Humankind has shown miraculous progress because human nature reasons to solve problems. We want our problems to be solved by employing the human mind, but it must be a *sober* human mind.

One must ask: Why does American society continue to shackle itself with the time-consuming and costly burdens of the self-inflicted injuries and illnesses of the nation's drug and alcohol abusers? If American society would approach the zero tolerance that the boozers use in dealing with the pro-sobriety crowd,

America could remove many of the very sorry aspects of alcoholic intemperance.

Thanks to the tidal flow of alcohol, the United States, today, witnesses the killings equivalent of a St. Valentine's Day massacre just about every four hours! This is senseless. Such unabated slaughter is outrageous, but we barely show even a hint of indignation!

Admittedly, Prohibition was a failure. However, the evidence overwhelms. Post-Prohibition is one of History's colossal flameouts! The *ignoble* experiment—the return to lawful binging—is a human tragedy of historic proportions! Annually, today's legally-permitted boozing kills thousands of Americans! Why can't we address this reign of terror? Why glamorize behavior that is so antisocial and so harmful to the drinkers and to their countless innocent victims?

Contemplate the irony: Prohibition greatly spurred the further rooting and growth of America's Mafia and the burial, alive, of the once robust American temperance movement. Tragedy doubled? Oh, no . . . tragedy compounded!

Chapter Five

Moonlight Sonata

The enduring illicit alcohol trade

Moonshining is a popular term for the illegal making of alcohol. Needed for the making of 'moonshine' are the cooker, the ingredients and the isolation. In the world of alcohol, legal has never meant ethical. Two forces were pushing alcohol during late 19th century America. The one was the regular, legal trade and the other was moonshining. While most moonshiners have shown concern for creating a drink that wouldn't poison the drinker; they seem to have had little or no concern for the immoderate drinker or with the many negative results of drunkenness.

Moonshining pre-dated Prohibition and it survives in post-Prohibition America. Moonshining and bootlegging have been glamorized enough to make them a lucrative part of the nation's folklore. While moonshiners and bootleggers are a dwindling segment of back-country America, they inspired, and continue to inspire, countless American books, movies, songs, and local legends.

The man from Nubbin Ridge

[This topic is the result of visits to this convicted moonshiner's relatives in both North Carolina and Pennsylvania. The result is a two-volume biography (2010 and2014) about this legendary moonshiner. A combined one-volume biography is currently being written and expanded for release in late 2018.]

Prince Farrington was primarily known to family members, a few neighbors and local lawmen while living at the family

Apparatus from an antique "still." Courtesy of Steve Neff.

homestead, Nubbin Ridge, in North Carolina; but he became a legendary moonshiner after he relocated to Clinton, County, Pennsylvania.

Between local and federal prison stays (more than one-half dozen spanning his life from his teen years to his later years) Prince David Farrington made a fortune by illegally manufacturing and selling moonshine. Locally, his name is legendary. His is likely the most famous name in Clinton County and among the top two or three best-known names in Lycoming County in north-central Pennsylvania. It was here that he died in 1956.

A quirky coincidence

In the early months of 2013, a very weird coincidence occurred within the Keystone State. After many decades of lying hidden and, eventually, totally unknown, two *unrelated* Prohibition-era liquor stashes, located about 150 miles apart, hit the news!

Idyllic former 20th-century woodland still site in Clinton County, Pennsylvania (Author's archives)

Those two news items might remind one of the 1986 television special hosted by Geraldo Rivera. On April 21st of that year, Rivera was hosting a live broadcast that was going to show a huge audience (estimated at 30 million viewers), the unknown contents of a Chicago-area subterranean vault that had belonged to the late mobster/murderer, Al Capone. What might be found? There might be a treasure in Prohibition-era liquor; an unseen fortune in mobster money or a few bodies of individuals who didn't survive the late mobster's business methods. Because of the tantalizing possibilities, Rivera had, on hand, a medical examiner and several federal revenue agents.

Geraldo Rivera, one should note, had earned a law degree (Brooklyn Law School) in 1969. One of the primary rules that attorneys learn: Never ask a witness a question unless you know the answer. For this much-ballyhooed television special, Rivera was asking, before the estimated 30 million viewers: What marvels

Stock-car racing: The exciting spawn of the moonshining/bootlegging culture of the Prohibition era. The highly popular sport has gone from privately-owned jalopies to the sleek, hurtling vehicles of the NASCAR circuit. Pictured: A 21st Century *stock-car racing re-enactment* near Auburn, Pennsylvania

lie within the unopened vault? He would learn the answer at the same instant as his rapt viewers: The vault contained nothing more than *several empty bottles and the dust of decades!* Rivera is living proof that celebrities can make absurd decisions and remain celebrated.

Let's emphasize, again: The two 2013 Pennsylvania news reports of recently-discovered liquor stashes were exceptionally co-incidental, but they were unrelated. However, the two events had several common aspects and several unrelated facets. Compare:

First: a seemingly inaccessible hiding place

The liquor stash that was found in Williamsport (Lycoming County), Pennsylvania was found right in what might well be labeled as "Farrington Country." Of course, Williamsport, Pennsylvania was once a nationally-known lumbering town and is, today, the home of Little League baseball; but for several decades, from the 1920s and through the 1930s and into the mid-1940s, Lycoming and neighboring Clinton counties were the living and operating grounds for Prince David Farrington, a moonshiner originally from Guilford County, North Carolina. "Prince" was his actual given name. Attracted to the very rural aspect of the two adjoining

Prince David Farrington, (1889-1956) a North Carolina "Tarheel," who moved to the forested hills of Clinton and Lycoming counties in Pennsylvania, where he moonshined and bootlegged and became a local legend.

counties—which are still three-quarters or more wooded in nature—Prince Farrington moved to the area of these two counties with his wife and the first three of his eventual four children. He also was accompanied or joined by a brother and several others of his moonshiner cohorts from North Carolina. He lived for several years near the town of Loganton (Clinton County) before moving to a riverside home across the Susquehanna River from Jersey Shore (Lycoming County). Prince David Farrington achieved the status of 'legendary' even before his death in the Williamsport Hospital in 1956. Over the years he had opened and/or reopened *several dozen stills* among the secluded hills and disguised buildings of the two-county area. Prince Farrington also became legendary for his many jail or prison terms, his generosity and for the *superb quality of his moonshine liquor.*

Steve Weaver, local history buff, at the woodland water
source of one of Prince D. Farrington's once-hidden 'stills'
in Clinton County, Pennsylvania [Author's archives]

Andy Harris is a businessman in Williamsport. Andy invests
in realty. One such property is at 428 Glenwood Avenue in that
city. Harris' investment program also includes renovation of the
properties acquired. He decided that the home on Glenwood Avenue could use some cosmetic work as well as a new heating
system, major plumbing, and major electrical work. To rewire the
kitchen outlets, the electrician had to break through one of the
walls in a closet. The electrician's flashlight illuminated a seemingly inaccessible, secret compartment holding a stash of dust-
covered, odd-sized bottles and jugs; each containing moonshine.
How was this compartment accessed? Unknown to the innocent
onlooker, a single, small panel, in the ceiling of the basement
beneath, could be lifted and slid to one side to allow access to a
slender invader. Apparently, it was unvisited for the many decades since the original storage of its once-contraband contents.
That would have been about 90 years earlier!

The random containers held sherry. Obviously, the persons
who bottled the liquor used whatever containers could be found.
That would have been a hodge-podge of medicine bottles, catsup

Prince Farrington cohorts at an ambitious woodland moonshining operation. From a private collection; courtesy of the owner.

From Williamsport, Pennsylvania: The Woodland Avenue stash. Courtesy of Andy Harris. Note that the once-secret horde of booze has been placed on modern shelves; but that the dust of decades still clings to the original containers.

bottles, a variety of jugs, etc. There was something helpful about the bottling: Dates and flavors were written on plain labels, where one might find such flavors as *strawberry, blueberry, grape, and rhubarb*. Andy Harris and a handful of appreciative friends opened a bottle for tasting. A pair of comments noted that the lovely liquid was: "Absolutely, fantastically delicious!" and "Contents were fantastic!"

Now short just a couple of bottles, the stash was put on temporary display in the Lycoming County Historical Museum in Williamsport. The stash has since been returned to its owner, Andy Harris, who faces the daunting chore of deciding the permanent future of Williamsport's Glenwood Avenue treasure trove. The quirky part? Elsewhere in the Keystone State, a second stash had been discovered a couple of decades ago; but it was also in early 2013 that this second cache hit the news . . .

The fox in the Scottdale henhouse

J.P. Brennen (1857-1919) was a wealthy industrialist who made his fortune in the coke industry, a field that was critical to the manufacture of steel. That explains the fact that he hobnobbed with the likes of Andrew Mellon, Henry Clay Frick and Andrew Carnegie, a handful of America's most affluent individuals. All four were related to the booming steel business associated with the city of Pittsburgh and its surrounding counties. [Brennen's wife, Ella, was from the Kehoe family, the same family that produced John Kehoe, the leader of the notorious Mollie Maguires, a secret organization of Irish mine workers of the anthracite fields of eastern Pennsylvania.] Brennen was later remembered as greeting visitors to his home while holding a glass of whiskey. He and his family lived in a modest mansion in the town of Scottdale, (Westmoreland County) Pennsylvania.

J.P. Brennen purchased some whiskey directly from a distiller in 1917. It came from the Old Farm distillery in the neighboring town of West Overton. That distillery was owned by Brennan's friends, Mellon and Frick. Apparently, with the approach of national Prohibition and the anticipated outlawing of booze, J. P. Brennen decided to make a quantity of this supply less conspicuous. Nine cases of his stock of Old Farm Pennsylvania Rye Whiskey were hidden. That was nine cases of a dozen bottles each. For the mathematically challenged, that would be a total of 108 bottles of quality hooch.

J. P. Brennen's Scottdale, Pennsylvania mansion. It also held a hidden stash of valuable liquor. Photo courtesy of Patricia Hill.

J. P.'s wife, Ella, died in 1913 and J.P. followed in 1919. After many decades had passed, one of Brennen's daughters offered the mansion at auction in 1986. The winning bid belonged to Patricia Hill, a New York City model. Her plans were to convert the mansion into a charming, antiques-laden bed-and-breakfast. Ms. Hill lovingly began to remodel the Brennen mansion. That is when workers uncovered a secret compartment in a basement stairway. That compartment contained the nine cases of Brennen's hidden store of Old Farm whiskey. Since John Saunders was an old friend of Pat Hill's family, it was natural that he should serve as the live-in caretaker of the former Brennen mansion and its Prohibition-era treasure.

In 2013, Pat Hill decided on the fate of her 104 bottles of whiskey. She would offer them to the West Overton Museum, a museum located in the town from which the old liquor had come. With museum officials present, Ms. Hill took a bottle from its old wooden case. She was shocked. That bottle was empty! So were the next several bottles that Patricia Hill lifted to display to her guests. These empty bottles were to have been under the watchful eye of her long-time family friend, the septuagenarian, John Saunders. Hill glanced in his direction. Although present in the same room, he seemed detached; but finally suggested that the alcohol must have evaporated. Saunders' explanation made no sense . . . particularly when the next bottle she lifted for display was totally full and untouched. Pat Hill's tally: 52 empty bottles and 52 untouched bottles, along with one trusted employee declaring his lack of knowledge about the missing sour mash whiskey!

Local police chief, Barry Pritts of Scottdale filed a complaint against Saunders. DNA samples taken from three of the empties were declared to match that of John Saunders. Saunders appeared before a local magistrate, Judge Chuck Moore. However, the case effectively ended when, in July of 2014, Mr. Saunders died. Would restitution have been reasonable? That would depend on whom one asked. When a New York liquor appraisal firm was consulted, they set a value on each unopened bottle. According to their appraisal, the amount of aged liquor that Saunders was charged with guzzling was valued at $102,400.

Is Prince D. Farrington tied to the Glenwood Avenue cache of moonshine?

How does all this connect to Prince David Farrington? There was no connection whatsoever between Prince Farrington and the Brennen stash in Westmoreland County, Pennsylvania. Also, there is no direct evidence that Prince Farrington was connected to the stash in Williamsport; *but a mountain of circumstantial evidence points in his direction.*

The Glenwood Avenue trove was in the heart of "Farrington country." Prince Farrington is known to have delivered moonshine to Williamsport. Farrington took his children to a Williamsport dentist because he had moonshining business with that same dentist. Farrington is known to have attended parties in that town. The Glenwood Avenue stash was bottled in whatever bottles the distiller could scrounge; a practice commonly exhibited by the moonshiner, Prince Farrington. Further, at the time of their 1920s' storage, someone put the dates on the bottles. Those dates fit comfortably into the time frame for Farrington's main years of activity. Also, the hidden compartment used for sequestering the illicit booze matched the hiding place found in Prince Farrington's brother's house, in nearby Lamar, Pennsylvania. Finally, when the discovery was found and a tasting event was held, the liquor tasted was enthusiastically declared to be of *superior quality!* That pointed directly to the master distiller from the Lycoming County town of Jersey Shore, Pennsylvania.

Copy of the notice placed on raided Prohibition era properties.

Lingering fascination

If the Prohibition Era ended in 1933, one of its pathetic activities didn't. Moonshining, still illegal today because it avoids proper fees and critical health standards, continues. Internet sites continue to track the practice. A site for Ferrum College, of Ferrum, Virginia, tells about *Franklin County, Virginia,* where moonshining was an especially robust occupation during the Prohibition era. When authorities counted the number of whiskey-storage containers sold in Franklin County, during just a one-half-decade period in the 1930s, they found that the number of whiskey containers sold would have held over *five million gallons of moonshine whiskey!* With such an astonishing figure, one can easily understand why Franklin County, Virginia is the self-proclaimed "Moonshine Capital of the World."

Copper to stainless steel

Whether they are part of the lingering culture of illegal moonshiners or among the state-licensed makers of 'moonshine', the activity remains and thrives. While major differences linger, the legal and the illegal trade remains similar: Both offer the lure of tradition and both have switched to better equipment, such as the replacing of the old copper stills with modern stainless steel. But there are important differences: The legal moonshiners have open marketing, the state license, and its accompanying regulations; the sale of souvenir items and less likelihood of violence in the distilling end of alcohol production, sale and consumption. The ugly violence has more fully shifted to the world of the consumer.

Sadly, it is from the world of modern 'moonshining' that we have collected a depressing quote, taken from an internet site (mountainx.com, downloaded 6/20/16) and quoting a North Carolina state official: "To suggest that we want to discourage people from drinking is silly. That's a moral judgment and really shouldn't be decided by the state." I find that to be a saddening observation. Of course, we should strive to keep legislation minimal; but where the welfare of many innocent citizens becomes threatened, the wisdom of legislation is recognized. Even with the 'state' doing some regulating, the citizens of this country are often victims of some 'unregulated' behavior. Where, better, to observe this than in the world of alcoholic excesses?

> ## Sober Slogan #10
>
> **Drunkenness smooths the road**
>
> **From riches to rags!**

Americans must escape their fascination with the clandestine, dark-of-night, back-mountain culture of moonshining. It's now time for every American parent, politician, church leader, civic leader, medical expert, educator and journalist to condemn drunkenness, whether clandestine or blatant. Let all Americans flout tradition and aggressively distill *sobriety.*

Chapter Six

Tying Our Own Blindfolds

The Scots like the Irish and the Irish love the Scotch
While discussing the Irish and the Scots, we might insert a short verse that has long suggested more about slaking sailors' thirst than about national drinking habits. That verse (from the Scottish writer, Robert Louis Stevenson's 1883 book, *Treasure Island)* proclaims:

> Fifteen men on the dead man's chest
> Yo-ho-ho, and a bottle of rum!
> Drink and the devil had done for the rest—
> Yo-ho-ho and a bottle of rum!

With apologies for painting with an undeservedly broad brush and with mean stereotyping, I offer the following:

SHAM ROCKS

> I spent two years a-searchin'
> From dawn t' dusk t' dawn,
> Before I fin'ly found one:
> A wily Leprechaun.

> Two decades more I've hunted
> O'er ev'ry inch of ground.
> A *sober* son of Erin?
> 'E's nowhere to be found!

I was penning an apology for composing and printing the above rhyme but then thought better of it as I searched the ether to get information on drinking songs. Hell . . . I found lists of drinking songs; with songs for every occasion and for any mood . . . other than sobriety. Even more revealing, *I found but one nationality connected with internet collections of drinking songs.* There was no collection of Canadian drinking songs or Dutch drinking songs or Japanese drinking songs, etc. Of all the world's one-hundred-plus nations, there was positively only ONE nation listed with its own traditional drinking songs: Ireland!

Does Ireland have a national drinking song? It would seem so. That country, dotted with shamrocks and pubs, and home to the very popular brewer, *Guinness*, has a keg full of truly popular drinking songs. Either of the following two would make an exceptional candidate for an Irish national drinking song: "Rosin the Bow" and "Whiskey in the Jar."

The lush of the Irish
The word *whisky* (without the 'e') comes to us from Scotland. If we add the 'e' we have the Irish version. The very term, whiskey, came to us from the old Irish, about 1715. For them, it meant "water of life." Sadly, for many Irishmen, and millions of Americans, that meaning lingers. We have no notion as to the origin of the claim that God created whiskey so that the Irish wouldn't rule the world. Nor do we know who suggested that a seven-course Irish meal consists of a six-pack and a bowl of stew. All we do know is that Ireland was converted to Christianity by St. Patrick, who, legend says, chased all the snakes from Ireland. The Irish would have been far better blessed if the good saint had allowed the snakes to thrive and had chased alcohol from the Emerald Isle. However, in fairness, it must be noted that Ireland once had some admirable temperance work being done.

The alcoholism that is rampant in Ireland has followed the Irish immigrants to America. How better to observe Irish tradition than by celebrating St. Patrick's Day, a booze-laden holiday.

Strangely, the 1929 edition of the *Encyclopaedia Britannica* (Volume 18, p. 596) refers to "the most drunken countries." Such labeling of a nation may no longer be acceptable. If one did that today, he or she might be smacked with a Shillelagh!

The United States and drinking songs
While there seems to be no drinking song attached to this binging nation, the U.S. has enough drinking songs to provide such *hymns to ethanol* to the entire community of nations. There are drinking songs for parties, drunks, country occasions, rock music lovers, folk music lovers and, of course, in their own national category, the Irish drinking songs. As an example, there is a list found on Wikipedia that lists, on the day it was downloaded, 71 songs (http://en.wikipedia.org/wiki/Category:Songs_about_alcohol). The mere presence of so many lists, some of which may overlap, tells the nation—drinkers and non-drinkers alike—that we must try to stay afloat in an alcoholic deluge. Clearly, we are foundering.

Freaky ain't funny!
The stand-up comedians, the cartoonists, and all others who use drunkenness as a basis for humor are contributing to America's cavalier attitude toward the terrible terrorist, alcohol. Where to begin?

A few of their names: W. C. Fields, Foster Brooks, Dean Martin, and Ron White. They are the pathetic comics who pretend that there is humor in drunkenness. Considering the mountain of negative results from drinking, these 'comics' are beneath contempt. They should have been booed from the stages. They seem to be trying to portray themselves as 'lovable drunks'. Let's be brutally frank. There has never been a likable lush.

Granted, I've only passed my eighty-fourth birthday; but I've never seen a 'lovable drunk'. I've seen pathetic drunks and puking drunks and abusive drunks and menacing drunks and killer drunks, but never have I seen a *'lovable'* drunk. Clearly, the two words, lovable and drunk are contradictory terms. I consider the phrase, "lovable drunk," to be an 'intoxymoron'.

Where there's a will . . .
Among the more distressing articles, I've encountered was the one which appeared (July 2008) under the byline of George Will. This prize-winning columnist tossed logic to the winds and jettisoned all journalistic responsibility when describing a bit of the long history of alcohol. He mentions the long-recognized evidence that people in past centuries had two choices: alcohol or polluted water. No matter what the threat of intoxication might be, polluted

W.C. Fields (1880 -1946), perhaps the granddaddy of
our several alcohol-linked comedians; a man dedicated
to entertaining audiences and to ruining his own
health.

water could be deadly. Therefore, he suggests, beer had a civilizing influence. He even quotes one of our best, Ben Franklin. Franklin observed, Will reminds us, that beer ". . . is proof that God loves us and wants us to be happy." But, if we go to a related website (http://beer.about.com) we read the statement of a "beer expert" named Bryce Eddings, who states (download of 12/10/15) that, "There is no evidence that Franklin ever said this." Employing the same irrational thought so oft attributed to Ben Franklin, the skilled writer and signer of both the Declaration of Independence and the U.S. Constitution, we should also infer that shackles were proof that God wanted us to have slavery. To make his argument, Will skips the entire history of humanity between colonial times and the present; that long period where humans created hundreds of different kinds of refreshing drinks that are NOT polluted and that do NOT intoxicate or alter behavior. One of those, of course, is pure drinking water. I would submit that if Ben Franklin were living today, he would write something like, "Potable water, carbonated sodas, pure juices and the countless other refreshing, non-alcoholic drinks, are proof that God loves us and wants us to be sober!"

I liked the writings of the late Andy Rooney. I particularly like the column (*TDI*, 9/6/9) which opens with this sentence: "If I had to limit myself to drinking just one thing for the rest of my life, there's no doubt my choice would be water. A glass of cool, clear water is unquestionably the best drink, although I start every day with a cup of coffee." Rooney then goes on to discuss a variety of drinks, mentioning that beer is the world's most consumed beverage after water and tea. He closes that piece with a modest lament: "It's really too bad that everything we do that isn't good for us doesn't have such a direct negative impact. It would certainly be good if we felt as bad after eating too much as we do after drinking too much."

Surely, the polka writers, Ernst Neubach and Ralph Maria Siegel, who wrote (1956) the polka entitled "In Heaven There Is No Beer," were closer than Ben Franklin to the theological truth when they created their Hedonistic lyrics. Among the greatest consolations we have in this vale of tears is found in knowing what the lushes have sensed: in Heaven there is no beer . . .

However, from Hollywood to New York, and from Brandon to Nashville, and to any other entertainment-generating center in the United States, the corrupt folks who want to fleece us of our entertainment dollars can't think of enough ways to use alcohol to help sell their monologues, music, and movies. Ah, to have such mindless audiences, who can't remember this morning's traffic report long enough to think critically about the garbage that tweaks their funny bones! However,

The humor eludes one

We know that the consumption of alcohol in America is approaching the tsunami stage. Alcohol's production, promotion, and consumption proliferate. Despite mounting evidence of the social and physical damages done by alcohol in our society, the glamorization continues. How can we respond? The following topic simply gives one individual's life with an alcoholic family member; and it should be acknowledged that laws and agencies have been created that now offer a bit more protection from the dangers of alcoholic individuals, such as the one described here. Let the reader reach his or her own conclusions regarding the size of the alcohol problem in America. Simply dwell on this thought:

While many entertainers use alcohol as a basis for much humor, it's the liquor industry that flashes the broadest smile! Also, bear in mind that the account given here could be duplicated thousands of times over. This account involved real people with real pain and true heartbreak.

Older residents of *Antes Fort*, Pennsylvania and some from its larger neighbor, *Jersey Shore*, Pennsylvania, can attest to the accuracy of this account; but I will use only given names out of respect for the living members of the family, whom I visited several times and interviewed by phone several additional times. I also came to consider Charles as a friend.

Charles was a man in his mid-eighties, who had been battling health problems for most of his life. He was born in the small village of Antes Fort, in the Keystone State's Lycoming County. Antes Fort's neighbor is the town of Jersey Shore, a couple of miles away and on the opposite side of the Susquehanna River. Although Jersey Shore has a population of about four thousand residents, Antes Fort's population is measured in the hundreds, only. The town, named for a colonial defensive 'fort', once had a primary school, which Charles attended; but which is now closed. It has a post office; but that, too, is destined to close, so Antes Fort will be served by the U.S. Postal Service through the Jersey Shore facility. Charles was a child of the 1930s, a child of the Great Depression and a child of a drunken father. I have yet to find anything humorous about the liquor in Charles' life.

Charles' dad, J.W., married a young woman named Ruth, who was a native of Williamsport, Pennsylvania [home town to the Little League Museum and the Little League World Series and once the home of the *GRIT* weekly national newspaper]. And, while some studies suggest that men who are alcoholic may be somewhat sexually impaired, such men often father small broods of children. Charles' father, J.W., fathered seven: Charles, his three brothers, and three sisters. J.W., says son Charles, was an alcoholic who regularly made his own beer and who, says his unfortunate son, lost every job he ever had because of his drinking. J.W. gathered used beer bottles from the generous owners of the two local taverns. He used these as receptacles for his homemade beer. From the time that he was about seven years old, it was Charles's job to cap those freshly-filled bottles. If Charles made a mistake, he could be slugged on the head by the family brewmaster.

Charles told of a time when his older brother, Henry, was working on a state road-building project. Their dad, J. W., was the foreman. J.W. regularly found people in the area who sold their own homebrew. He purchased more than enough to get him through each day. Thus fortified, J.W.—by the end of the workday—was no longer ambulatory. His son, Henry, would lift his inebriate form onto a truck and take him home.

At home, the drunken patriarch could become a terror. A singular example: On one 'memorable' occasion, a major dish for their supper was a bowl of freshly-picked garden peas. The father's drunken behavior at this family meal included grabbing the bowl of peas and hurling it toward the kerosene lamp in the center of the table. One of Charles' older siblings grabbed the lamp and kept it from falling, but many dishes were scattered and shattered! As was always the case, Ruth had to 'soldier on', trying to restore order in a drunkard's domicile. She was finally able to separate the children from J.W. for their meals.

Where there are seven offspring and an alcoholic father, the mother's ongoing role is to work at raising eight children, one of whom is destined to never reach maturity and to rarely know sobriety. It was Ruth who had to struggle to find enough food for the family. It was Ruth whom her children would hear saying that she wasn't hungry when the entire family knew that she was simply denying herself a share in order to feed others. It was Ruth, with young Charles' assistance, who did the washing and ironing of neighbors' clothes in order to earn extra funds for the family. It was she who taught her children to be compassionate. Charles recalls the time when a moonshiner neighbor was arrested by federal Revenue agents. Ruth gathered all the children and admonished them to say nothing that might embarrass the neighbor's children. And it was Ruth who got her children off to weekly Sunday School services, after handing each of them a penny for the collection plate. Still, it was the drunkard's tyranny—J.W.'s drunken anger and his mistreatment of the siblings and their mother—that led each of the children to leave home at an early age. All except Charles.

One of Charles' older brothers got married, but later divorced and returned home for some time. The brother's ex-wife remarried over and over again for a full seven marriages. When she was still the mother of just two children—a young boy and a two-month-old infant son—the ex-wife suddenly brought both fruits of her loins to Ruth's house and abandoned the boys on the doorstep, with the baby being delivered in a cardboard box. She brought no formula and little else for the momentary foundlings. So their grandma, Ruth, and their uncle, Charles, immediately became the youngsters' principal caregivers.

J. W. eventually had a crippling stroke. He could no longer take care of himself, much less hold a salaried job. There was no insurance, no welfare, and no income. That's when Charles' mother began doing menial jobs that generated a pittance. The children, especially Charles, found menial jobs as well. Charles cared for invalid neighbors, scrubbed and polished floors and helped his mother to do neighborhood washing. She also cared for her invalid husband, who could no longer feed himself. The once-hard drinking family head lived for five years in that dependent condition, before dying and being placed in the family plot in the Jersey Shore Cemetery. Charles mother, however, went on to live for another 30 years and to reach her nineties before being placed in the earth beside C.W.

Despite the daily suffering, Ruth remained with her drunken husband and Charles remained with his mother. Although they changed houses, Charles and his mother remained in the village of Antes Fort. He worked for a couple of years as the freight clerk at the old Antes Fort railroad station. Then, he got employment at the famed Piper Aircraft Company in nearby Lock Haven. He worked for Piper Aircraft for nearly forty years. When the company moved to Florida, Charles rejected their offer to accompany the firm, preferring to remain with his then-invalid mother. After her passing, he lived either in neighboring Jersey Shore or in his hometown of Antes Fort.

Does the parent have a right to discipline an annoying son? We know that some children rebel; but what of Charles' need for punishment? It was during one of J.W.'s many drunken fits of rage that he once attacked Charles. He savagely kicked his son and continued the assault until Ruth could restrain J.W. Why didn't Charles more aggressively defend himself? It is difficult for a boy, who is not yet six years old, to mount a defense against a drunken bully. In fact, it was during this alcoholic rampage that five-year-old Charles was repeatedly kicked in his groin!

Charles' mother applied ice bags to his scrotum for about a week. The doctor said that one of his testicles had to be removed. However, the remaining one was also permanently damaged.

J.W., the boozing father of seven children, had condemned his son to remain forever childless.

How young was Charles when he first encountered his dad's drunken behavior? Actually, that's hard to explain. There was the day, in the midsummer of 1927, when a liquored J.W. again got angry with his wife. Ruth was expecting again and was far along in the pregnancy. He proclaimed that he wanted no more squalling kids around. Then he knocked his wife off the porch and onto the ground!

The next day, Charles was born.

Because of his dad's humiliating and brutal attack on Charles' mother, the neonate was born with a slightly deformed head that took months to slowly return to normal. However, Charles was still suffering from an uncontrollable shakiness and restlessness that he carried into his early school years, to the annoyance of some unsympathetic teachers. Despite the agony of years of living with a drunken bully, Charles persevered and, by the time he was in the Jersey Shore High School, he was a capable athlete and an actor in school productions. He remained slender of build and was a pleasant conversationalist. Despite many cancer treatments, the octogenarian's hair remained black and nearly full, a condition that he attributed to the fact that he had American-Indian ancestry, from a native Cree who was his great-grandmother.

Charles, who never married, once observed about his mother's pathetic life: "Some marks that he gave her, she took to her grave." Surely, *emotional scars* will also have been or will be carried to the grave by every one of J.W.'s hapless family members. Charles also carried the permanent wounds of a senseless childhood attack. Yet, undaunted, Charles could be seen at meetings in the Antes Fort museum [of which he was the principal founder], or visiting his ailing sister in a local nursing facility, or going for regular cancer treatments or sitting in the pew for Sunday morning worship service at the Antes Fort United Methodist Church, a house of worship that Charles attended for those many decades since his suffering mother used to distribute their coins and see her children off to church.

Within weeks of my last telephone interview with Charles, for the above account, an advice columnist, Carolyn Hax ("*Tell Me About It*") responded to a query with a column (8-4-15) telling readers that "growing up in the shadow of a parent's drinking problem. That's the beast, where the drinker's problems devolve to the family members . . . A drinker makes a mess, the family cleans it; a drinker does something embarrassing, the family covers it. The drinker is easily provoked, the family tiptoes around." Obviously, if the budget for an alcoholic's family is tight, booze will replace bread and intoxication will replace a reasoning intellect. I was deeply saddened by a note from a friend in February of 2018. Charles finally took his paternally-broken body to a grave near the graves of his parents.

Daniel Okrent, quoted elsewhere, can be quoted once more regarding reasons why the women of 19th century America wished to see temperance become fashionable. He summarizes, quite nicely, (p. 16) the genuine alcohol-spawned travails of women in 19th century America. A passage follows:

"A drunken husband and father was sufficient cause for pain, but many rural and small-town women also had to endure the associated ravages born of the early saloon: the wallet emptied into a bottle; the job lost or the farm work left undone; and, most pitilessly, a scourge that would later in the century be identified by physicians as "syphilis of the innocent"—venereal disease contracted by the wives of drink-sodden husbands who had found something more than liquor lurking in saloons."

As the preceding paragraphs suggest if a boozer has a frugal mate, that mate must endure the hell of seeing his or her frugality wasted in a struggle that lasts throughout the entire length of a marriage, while the boozer uses his tummy as a bottomless tankard. Pathetic? Yes. Inane? To be sure.

Society's responses?

After decades of absurd behavior by drunkards, Prohibition came and went. Those who admired sobriety were chagrined that we were putting our fragile craft back into the swirling ethanol currents once more. There were changes, of course. Today, there are laws and agencies that have been established to protect family members from physical and emotional abuse, such as that described in the above account from central Pennsylvania. One can also recognize that the very laws that are designed to prevent impaired drivers are also the laws that cause large numbers of hit-and-run victims. Further, it's especially disheartening to observe that all our laws and all our agencies must squander most of their resources in *reactive*, rather than *preventative* works. There are fine efforts, like alcohol checkpoints; but we face a sorry fact.

The bulk of our efforts go to responding to the ills of alcohol, rather than to the prevention of those ills. There is another modern phenomenon: the proliferation of clinics and rehab centers. In view of the crushing numbers of dipsomaniacs and drunken drivers, we can be grateful for all efforts to reduce alcoholism; but such efforts are still not doing enough *dissuading and preventing.* Meanwhile, the drunkard lingers as a major celebrity and dangerous fixture in our modern American society . . . and alcohol's intoxicating deluge continues to saturate our landscapes and to disrupt our lives.

Literary lions and the lapping of liquor

My cousin, Glen Graybill, lives in Emmett, Idaho. Citing local lore, he has mentioned that Ernest Hemingway "closed a lot of bars around here."

Was this the rugged American author, Ernest Hemingway, who was lionized by the literary world and given a Nobel Prize for his literary endeavors (writings which alienated his own parents)? Was this the man who was a World War I ambulance driver and, later, a big game hunter on the African continent? Was this the man whose published books were transformed into several popular movies? Yes, this was the literary giant who was husband to a series of four wives and father to three sons and who, at the age of 61, could no longer face life's challenges and who took his loaded rifle and sought the biggest of the earth's big game, one's self. His Wikipedia biography (downloaded 12-10-15) makes several references to his abuse of alcohol. They include mention of "alcoholic sprees," and (in the 1950s) medical advice to stop drinking, advice which was only briefly heeded, and the assessment, "Added to Hemingway's physical ailments was the additional problem that he had been a heavy drinker for most of his life."

However, of all those people whom one might condemn for their alcoholism, Ernest Hemingway is one who might require some genuine sympathy. The man had experienced, and survived, domestic accidents, several automobile crashes and a pair of serious airplane crashes. Ernest Hemingway was a walking bundle of genuine physical agonies. Even a strict teetotaler might be driven to suicide with such a record of serious injuries.

For those of us who relish sobriety, in ourselves and in the society in which we wish to move, the drinking records of many of our author celebrities are disgusting. Writers like Dashiell

Hammett (1894-1961), F. Scott Fitzgerald (1896-1940), Dorothy Parker (1893-1967), Edgar Allen Poe (1809-1849), Carson McCullers (1917-1967), John Cheever (1912-1982), Truman Capote (1924-1984), and others have biographical accounts that all reek of alcohol.

One could argue that alcohol might have brought forth their literary genius. I submit that a counter argument would be just as valid. Those literary giants were geniuses *despite* their minds being lubricated by booze. There is another consideration. All their ages at death fall between 40 and 73. To me, this *suggests* that most, if not all, of these celebrated writers reduced their literary life spans by being liquor's lackeys.

Some pundits never seem to overtake current trends. *The Weekly Standard* (5/21/18) tells of a recent study that proved that being "one sheet in the wind" (my choice of phrases) enhanced creative thinking. I thought an April 2018 item by Emily Temple had already laid that notion to rest. Ms. Temple, writing for an internet site, *Literary Hub*, quotes (downloaded 4/17/18) the Colombian novelist and Nobel Winner, Gabriel Garcia Marquez, as follows: "One thing that Hemingway wrote that greatly impressed me was that writing for him was like boxing. He took care of his health and his well-being. Faulkner had a reputation of being a drunkard, but in every interview that he gave he said it was impossible to write one line when drunk. Hemingway said this too." Really? "Impossible to write one line when drunk." Humph! What would Hemingway and Faulkner know?

Zane Gray (1875-1939), the very popular writer of "Western" stories gave this writer a feeling that he, too, was for temperance. In his one book, *Raiders of the Spanish Peaks*, he mentions a man feigning drunkenness. Elsewhere (page 13) he identifies liquor as "that bane of riders." On page 93 he writes that a newly-hired cook "had a weakness for the flowing bowl." Lastly, Gray observes (p. 84), about his hero: "There were reasons why his nerves should never be unsteadied by tobacco or liquor."

We need to take a glance at another recent writer, Sue Grafton (1940-2017). This author of a very successful series of mysteries ("C is for Corpse," etc.) had a truly pathetic childhood and an early life that was made worse by alcohol. The tragedy of her life was that she had two parents who were alcoholic. She has described a long and painful youth that included her mother's suicide following an operation for throat cancer.

To close any discussion of alcohol-fueled authorship, let's read a quote that Philip Krass used to open his biographical work on the distiller, Jack Daniel (*Blood and Whiskey*). The quotation is attributed to "A Tennessee Aristophanes," and reads as follows: "Quickly, bring me a bottle of whiskey, so that I may wet my mind and say something clever." I submit that that is neither clever nor profound. Clearly, the alcohol-dampened mind formulates and utters statements that would make the braying of a jackass seem profound.

If Oscars were given for drunkenness (Alcoholly-wood)
Hollywood has often used alcohol in movies to create more appeal to moviegoers. Too many actors and actresses aggravate the problem. Here is a sorry sampling.

The plastered chimney sweep
Dick Van Dyke is among the most talented and admired of American movie stars. Yet, in his later years (he is 92 years old as this is being written, in April of 2018), he admitted that he was, for about a quarter century, an alcoholic, whose co-star was often a troubling hangover. He sought clinical support and—it is a joy to note—eventually regained control of his personal behavior and the late stages of his illustrious career.

The bombed Beedle
Billy Beedle, Jr. became one of Hollywood's most successful actors, where he used the stage name of William Holden. He was *best man* at Ronald Reagan's second marriage and he starred in frequent hits, winning an academy award for his role in one of the great 'war' movies, *Stalag 17*. One of his last films was also considered to be one of his greatest, *The Bridge on the River Kwai.* He was also known to be an alcoholic, a situation that complicated his work and his romantic relationships. In 1966 he earned an eight-month suspended sentence for causing the death of another driver in a drunk-driving accident in Italy.

On November 12, 1981, William Holden apparently slipped and fell while alone and drunk in his Santa Monica apartment. His forehead was cut open when his head struck a teak table. It was believed that he may have been conscious for a half-hour or more but was unable to summon help. Alone and intoxicated, he bled to death. His corpse was found several days later.

Jason

Jason Robards, Jr. was the son of an actor; but he far surpassed his father in thespian fame. He was recognized as an alcoholic, but he was one of those topers who functioned exceptionally well with that affliction. He was a highly-regarded stage actor and made dozens of movies for theatres and television. He was one of those actors who impressed the public just from the roles in which he portrayed real historical figures. Jason Robards, Jr. had about a dozen roles where he played such luminaries as Abraham Lincoln, Ulysses Grant, Franklin Roosevelt and Richard Nixon; yet he also successfully carried off such challenging roles as Al Capone, Doc Holliday, George S. Kaufman, Howard Hughes Andrei Sakharov, Dashiell Hammett, Armand Hammer and Ben Bradlee.

However, among his four wives was Lauren Bacall, who once observed, regarding his alcoholism, "I don't know if he enjoyed it, but he was hooked on it." Their marriage—according to a Wikipedia download of 4-25-2015—ended thusly: "They divorced in 1969 in significant part because of his alcoholism." His biography, on IMDb (4/25/15 download) records that "In 1972, he was in a horrifying accident on a winding California road. He drove his car into the side of a mountain and nearly died. His acute drinking problem contributed to the accident. He slowly recovered after extensive surgery and facial reconstruction."

Christian Slater

By perusing a fistful of internet sites, one might observe that the actor, Christian Slater (b. 1969) is, or is not, dead; is, or is not, maturing and is, or is not, the sexiest man alive (or dead) etc. A victim (or perpetrator) of hoaxes, makes much data about Slater unreliable. He has had several arrests, at least two of which involved alcohol. The only thing that seems reliable is his reputation as a polygamist, lawbreaker, and alcoholic. These seem to be the sure things for many modern American celebrity types.

Robert and Randy

How refreshing: They say that Robert Duvall doesn't drink or smoke outside of the movies. On the other hand, country singer and film star Randy Travis does appear to drink outside of his office, outside of his home, and even outside of his clothes! Travis is great fodder for the tabloids; but not the role-model essays. He had two driving arrests in 2012. He is about 5' 9", according to a very unflattering mug shot.

Alcohollywood might be a more appropriate name for the world's busiest movie-making center. The Hollywood Crowd [Ray Liotta, Lindsay Lohan, Nicole Richie, Mel Gibson, etc.] keeps the liquor flowing and the tabloids humming. Sadly, *Time* magazine, which should be one of the journalistic leaders in the search for sobriety, simply goes into its cutesy routine, advising "Gang, when you can afford a limo, party night's the time to use it." (3/5/07, p. 79)! *The Week* magazine (2/2/07) informs readers that Matt Fox, a television star, was drinking at 14 and tries to get his co-workers drunk. One must believe that many celebrities use alcohol and drunkenness to stay on the front pages of the mindless entertainment magazines and the tabloids. Sylvester Stallone, who made a fortune by pummeling Russian boxers in a series of films, has picked up another small fortune as a spokesperson for vodka.

Lindsay Lohan has kept the tabloids and the normal news outlets busy tracking her party-girl career. The New York-born actress has spent her entire first three decades, since she was three years old, as an actress and the last decade as one of the nation's most-known party girls. She has had multiple DUI arrests, multiple car crashes, multiple rehab stints and multiple court appearances. Her major award during her most troubled years was the alcohol-detection bracelet that graced her slender ankle. In one of her films, *The Parent Trap*, Lindsay portrayed twins. "Lilo" should really have been born as triplets, to cover her many party-girl roles. In her defense, she seems to have spent the last several years in actual, trouble-free, acting activity.

In 2012 (Feb. 6), *Time* magazine offered readers some earth-shaking news. Pat Sajak was bragging about his alcoholic exploits. *Time* noted that Sajak, host of the vacuous T.V. game show, *Wheel of Fortune*, admitted to leaving the set of his show, between tapings, with his co-host, the mannequin-like Vanna White, for "two or three or six . . ." margaritas. Thus reinforced, they returned to the set but could have trouble recognizing the alphabet. Obviously, *Time* reporters have similar trouble recognizing newsworthy material. *Time* could have shown a modicum of maturity by simply telling its readers that, annually, in this nation, alcohol slams on the brakes on the wheels of fortune of countless alcohol lovers.

(From *The Daily Item*, 1-23-13) When celebrity television hostess, Barbara Walters took a tumble at a party and was away from her show, *The View*, for some days, a co-host, Joy Behar—who has been improperly identified as a 'comic'— offered the thought that Barbara should "lay off the Grey Goose." That's a brand of vodka. Where's the humor?

Names of entertainment celebrities who have had alcohol problems abound. The list is nearly endless; but here are some that one easily encounters in the most cursory scanning of the regular newspapers, the tabloids, the television broadcasts or the internet. The list includes Richie Sambora, a long-time guitarist for Bon Jovi; David Hasselhoff, Nick Nolte, a very popular star, Johnny Depp, Diana Ross, Jamie Lee Curtis, Lynda Carter, Ben Affleck and Michael J. Fox (who is reported to have abandoned alcohol after his diagnosis of Parkinson's disease).

It is often a 'toss up' as to whether a celebrity is celebrated for his or her talents or is celebrated for his or her drinking. One must lament the situation where society helps prop the celebrity's pathetic drinking record by further glamorizing the behavior. Those Hollywood types who deserve special awards for their very intemperate off-screen lives would include the following nominees:

1. Mel Gibson
2. The late Whitney Houston
3. Lindsay Lohan
4. Charlie Sheen

Among Alcohollywood's most pathetic figures has been Charlie Sheen, former star of *Two and A Half Men*. That was a show that used vulgarity, flatulence, masturbation, hard drinking and prostitution to prop the egomaniac who was its 'star'. Sheen is a national joke. As with so many entertainment celebrities, one must ask of Sheen: Which came first, the matrimonial problems, the arrest problems or the booze? He might have been a bit more appealing if he hadn't pretended that he could get by without his canned laughter, his skillful scriptwriters, his piano-playing double, and his primary co-star, a bottle of scotch.

While Charlie Sheen is a national joke, Whitney Houston was a national tragedy. For the entire boozing crowd in Hollywood, the behavior is totally senseless. How distressing that these sotted celebrities often become role models for the masses.

Oscar
As a life-long rustic, I've only been to a half-dozen-or-so events to see celebrated performers of one sort or another. However, two of the paucity of such performances featured the same artist. Once—about 1950—while visiting an aunt who lived in Philadelphia's burbs, I went to the Robin Hood Dell to hear Oscar Levant (1906-72). In the same time frame, my then-fiancée and I drove the 50 miles to Harrisburg to attend a performance of Oscar Levant in the capital city's Forum building. I recall his delightful wit and his rendition of "*Rhapsody in Blue.*" I feel especially privileged that I saw not just one of his performances, but two. I am saddened to read that he was "an unreformed alcoholic." I'm also saddened to have searched the internet for details of his personal drinking problem, but find nothing beyond that general description. Still, I must list him as one of our national musical treasures who was troubled by the use of alcohol. I suppose that it's a personal weakness that I was so in awe of his musical and intellectual genius that I tend to overlook whatever it was that lured him into alcohol's damning influence. I must ask . . . how can one remain unimpressed by a man who declares "What the world needs is more geniuses with humility; there are so few of us left."?

A suspected crime, like good whiskey, gets better with age
The actor, Robert Wagner, can easily be envied by some of us who are nondescript men. He hasn't seemed to lose either his handsome appearance or debonair manner. We've seen him in a television series with Stephanie Powers, then offering us a reverse mortgage and adding charm to the now-defunct Charlie Sheen vehicle. However, despite the passing of more than three dozen years, the suspicion of a crime hangs over him. The 1981 drowning death of his wife, Natalie Wood, leaves an air of suspicion clinging to Wagner. New witnesses have appeared with tales to tell, but their stories have a tiresome ring. *The Week* magazine reports (2-16-18) that "Wood and Wagner had a blazing, alcohol-fueled argument . . ." Nothing new has been reported as of this date (4-18-18). Natalie Wood might still be with us *if only* . . .

The comic strips
Neither we nor our children can even read the comics without encountering our nation's terribly cavalier attitude towards boozing. Among these purveyors of pro-alcohol comic strips are *Hagar the*

Horrible, Andy Capp, Non-Sequitur, and *The Wizard of Id*. Demonstrating the longevity of a pro-booze comic strip is the very long-running *Barney Google*. *Barney Google* may be the granddaddy of the alcohol comic strips. The setting for the strip is some isolated mountain where Snuffy Smith runs a still and where the liquor jug is a primary character. This strip has been selling since 1919!

One would think that anyone who appreciates a sober society would be offended by the following:

Dik Browne's *Hagar the Horrible* (*TDI*, 1-16-15) has just two blocks. In the first, Hagar and his wife are seated by the lighted fireplace. He says, "Ah! A toasty seat by a roaring fire!" Then he adds, "It doesn't get better than this!" Then [Second block] he turns to his wife, to add, "unless you want to fetch me another beer!" Within a single week (10-23-15 and 10-28-15), Hagar twice entertains the readers with alcohol-based wit. In the first, his wife is wheeling him home from a tavern, while he describes his condition ("I'm drunk as a skunk") and a few days later we see a bartender listing Hagar's choices: Vodka, Rum, Beer, Wine, Scotch, Ale, and Brandy. The hilarious last panel has Hagar declaring, "I'll take them in alphabetical order!"

In another edition of the same paper (11-29-15), the Sunday strips show only gluttony creating the humor for Hagar, while the opening two blocks for *The Wizard of Id* reveal a bartender asking the resident lush, "Which political party do you support?" The conclusion to that segment is in the very next panel, where the lush gives a profound, six-word response: "Whichever party had the most booze" One must fight to control one's laughter long enough to giggle when Andy Capp's wife berates him for suggesting that he and the vicar "arm wrestle to decide who's going out for the beers." We can be grateful for those who import the British cartoon; otherwise, we'd have missed that hilarity in our mundane lives . . .

It is mildly interesting that the Andy Capp strip, according to a Wikipedia article (https//en.wikipedia.org/wiki/Andy Capp), downloaded 12/6/15, has evolved somewhat in keeping with changing mores. Capp no longer beats his wife and no longer smokes. If the cartoonists can imagine Capp with such phenomenal changes, why can't they show Andy Capp doing the truly noble thing and embracing sobriety? More recently one is brought back from daydreaming about a truly reformed Andy Capp. His strip of 11-27-16 (*The Daily Item*) has a doctor asking Capp, "Did you take my advice and cut down the booze by 90%?" To which the incorrigible Andy replies "No, not yet. Give me a chance, Doc. That was only three months ago. It's still sinking in."

My local newspaper has had some letters complaining about the presumably liberal comic strip, *Doonesbury* (Garry Trudeau) and, conversely, some letters complaining about the presumably conservative comic strip, *Mallard Fillmore* (Bruce Tinsley). My impassioned query: Why is no one—liberal or conservative or any other political shading—registering complaints about the steady pro-alcohol 'humor' that some comic strip creators so regularly offer their readers?

Locker room or liquor cabinet?

While some athletes seem to be too busy injecting steroids to do any heavy drinking; many surely try. Many sports legends were also legendary drinkers, not the least of which was George Herman "Babe" Ruth. His dad was a barkeep who died in a barroom brawl when Ruth was in his early 20s and playing major league baseball with the Boston Red Sox. The Red Sox, who still blush about the act nearly a century later, peddled Babe Ruth to the New York Yankees. Ruth, who created new standards for judging power hitters, became the best-known player in the major leagues. Ruth's single-season home run record (60) lasted for 34 years, while his lifetime record for homers (714) lasted 39 years. "The Babe" was not the first lush in sports; just one of the earlier giants of the game who also had a Gargantuan thirst, too regularly slaked in an age when alcohol was illegal. Many other athletes were alcoholic. Some were seemingly able to cope with athletic opponents and alcohol at the same time; while others had their careers ruined by their excesses. Just one further example: Consider Mickey Mantle. This New York Yankees star hit over 500 home runs, including some among the longest homers ever launched. Yet, he also seemed eager to get into the record book of hard drinkers. Mantle barely made it into his 60's before he was shopping for a liver. He got one, but it was too late. He died at 63. Mantle's plight also raises a whopping ethical question: Should wealthy or celebrated (or both) individuals—who showed no concern for their own livers when younger—be given any special consideration for organ transplants?

In October 2015, it was revealed that a New York Yankees pitcher was going into alcohol rehab. This was the 35-year-old, lanky (6'7") Californian named Carsten (C.C.) Sabathia. A former hurler for the Cleveland Indians and Milwaukee Brewers, Sabathia was a Cy Young Award winner (2007), In 2009, he became the highest-paid pitcher in major-league baseball, when he signed a seven-year contract for a modest $161,000,000. That sum can buy a lot of booze and a stadium full of rehabilitation. His announcement reminds fans of his guzzling predecessors on the Yankee roster: Babe Ruth and Mickey Mantle. Regarding Sabathia's quest for sobriety, one must wish him well and hope that he can fulfill his wish to return to the mound.

Keeping the topic of alcohol and athletes current: Josh Brent was a member of the Dallas Cowboys professional football team, who had a prior arrest for Driving Under the Influence of Alcohol. In 2009 he offered a guilty plea in response to a DUI charge. Then, on a December night in 2012, Brent—again drunk—was driving along a Texas highway near Dallas. A couple of hours after midnight, he lost control of his 2007 Mercedes Benz S60, which skidded several hundred yards and flipped several times! When police arrived, they saw Brent trying to pull his Cowboys teammate, Jerry Brown, from the burning car. Josh Brent suffered minor injuries. Jerry Brown was pronounced dead at the hospital. The charge against Brent? Intoxication manslaughter.

Another one-time sports star is Carlton Fisk, who spent a couple of dozen years pitching in major league baseball, with the Red Sox and the White Sox. His DUI arrest in December of 2012 reminded fans that he also had an alcohol-related incident a few months earlier. It was in October of the same year that police found Fisk in his Ford F150 pickup truck. The truck left the highway, drove through a ditch, got a flat tire and came to rest in a cornfield. When police arrived, they found that the truck's engine was still running; but the driver was passed out. There was also an open bottle of vodka on the floor.

A popular song recalled

While one can easily complain (see below) about modern country-western music dwelling on alcohol to a degree of absurdity, there is just one popular song that haunts. One wonders, even after the many decades, whether it was the music or the lyrics that made it popular. The early Rock-and-Roll group, "The Champs" had a million-seller recording in 1957. Their hit, "Tequila," had lyrics consisting of just 'three' words: "Tequila . . . tequila . . . tequila."

The Mashville sound?

As an aged lover of most forms of music, I remember, as a youth, hearing and seeing, in live concert, Roy Acuff; while, as a septuagenarian, it was Alan Jackson. I do appreciate most of the old-time country-western songs and many of today's forms of the genre. From the renditions of Roy Acuff, the Carter family, and Hank Williams, down through Porter Wagoner, Loretta Lynn, George Jones and into the music of today's country vocalists, I find country music to be both tuneful and pleasant to my ears. That only makes the "however" that much sadder.

However, while early country music touched on alcohol as a theme, it was from a truly different angle than it is today! In that historic old town of Nashville, Tennessee (which should be renamed 'Mashville' in honor of the alcohol-loving mentality of so many of *today's* songwriters and stars), there is no evidence that current stars have any qualms whatever about inspiring the young people of America with *hymns to hooch.*

When early country music dwelt on alcohol, it was generally presented as a form of decadence for which one should feel shame.

This nation needs to fill the air with songs of sobriety and sanity and to stop writing songs that suggest that the utterly shameless songwriters are the paid pitchmen and pitchwomen of Old # 7 of Lynchburg, Tennessee.

Scotch and scatology

Beyond its musical contributions to the terror of alcohol, there is the push to sell booze in other things *country.* Should you be one who follows country comedians, the topic title, "Scotch and Scatology," should promptly bring one individual to mind: Ron White. This Texan got national notice as part of the country quartet of traveling comics known as the "Blue Collar Comedy Tour." Ron White, a thrice-married comic, is easy to recognize, even if one doesn't recognize the face. He's usually gripping a cigar and a glass of Scotch. He is also one of a league of comedians who rely on lines about dogs licking their bottoms to squeeze a few laughs from their 'laugh at anything' crowd. It seems likely that, while with the "Blue Collar Comedy Tour," the four comics would start each new week with the discussion about whose turn it was to use the bottom-licking canine joke.

As with the late Dean Martin, much of Ron White's humor involves his intemperate drinking. White has moved into the high income-tax brackets with such revelations as, "I can't do it much longer . . . my liver won't hold out." [CMT broadcast 10/16/08, about 10:30 PM]. Alcohol is a standard prop for White, a rustic role model who bragged (1/8/13) on a television show, "I've been drinking like a fish for thirty years . . ."

Sadly, Ron White can find enough self-conscious audience members who will titter and laugh at the most humorless lines if they are laced with terms that might be known as "Texas Crude." Should you ever have the opportunity, observe the act that has a Scotch glass and a cigar attached to a so-called 'comedian'. White has joined such celebrated jackasses as W. C. Fields, Foster Brooks, Dean Martin, Charlie Sheen and others who portray themselves as charming bad boys. At least, Dean Martin was a fine singer; but all should be ashamed of themselves for pretending that alcohol gives them some sort of charm. If any of these fellows had real charm they could exude that charm without the prop of alcohol.

As noted earlier, in recent decades there's been a pathetic, pro-booze approach to country music lyrics. Early lyrics seemed to tell of alcohol's impact, in clearly *negative* terms.

Some examples, from older country songs, would include the words from a Porter Wagoner song ("Cold Hard Facts of Life"), referring to the singer, before attacking an unfaithful wife and her friends with a knife, becoming fortified by drinking a "fifth of courage." Another of Wagoner's songs spins a pathetic account of "Skid Row Joe." There is George Jones singing, "With the blood from my body, I could start my own still. If drinking don't kill me, her memory will." (Cassette # EGT 38323). The old Tex Ritter song, "Rye Whiskey," suggests that the singer hates the liquor on which he thrives. He warns others that, "If I get drunk, madam, it's nothing to you" and he closes the song with "Rye whiskey, rye whiskey, you're no friend to me. You killed my poor daddy, God damn you, try me." A 1940s era musical group that satirized much ~ *Spike Jones and the City Slickers* ~ had a song ("Behind Those Swinging Doors") that satirized the theme of the book, *Ten Nights in a Barroom*. In their song, a little girl from a mining town fails to get her father to return home from a saloon at two o'clock in the morning. The closing chorus follows:

> Oh . . . Oh!
> The doors swing in, the doors swing out
> Where some pass in, and others pass out
> This story is told of a fool and his gold
> Behind those swinging door-or-ors,
> (Hic—Burp)
> Behind those swinging doors.

Another of the older country tunes performed [LP album CAS-793(e)] by comic musicians Homer and Jethro warns everyone to beware of "Cigareetes, Whusky and Wild, Wild Women"

Far more somber is a song by Hank Snow, a Canadian-born country star who was well-received in the United States. His lament-style song captures the feeling of despair over the influence of alcohol. Snow's song, "The Drunkard's Son," tells of a scared boy, shortly before his death, hiding from a drunken father. That song, with its touching lyrics was recorded by RCA Camden (CAL-722) records in 1962.

I appreciate both the music and the lyrics to country legend, Loretta Lynn's 1967 hit: "Don't Come Home a-Drinkin'." Her song expresses thoughts that one would likely find to be common among wives of boozer mates.

The Canadian singer, Shania Twain, has a voice that has earned her several hundred million dollars. Ms. Twain is, in this man's opinion, the most naturally attractive (sans cosmetics) of the country singers. *The Week* news magazine (5/18/18) tells of her harrowing life, in part because of a step-father who was sexually abusive, "mentally ill and an alcoholic." That article tells us that Shania relates that the survival skills she learned in childhood "really helped me through."

Along with the shameful pro-booze approach to country song lyrics, one country-singing star, Randy Travis, has brought another helping of shame to Nashville. Travis would be well served if he applied one of his early song titles to his alcohol problem. He might sing, "I Won't Need You Anymore" (Warner Brothers Records, Inc., 1987). However, Randy Travis made sure he'd not easily be forgotten when, in 2012, he allegedly walked into a convenience store for cigarettes; but he lacked cash or the clothing to hold cash! Shortly after that naked effort to buy cigarettes, Travis crashed his car and was arrested for driving while intoxicated and for making a terroristic threat. He still hadn't covered his naked body. His drunken behavior got him a suspended jail sentence, a fine and two years of probation.

Coincidentally, perhaps, Travis recorded a 1990 hit ("A Few Ole Country Boys") with a compatriot, mentioned briefly above, in country music and in boozing: George Jones. Although Jones (1931-2013) indulged in both drugs and alcohol, he didn't seem to let his disregard for his own health or his changes in rehab programs or recording companies or marriages prevent him from recording hit after hit. He was among the giants of country music, leaving his mark on Nashville as well as on the Nashville bridge into which he wrecked his car in 1999. That crash left Jones badly injured and with a return to rehab. This book, *Intoxication Nation*, obsesses about the many unhealthy results of alcohol abuse; but George Jones' life seems to be the exception that proves the rule. George, who is regularly identified with alcoholism, was 81 years old when he died. Also showing terrific longevity was one of his many hit songs: "He Stopped Loving Her Today." That song can be found on YouTube. On the morning of May 8, 2018, I checked the number of viewers for "He Stopped Loving Her Today." Within just one-half hour, the song had gained another 100 viewers! That gave the song a total of 9,244,451 YouTube viewers! That's not too shabby for a 38-year old ballad.

The truly legendary old country singer, known for his songs and his alcohol intake, was Hank Williams, who was identified as a major influence on George Jones. Williams (1923-1953) wrote and recorded one of my favorite country tunes, "I'm So Lonesome I Could Cry." But, he had succumbed to the lure of alcohol and drugs. He died in the back seat of his Cadillac while being driven to a singing engagement. A Yahoo listing (4-5-18) offers this cause for Hank Williams' death: Drug/alcohol-related heart attack." He didn't make it out of his twenties.

Of course, songs about a drunkard's son or a drunken skid row derelict stand in sharp contrast to the booze-loving ballads of today. Read, or listen to, the liquor-worshipping lyrics of today's country artists.

Any of the following names could draw endless ticket lines at entertainment centers across the U.S. It's a repugnant situation: Some of those same entertainers either use alcohol to make an entertainment buck, or use alcohol to make themselves drunk, or both. Either approach should be condemned for the hellish negative messages of their actions or their songs.

A modern magazine, *Men's Journal*, ran an article (12/15) about one country hunk, singer Tim McGraw. As the magazine tells it, the 48-year-old McGraw has "traded late-night boozing on tour for intense daily workouts . . ." The journalistic piece quotes McGraw as declaring that "In 2008 I stopped drinking, and that turned everything in the right direction." This suggests that it took him about four decades to reach maturity. Still, that is much better than many entertainers, who seem determined to have booze served at their funerals and to have their corpses packed in booze for that final journey. One might wish that Tim McGraw's above quote could be placed on a few billboards along our interstate highways for a few weeks. How refreshing it would be to be able to go tooling down the interstate and suddenly see those words of wisdom: "I stopped drinking, and that turned everything in the right direction."

Sadly, *Men's Journal*, that same magazine—and same issue—has very classy liquor ads, with all things upscale. It also has a piece ["Tarantino Takes Telluride"] about Telluride, Colorado. In this article, I learned some things I will never forget. I learned that when a motion picture is shot in the Telluride area, it will have magnificent scenery and self-indulgent actors and artists. I learned that Quentin Tarantino "favored honey-flavored Jack Daniels" and that there's a cockeyed tradition that requires the breaking out of champagne "after every 100th roll of film that is shot." Also, "it was no surprise that when the crew . . .arrived in the town in late 2014, things got a little out of control." The state apparently used a five-million-dollar tax incentive to lure the producers to the Centennial State, knowing that (as producer Richard M. Gladstein noted) "we spend a lot, eat a lot of food, and drink a lot of booze."

We needn't belabor the issue; but I'd ask any reader who wants to properly judge the alcohol problem in America to at least expand this topic on his/her own by reading adequate accounts of the likes of George Jones, Hank Williams, Keith Urban and, the high priest of booze ballads, Toby Keith.

A distaff disciple

Mindy McCready made it in country music with frequent hits, but she couldn't avoid the law and she abused both drugs and alcohol. After several arrests, two out-of-wedlock pregnancies, and a well-publicized abusive relationship, she bore her second child, with a different father than that of her first child. During these problems, McCready made several attempts on her own life. Then, so say the allegations, her current boyfriend, and the father of her second son, committed suicide. Mindy McCready never reached her 40th year. On February 17, 2013, about five weeks after the loss of her then-current boyfriend, McCready shot herself in a successful suicide effort.

The man from Margaritaville

It's one man's opinion (this man) that every Parrothead is a dimwit who has hitched his wagon to a star. The star is Jimmy Buffett.

Las Vegas, Nevada—city of slots, sluts, and suckers—is one of many slick places for the weak-willed to download their wallet and to upload their livers. Thanks to the magic of Jimmy Buffett's name, booze and gambling are combined at the Flamingo Casino. There, visitors can sit on the patio of the *Jimmy Buffett's* Margaritaville restaurant and watch the crowds move from one dive to another while listening to the music of hundreds of nearby slot machines.

Exceptions?

There are several references in the Bible to a "voice crying in the wilderness." That is what one must feel is true regarding country music and the rare anti-alcohol songs coming from contemporary artists. In 2015, one of those rarities appeared. Alan Jackson—a top American country-western singer and/songwriter—released a new song with lyrics that clearly challenged the regular thinking in Nashville. The title, itself, tells us much: *"Angels and Alcohol."* That song's four verses all suggest that sweethearts and drinking run counter to one another. That is a very refreshing bit of musical art.

What of two voices crying in the wilderness? There is also that of Brad Paisley, another country singer and songwriter who has garnered many awards. Similarly impressive, Paisley is also on the Advisory Board for Mothers Against Drunk Driving.

Are there any other anti-alcohol songs out there? Yes, I found several; although one song, with a 1991 release date had just 60-some words and eight of them were some variation of the "F" word; evidence of another artist with a one-word basic vocabulary.

A single-incident horse thief?

Kenny Chesney's career as a country-singer and bad boy likely didn't begin near Buffalo, New York; but the event suggested an ill-mannered artist. On the night of June 3, 2005, Chesney and fellow country music star, Tim McGraw were performing at a stadium near Buffalo. One of the Erie County, New York deputies was honored to get a request from Chesney. Could Chesney mount the deputy's horse? The deputy consented. That should have been a good public relations gesture for both parties. However, once mounted, Chesney rode away with the deputy's mount! According to accounts, the deputy ordered Chesney to stop; but the celebrity rode on. According to the Sheriff (Patrick Gallivan), the deputy went to remove Chesney from the horse. When another deputy moved to help remove Chesney, Chesney's buddy, Tim McGraw, grabbed the second deputy from behind. The second deputy needed help to get free from McGraw's clutches. McGraw claimed that he was only trying to prevent Chesney from falling to the pavement. However, one might feel that a person who rides away with a police deputy's horse deserves a bump on the pavement.

One thing was clear: Alcohol was not mentioned as being in any way connected to this case. It might also be suggested that the appearance of *celebrity influencing justice* was present in this case. In addition, Kenny Chesney is also invested in a liquor company that produces a rum named *Blue Chair Bay*. Their website (http://bluechairbayrum.com) boasts that it is "The rum inspired by the island life of multiplatinum singer-songwriter Kenny Chesney."

More recently (*TDI*, July 4, 2016 edition) a Kenny Chesney concert in Pittsburgh, Pennsylvania, made news because several dozen people were cited for underage drinking, while 25 people went from the concert to hospitals to be treated for problems created by "intoxication or intoxication-related injuries."

Still, when comparing those whose life seems to be to promote alcohol, Kenny Chesney is a piker compared to the musical artist named Toby Keith.

Keith: king of the booze boosters

Should the United States ever adopt a national drinking song, it could easily be provided by Toby Keith, another country singing star who has amassed a fortune by mining that great mother lode of country music lyrics, alcohol.

Country music artist and actor, Toby Keith, has also offered support for the nation's diplomats. One of his songs cautions:

"An' you'll be sorry that you messed with the U. S. of A.
'Cos we'll put a boot in your ass, it's the American way."
[from "Courtesy of the Red, White, and Blue", 2002]

The U.S. liquor industry is among the nation's richest and most potent segments of American society. Sadly, Toby Keith has been especially supportive of that powerful group. The brewers and distillers couldn't have a better friend than Toby Keith. This talented songwriter is worth millions of dollars to the liquor industry. Toby Keith Covel (born 1961) is a native of Clinton, Oklahoma. He has written many hit songs, including a disturbing number in which he gushes over alcohol. It's easy to get the impression that the only sober words on his music are those of the FBI anti-piracy warning. A quintet of his boozy country ballads could include "Beer for My Horses," "My Little Whiskey Girl," "I Love This Bar," "Drinks After Work," and "My Little Red Solo Cup." If the bulk of one's income comes from the production or sale of alcohol, one cannot thank Toby Keith enough! And Keith, himself, has become a very wealthy man and one who has garnered some of the top awards in music. Thus, fame and fortune have come to Keith, in large part, because of his willingness to dip his pen's nib into a shot glass of the hard stuff to write his songs. This nation is mired in misery because of the abuse of alcohol, which only makes Toby Keith's pandering that much more disgusting!

Toby Keith is the ideal case study. This musically-talented man is so popular today that he can write any sort of song and it becomes a hit. His lucre and his professional awards accumulate. Surely, it's time for the stars of country music to publicly acknowledge the whole national problem of drunkenness and to take the lead in deglamorizing alcohol. Sadly, that's utterly unlikely. In one single year, 2012, Toby Keith's musical Midas touch was evident. In that year, Keith added a couple more hits to his resume. *Both glorified alcohol.* These two hits were "I Like Girls That Drink Beer," and "Beers Age." According to the lyrics for the second song, the singer is boasting of the huge number of beers he has downed since his teen years. Two hits in just one calendar year? Surely, Toby Keith is America's leading booze balladeer. 2012 was just one of several fabulous years for Keith. It must have been a fabulous year for American brewers, as well! The satisfaction that Toby Keith must be enjoying, as this is being written (2017-18) is surely enhanced by the information offered by the July 2014 copy of *Forbes* magazine. That issue told the world that the man who may be alcohol's greatest hymnist now has swill-gotten gains that hover around $500 millions of dollars.

Keith is among a bevy of country-music stars who push booze to the point of absurdity.

Chapter Seven

The Gonads to Govern

"One nation, under alcohol, with anarchy and mayhem for all."

Rebellions often fail. Americans have been quite fortunate in their record of attempted rebellions. Most have triumphed. After considerable sacrifice and dedication, the American rebels gained political freedom (1781) from the tyranny of English royalty.

The newly forged American nation was tempered in the furnace of political revolution. During and following that revolution the greatest collection of thoughtful men that the world has ever seen, gathered in deliberative assembly. That assembled pantheon then developed democratic institutions and forms of government that, if respected, would ensure that America would remain forever free of tyranny. Following considerable sacrifice, American rebels triumphed another time, in the 1860s, to crush the tyranny of slavery and to begin plodding the path toward racial equality. Again, in 1919, the American rebels finally overcame gender tyranny.

All these victories required serious honing over the decades, but the victories held and the results of each rebellion endured. Tragically, the rebellion that was concluded in 1933 ended in failure, with the easy triumph of a resurgent—and very vengeful—tyrant, alcohol. *That tyrant remains at large.*

The author once attended a wedding reception where the couple had decided—in deference to the non-drinkers among both their families—that there

> **Sober Slogan #12**
>
> Lovable drunk?
>
> An intoxymoron!

would be no alcohol at the reception. Obviously, they didn't understand that a three-hour span without alcohol was insulting to the few who needed their liquid life-support. Someone blatantly brought booze to the reception and shared it with a few people, including the gentleman who may have been the eldest attendee. When he was reminded of the expressed wishes of the newlyweds, he gave an answer that was dripping with filial love and the wisdom of age. His patriarchal reply: "I don't give a damn!"

The evidence unending

For anyone who thinks a sober nation might be superior to our national binge, the daily newspaper or internet accounts become tiresome as well as depressing.

Unless otherwise identified, all the following 'news' items are from a lone newspaper, *The Daily Item*, of Sunbury, Pennsylvania.

A news report (*TDI*, 7/19/13) raises this question: Is it legal for a fellow to cook a pizza in his friend's house at 3:45 in the morning, wearing only his boxer shorts? The man involved was charged with criminal trespass. All of that might have been legal enough; but the friend's house was about 13 miles away and the fellow who was making himself a pizza had no notion as to where he was, where his clothes were or how he arrived at that location. Such are the results of having had, as the man admitted, a "large quantity of alcohol." Unlike so many actions that result from having had a "large quantity of alcohol," this one was simply absurd, except to the owner of the house who awoke to find the stranger visiting his kitchen a few hours after midnight. Annually, however, alcohol-fueled incidents have tragic results for thousands of American citizens.

(10-5-12) A 62-year old woman allegedly drove into a parked car and scraped against a light pole. She was charged with *driving under the influence*, which was her second DUI charge within three days. Among the several telling signs of intoxication: "she smelled like alcohol." Perhaps a driver should be charged with a crime just for smelling like alcohol since many forms of alcohol emit a stench that is offensive with or without the absurd behavior that often accompanies it.

(1-9-13) A woman in Yelm, Washington had a repairman check her home's faulty heating system. The problem, he discovered, was that someone had been living in the crawl space beneath her home and had been stealing the heat for himself. Evidence of the squatter's presence, other than the modified heating system: A liquor bottle and some beer cans.

(1-5-13) A man at the Minneapolis airport was detained for a Breathalyzer test on January 4, 2013. When he was found to have an elevated blood/alcohol level, he was arrested. This delayed the flight for a couple of hours since a replacement pilot had to be found. Another flight (Detroit to Philadelphia) was reported (3-30-16) to have been *canceled* because the pilot was found to have double the accepted blood-alcohol level. Despite the two aforementioned incidents, pilot DUI's are running to less than a dozen a year; a major improvement since the 1990s incident when a jury convicted three pilots of DUIs. All three were on the same flight.

(2-16-13) A woman in Florida wrote to "Annie's Mailbox" advice column to lament, "I, too, married a wonderful guy who was an alcoholic. When sober, he was kind, funny, intelligent and a good father. After years of declining health, my husband made a reality of all his doctors' predictions. He wasted away, every organ and every inch of his body affected by cirrhosis and myriad complications, and he died a slow, painful death in his 60s."

From the Providence, Rhode Island *Journal*: (10-2-12) A 25-year-old driver, already on probation on a domestic disorderly charge, shot past a construction site at 120 miles-per-hour. When police stopped him, they also found that he had three passengers: his 2, 3, and 4-year-old children. This menace was charged with a DUI.

(6-1-16) Because of a DUI incident in his past, 49-year-old Frank Beitz of Milton, Pennsylvania decided not to stop for his latest alcohol-driven encounter with the police. This led to his reaching speeds in excess of 90 miles-per-hour. Even when an officer placed stop sticks in his path, Beitz pushed on. He ran over the strips and nearly hit the officer. One of his tires flattened;

but he kept driving, despite having just three inflated ones. When the flattened tire flew off its rim, he kept driving for a distance. Finally, he stopped the car and began running, until overtaken by two officers. His blood-alcohol reading was listed at slightly more than double the legal limit. The lesson for the public: Once again, we are confronted by very convincing evidence: We must stop trifling with repeat offenders. When driving a killer machine on a public road, isn't once one too many times? Shouldn't every sot be terrified that he or she might be caught a second time? Such is not the case in this land of tipplers. Our legislators should provide laws that make even the hardest drinkers fear getting caught even once. To do less, as we do in America, is to invite the inevitable: Needless mayhem and death. Blame the legislators and all others who can't get serious about one of our nation's most serious and frightening problems.

(2-15-13; 2-16-13) Christopher Wirth had no license to drive in January 2012 since it had been suspended for a DUI conviction. However, he was driving anyway. He was also drinking alcohol at a rural Pennsylvania bar, Boomerang's Bar and Grille. Long after midnight, the drunken Wirth climbed behind the wheel of his 1999 Mercury Cougar. His girlfriend, who was also the mother of his daughter, climbed into the front passenger seat. A female friend climbed into the back seat. One of the three was destined to die suddenly and ignominiously. The backseat passenger testified that she realized that the car was speeding and looked at the speedometer. She yelled at Wirth to slow when she saw the speed registering at 87 miles per hour! The Mercury soon shot from the roadway and into trees. Wirth and his girlfriend were both thrown from the car. The friend was trapped in the backseat and was not freed from the mangled vehicle until the roof was removed. She survived with serious injuries. Wirth, who was found to have a blood-alcohol level of .136, was hospitalized. The horrific impact of the collision tossed his front seat passenger, girlfriend, and the mother of his young daughter, into the air. Her lifeless body hung about 15 feet from the ground, stuck in tree branches. The five felony charges could require Wirth to pay thousands of dollars in fines and serve up to 27 years imprisonment. Comments from two other parties are telling: "Sometimes tragedies happen. It doesn't mean someone is criminal." and "He [Wirth] made a mistake that could have happened to anyone." Of course, both statements miss the point. Both seem to suggest that it was the fault of the alcohol. Obviously, such alcohol-related 'mistakes' don't happen to the sober. We'll address that phenomenon in a later chapter.

In late March 2012, 38-year-old Victor Swabolski, driving his Jeep Liberty near Mount Carmel, Pennsylvania, struck five teen-agers. The teens, 13, 14, 16, 17, and 18-year-olds, were sprawled like bowling pins, with one being unconscious. Two were hospital-ized, one with a fractured pelvis. This was another alcohol-fueled hit, and hit, and hit, and hit, and hit and run. Swabolski allegedly drove another seven blocks to the area of his own home, where he retrieved an open can of beer and an unopened one and ran into some bushes. A witness was quoted (*The Daily Item*, 3/29/12) as saying that the driver hid in nearby bushes, pretending to be a tree!

That same witness said that the recently-abandoned vehicle also had a flat tire. The Jeep also had two spare tires, but they wouldn't be helpful since they were on one of his victim's bicycle; a bicycle that had been dragged along by the Jeep. Swabolski was a sixth-grade teacher in a nearby school district. Charged with nine assorted crimes, he pleaded not guilty. Later news items in the same paper, in early 2015, mentioned Swabolski's blood-alcohol level as having been 0.225 at the time of the incident. Since then, all his victims have recovered; he has resigned from his teaching job and entered a last-minute guilty plea. On January 5, 2015, he was sentenced to state prison for a minimum of two years.

She was a former elementary school principal in Sunbury, Pennsylvania (*TDI*, 9-11-15); but was asking for an early leave from court supervision so that she could interview for another job elsewhere in the state. It was granted. Her initial sentence and her resignation from the Sunbury position stemmed from an incident in 2014 that led to her arrest and resignation. In that incident, her arrest resulted from having been driving while she was "four times over the legal limit of intoxication."

(1-10-13) The 28-year-old patron, Mr. Ogando, was expelled from an Allentown (Pennsylvania) strip club. When he tried to get into a nightclub in the area, he was refused entry. At that point, he was ready to return home, but he lived south of Allentown and had to take the road to Emmaus. Ogando then tried to get into someone else's car and insisted that the driver take him home. Emmaus is just a few miles south of Allentown. When the driver told Ogando to take a cab, Ogando began shaking the car. He then began screaming and poking at the driver. All this activity got Ogando arrested and charged with aggravated assault, disorderly conduct, resisting arrest and public drunkenness. His destination for the morning's behavior: a jail cell. Perhaps, the next time, he won't commit so many acts of mayhem when the car he approaches is a patrol car driven by a member of the Allentown police force.

Excuse me. It's two o'clock in the morning! Do you know where your child-like boozers are? According to a news account (*The Daily Item*, 10-9-12), a large group, consisting of attendees at a couple of wedding receptions at a Philadelphia area (I believe it's called *Sobriety Hill*) hotel, got involved in a brawl. People from the "City-of-Brotherly-Love" obviously know how to brawl. An innocent out-of-towner caught the tuxedo-clad gentlemen and their gown-clad ladies duking-it-out and it is now part of the great international archives of jackassery known as YouTube. Police were summoned; several participants were cited, and officials noted that they didn't know the cause of the melee, but that alcohol was involved.

A marriage in extremis

In fictional accounts, it's the man who faces a shotgun and accepts marriage under threat of death. Real life can be much different. According to police and news accounts, a Lackawanna County, Pennsylvania, woman took the marriage vows under threat of having her throat slashed by her 36-year-old pursuer.

At the wedding reception, the groom grabbed his bride by the neck. Later, on their wedding day, he punched her in the face, leaving her with a bloodied nose. The groom, once arrested, declared that he was taking full responsibility and *promised to stay away from alcohol.* He likely will, for at least the next 33 months to six years.

The groom went to jail. The bride moved from the state. The wedding was annulled.

It so seems

With each passing year, nuptials seem to have shorter vows and stronger drinks. One can easily imagine the officiating individual intoning . . . "through sickness and through health; through sobriety and through intoxication . . ."

The sub rosa life

In 2014, the anchor for the ABC program, *20/20*, Elizabeth Vargas, was reported to have twice been in rehab for her long-lasting alcoholism. According to an internet article by Erik Sherman (10/23/14), Ms. Vargas admitted that: "I am an alcoholic. The amount of energy I expended keeping that secret and keeping this problem hidden from view—hidden from my family, hidden from friends, from colleagues—was exhausting. It's a staggering burden to walk around with, and you become so isolated with the secret and so lonely . . ."

Likewise, consider the case of an American first lady, Jackie Kennedy Onassis. She was, for several years, the most popular woman in the nation. However, the author, Kitty Kelley tells us (*Jackie Oh!,* p. 251) that Mrs. Onassis "wanted no mention of her chain smoking or her drinking."

Relating to our chapter on "Frats, Vats, and Stats" (Chapter Two), one might observe that nearly 8 of every 100 college students have a natural propensity for a career in espionage. At least that is what one can surmise from the number of incoming students who already carry fraudulent I.D. cards. An impressive internet source, *EverFi*, offers visitors an "Insight Report" that informs the public of the statistics related to the college-level fake-ID carriers. There we learn that students with fake ID's are twice as likely to be planning on becoming frat or sorority members. With studies based on a sample of more than seven thousand students, the study results indicate that, among fake ID carriers, one-third admitted a willingness to drive after having downed at least four drinks! That suggests a huge contribution to the nation's *sub rosa* tippling.

So, let us add another immense 'negative' to the ugly story of alcohol. A need to live much of one's life in secrecy, so that society doesn't recognize that one is the pitiful subject of an often uncontrollable and frequently debilitating urge to consume alcohol. The need to keep one's alcoholism a secret from friends, co-workers and loved ones is an abysmal way to live. That fact, alone, should be emphasized to every young person who is about to embark on his or her adult

---

Sober Slogan #13

We've seen the drunken sailor . . . And he is us!!

journey. To do less is to expose them to the enslaving chains of the tyrant, alcohol. But, don't panic. There are hundreds of rehabilitation centers with doors open wide and with accountants at the ready.

In the old cliché, it is noted that "we turn a blind eye." The refusal to look at our outrageous alcohol problem is far more absurd than simply turning a blind eye. We blindfold ourselves regarding the horrific results of widespread intoxication. Refusal to see a problem is the surest evidence of immaturity.

Among peer nations, Americans get involved in the most vehicle accidents that involve alcohol.

Where numbers should reveal pathetic patterns of danger and damage in America's society, we avoid the revealing tallies. And so, it is with the topic of where alcohol creates huge numbers of victims. Aside from the highway carnage, we are far too selective in what we see. We need far more tallies relating to sporting events, the topers' homes and that great venue of violence: The bar and its environs.

> For lushes to lush, there's little it takes.
> True tipplers will tipple at weddings or wakes.

Alcohol helps patrons dig deeper into their dwindling resources. (Author's archives)

Just the inducements to drink alcohol can form a deluge. If one were to make a list of such inducements, it would likely include most of the following:

It's often free at slots parlors, where fools are conned into losing millions of dollars a week at the proliferating slots parlors throughout the land. The wild cry of a jackpot winner a few slots down should be enough to sucker the gamblers into investing more and more, but parlor owners appear to have found that suds and slots are a potent pair. Of course, these muttons need no inducement to gamble, nor will they ever accept the obvious: *There is no gambling in slots parlors since gambling requires all parties to be at risk.* Since the state and the owners never lose, there is only the wholesale fleecing of the slots players!

One man is quoted in *The Readers Digest* (10/11, p. 175) as follows: "Winning $700 in Vegas had me feeling rich and happy. So did the free drinks. Maybe they were a big part of it."

Temptations put before potential imbibers might include:

■ The free drinks offered by slots parlors.

■ The keeping of bar tabs, a practice which encourages drinkers to have another and pay later.

■ Booze-worthy observations would include the celebrating of births, weddings, funerals and the ticking of the clock.

■ Parents celebrating the 21st birthdays of their hapless offspring. The parents and their pride-swelling children would do well to agree to a new car for each child who chooses sobriety for the next three or four years.

■ The alcohol industry's expenditure of *billions* of dollars annually on the promotion of alcohol.

■ Peer pressure.

■ Fear of an alcohol-free hereafter, as suggested in various ways, such as the polka lyrics and the request of singing idol, Frank Sinatra, to have three mementos buried with him, one of which was a bottle of his favorite whiskey.

■ Sporting events.

■ The winning of special sporting events.

■ The hunting-camp environment.

■ Taking a cruise.

■ Becoming a college student and being on campus during rush week.

■ Being born Irish and male

■ Free salty peanuts and pretzels.

■ As a legendary inhibitions killer (Absinthe makes the heart grow fonder?).

■ The absurd notion that the pressures of life are erased by one of life's worst anarchists, alcohol.

■ Removing the cover charge for women.

■ Allowing any jackass in the crowd to proclaim, "I'll drink to that!"

If all the husbands who have created chaotic lives for the wives and children, had wives who decided to match their husbands' alcohol consumption and behavior, the American institution of marriage would be even more of a farce than it is. Sots need enablers, and heavy drinkers have a knack for blindly ruining the lives of others.

Save all your celebratory drinking until scientists discover an effective cure for dipsomania. Many of us are sick of being expected to blindly accept the behavior of dipsomaniacs, who are among the craziest of America's assorted crazies.

Get real! Every flimsy excuse for drinking that one can imagine is trumped by the stability of sobriety and the sanctity of life!

The knowledge that our society suffers immensely because of alcohol hardly sways our foolishness. A recent news item (*The Week*, 10-23-15) reveals that a survey taken by the Brits found that over one-third of the vegetarians surveyed admitted that—when drunk—bacon, burgers and shish kebobs are common fare. That same issue of that same magazine also reported that a woman in Florida 'live streamed' herself driving while admitting to being very drunk. Other motorists, who seemed concerned about driving on the same highway as the drunkard, contacted 911 and the responding police momentarily cleared another pathetic driver from the roads of the Sunshine State.

Remember, alcohol has a built-in mechanism for inducing more and more consumption. That mechanism is the narcotic nature of alcohol. Alcohol is assured the slavish devotion of a high percentage of all those who try alcohol a few times in their youth.

Damn sobriety day

With utter disregard for all the anti-alcohol statistics, the boozers push ever onward. The United States brewers and boozers have even teamed to create a national day of drinking as a show of their great devotion to alcohol and their utter disdain for sobriety. There is cute gear to buy, funny sayings to circulate . . . and much alcohol to consume. It is called St. Patrick's Day. Or Super Bowl day. Or wedding day. Or homecoming day. Or is it New Year's Eve, or one's birthday, *or whatever*. We should combine the absurdity of all these celebratory days into a single event; April Fools' Day?

The Super Bowl 50 event of February 11, 2016, was interesting for two related developments. The highly-regarded British actress Helen Mirren appeared in a Budweiser ad, chastising anyone who would drive drunk. Then, at game's end, the legendary Peyton Manning, the game's winning quarterback, made this dim-witted observation to the interviewer: "I'm gonna drink a lot of Budweiser tonight, Tracy, I'll promise you that." I added the preceding data to this book the day after I watched the closing developments on television. However, I found it interesting that *The Week* magazine (2/19/16) referred to that same quarterback declaration. That magazine even added the information that Manning is part owner of a couple of Budweiser distributorships. So much for allowing your children to view a wholesome sportscast. That unpaid and unethical 'testimony' was worth a few million bucks to the company in which he has a financial stake. Such behavior is even worse than deflating a football.

Venue, venue, and venue: dangers at the watering hole

Typical of the endless record of crimes committed within, and in the proximity of, America's 'watering holes' are the following:

Louisiana State University's leading rusher pled guilty to a misdemeanor charge of carnal knowledge of a juvenile. Before the next season had begun, he had already acquired new charges based on a 2013 *"scuffle in a bar parking lot."*

From New Brighton, Pennsylvania we learn (*TDI*, 4-26-14) that the 30-year-old woman was a new bride for mere hours when there was an argument later in the evening about who was going to drive. Her 21-year-old niece disagreed with the bride; but, thankfully, the bride's new husband had a handgun. According to allegations, the bride used the handgun to win the argument. She allegedly shot and killed her 21-year-old niece. This finale to her wedding day unfolded within, and in the parking lot, of a New Brighton bar.

The man is a hero. Airman 1st Class Spencer Stone helped to disarm a terrorist on a European train during the summer of 2015. He was properly hailed as a hero; but back in the United States, in his hometown (Sacramento, California), he received several non-life-threatening stab wounds in a different altercation. No terrorist attack, here. This was just your everyday American scuffle at your everyday American setting. Police described the incident as "an alcohol-related fight." In fact, the introductory heading for the news article told the tiresome story: "Guardsman Stabbed Outside Bar."

One doesn't realize how much socializing involves until he or she reads accounts of events unfolding within or near a bar. Thus, we read (3-27-16) a web page (www.pennlive.com/news/2016/01/pa_man_charged_with_killing-wo.html) that tells of a man, Charles McKinney, who shot and killed a woman who had just rejected his advances at a Pittsburgh bar. Police arrested the shooter after a car chase during which McKinney's car nearly hit two police officers and headed toward several others. McKinney's attorney said he didn't seem to be the type person who would do such a thing, even though police officers had already described him as being "extremely intoxicated."

A news item (*TDI*, 12-8-14) opened with these words:

"The reward for information leading to a missing 21-year-old West Chester University student has reached $50,000. Shane Montgomery, a senior at the suburban school, was last seen leaving a Philadelphia bar . . ."

Another account (*TDI*, 8-30-15) relates that a man who had been serving time in a halfway house for a drunken driving offense had escaped and was now convicted of a third-degree murder as the result of last summer's stabbing death that occurred outside a bar.

Once more (*TDI*, 4/2/13) we read of a celebrity-type, a cast member of the MTV show, *Buckwild*, who—along with his uncle and another person—was found dead in a sport utility vehicle in a ditch in West Virginia. To quote: "Authorities had been searching for the men since early Sunday morning. They were last seen around 3 a.m. Sunday at a bar . . ."

Whacko in Waco

A variety of motorcycle groups have impressed us with their charity causes and patriotism. I heartily applaud! This was not the case in Waco, Texas in May of 2015. In that instance, several members of several motorcycle gangs began by throwing punches in a restaurant. Knives and chains were also part of the bikers' arsenal. Then the fight spilled into the parking lot, with guns replacing fists. More bikers rushed to the scene, as did a bevy of state and local police. Before the bikers were finally brought under control, nine bikers were dead! The venue was, once again, a 'watering hole'. The incident spurred this caustic comment from the local Justice of the Peace.

"We have nine people dead because these people wanted to come down and what? Drink? Party?"

Does it distress no one that the interiors of bars, the parking lots of bars, and many other parcels of real estate associated with American bars, have a hellishly high number of tragic stories to tell? How can this be happening if no one is ever served alcohol to the point of inebriation? Every bar owner and every bartender and every bar patron is supposed to refrain from serving or slugging those final drinks that nudge the customers into drunkenness.

Sober Slogan #14

Nondrinkers are
Never alcoholics!!

Try not to become a
V O I D
Victim Of an Intoxicated Driver

So: stay off streets, sidewalks, lawns, houses.
Stay out of cars, trucks, vans, limos and street-side shops . . .
Living in a national binge can be hell!

Chapter Eight

Shunning All Science

Beware the bloglodytes

Scan the magazines and newspapers and, oops! Here's another one: The headline (*TDI*, 3-26-13) proclaims: "Seven anti-aging superfoods can add years to life" The presumably invaluable information that follows comes from a website that tells of the life-extending values of olive oil, yogurt, fish, chocolate, nuts, blueberries and (You've likely guessed it.) wine. Why wine? Because, the source proclaims, "Drinking alcohol in moderation protects against heart disease, diabetes, and age-related memory loss." The report also proclaims, "Any kind of alcoholic beverage seems

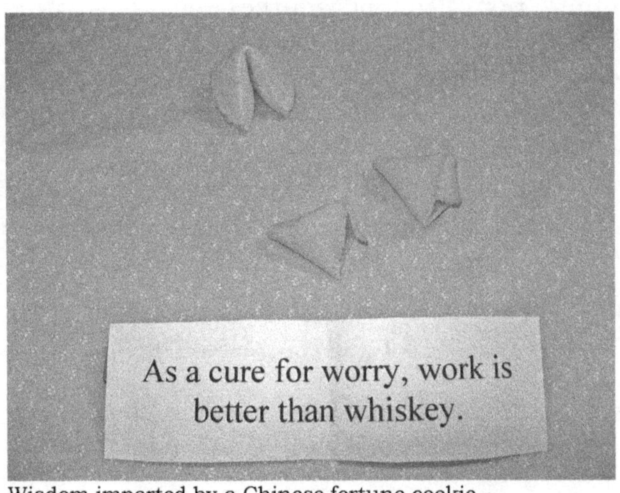

Wisdom imparted by a Chinese fortune cookie.

to provide such benefits, but red wine has been the focus of much of the research." Bullscat! A scientific report surely doesn't need the words, "seems to," to give it authority. Further, the only support the site (EatingWell.com) can even give to red wine is the presence of resveratrol in the wine.

More recently (6-16-15), a newspaper offered a health-related article telling of three drinks that are beneficial for the human skin: green tea, coffee and [once again!] red wine. The reason for humans to consume red wine? Preliminary research [note the qualifying term, 'preliminary'] from the University of Barcelona suggests that something called "proanthocyanidins" are in red wine and, the article informs us, these proanthocyanidins "may help prevent oxidative reactions in your skin." May? The author(s) of that advice column do show some integrity, by closing the article with the following: "Before you pour yourself another glass, though, remember that the recommended cap on alcoholic beverages is one a day for women, two for men."

Among the absurdities of America's binging society is the 'trotting out' of flimsy 'health' statistics that inform us of alcohol's modest health benefits. Perhaps, one can find the occasional benefit that may be gained by consuming a modest amount of wine, beer or whiskey. There are two follies with that approach to consuming alcohol.

■ It is likely that the benefit promised can also be obtained from other, non-alcoholic sources, which go unmentioned. The proanthocyanidins, for example, are readily available in the dietary supplements marketplace. If that approach has no appeal, one might try another novel path: consume a handful of coffee beans or grape seeds.

■ Even if one accepts the promised health benefits, one must also face the Denali of risk factors from alcohol's use.

Time magazine (9/29/14) offered a more general observation: Watch your alcohol and amplifies the message:

> "Cutting back can lower blood pressure. Heads—not bottoms—up: moderation means a drink or two a day at the most."

And what of the much-vaunted resveratrol?

The internet site, www.webmd.com, notes that "Early research, mostly done in test tubes and in animals, suggests that resveratrol might help to protect the body against a number of diseases . . ." Mostly done where? "Might" help to protect the body . . .?" For this flimsy reassurance, we must imbibe?

If there are true health benefits to be gleaned from products containing resveratrol, why must we go directly to *alcohol* for the benefit? Why not make the sober choice? Why not go to Nature's well-stocked pantry? The same website (www.webmd.com) that first drew our attention to resveratrol's *'possible'* health benefits, also identifies some natural sources that are not converted to liquor. "Resveratrol is found in the skin of red grapes, but other sources include peanuts and berries."

A truly forthright website (www.jerrybaker.com) is refreshing. In the "jerrybaker" website's print edition, *Healing Gazette* (Special Issue, mailed during May of 2015), one can read this headline: How much wine is divine? The headline is then followed by this gem of honesty: "Don't overdo it—one drink a day for women and two drinks a day for men will maximize the health benefits. Drinking more than that actually increases the risk of some cancers, as well as high blood pressure, stroke, birth defects, and other health problems." [Emphasis added.] Wow!

One more source worth quoting: Should I eat this? (a 2012 booklet, published by *Consumer Reports*).

The authors' summarizing remarks related to alcohol, from page 24:

> Even a drink or two a day of wine, beer, or liquor may slightly increase a woman's risk of breast cancer; two to five daily drinks ups the risk 1.5 times that of teetotalers. Moderate consumption may also contribute to colon cancer; high intakes can cause liver disease and cancer. On the other hand, moderate drinking can help protect the heart by raising the levels of HDL "good" cholesterol and prevent blood from clotting.

> Recommendations: Consider avoiding or rarely drinking alcohol if you have a personal or family history of breast or colon cancer. But if you're at high risk of heart disease, a

> drink a day for women or two for men is probably helpful.
> Just be sure to keep it separate from driving."

Here, once again, one might question the need to recommend a daily drink for women and two for men if there is a "high risk" of heart disease. Also, once again, this author shouts to the health gurus that there are other effective, non-alcoholic, drinks readily available.

Appearing after the previous paragraph was written, *The Week* (2/16/18) took on the issue of reducing the risk of cancer. "Some 595,930 people died of cancer in the U.S. in 2015, according to government statistics, making it America's second biggest killer after heart disease. While some of those cases involved cancers driven by genetic mutations, [our emphasis added to the following] *the majority of sufferers were diagnosed with common cancers directly linked to Westerners' sedentary lifestyles, high-fat diets, and tobacco and alcohol consumption.*" The report further amplifies with a quote from Alice Bender, the head of nutrition programs for the American Institute for Cancer Research: "Alcohol is a recognized carcinogen . . . It can damage DNA. It can increase hormones in your body, like estrogen, that can fuel cancer." Once again, *The Week* misses the opportunity to suggest that abstinence might be of value to Americans. Instead, it promptly adds the tiresome advice:

"Women should aim to drink no more than 5 ounces of wine or 12 ounces of beer a day; men can double that limit" Again, why in hell must they advise drinking in any amount at all when they could let the readers do just the tiniest bit of thinking for themselves. Perhaps it's that damned money factor again, since that very issue of *The Week* (2-16-18) carries a cover ad showing the bar of an airline, a report on the trebling of craft breweries within the past decade; a paean to Buffalo, New York where one can find that nearly "every block has a corner tavern that stays open and buzzing until 4 a.m." and a "park where you can grab a beer and then zip-line . . ." And, the reporter gushes, "everywhere I went, regulars struck up conversations and bought me drinks." This same issue also has a restaurant review where the wait is long, but neutralized by "the bar's delightful gin-and-tonic variations . . ." There is, of course, the regular liquor feature, the wine review. And readers of this issue, as revealed earlier in this book, are lucky enough to get the latest poop on the tragic death of Natalie Wood in 1981, an account that tells us that new witnesses "confirm reports that Wood and Wagner had a blazing, alcohol-fueled argument . . . before her disappearance." Reading just a lone issue of such a liquor-sloshed magazine is enough to make even a sober person puke. The once-influential group, the Womens' Christian Temperance Union (see Chapter 3), has almost no pulse today when anti-alcohol voices are nearly gagged; but that group reprinted (9-28-15) an item written by JoNel Aleccia of NBC News (NBCNews.com). In that document, we read, "When I talk about heart-healthy diets, my first words are not 'Have a glass of wine, '" said Dr. Suzanne Steinbaum, director of the women and heart disease program at Lenox Hill Hospital in New York. She says she has been known to recommend having a glass of wine with dinner, but "we can certainly get the health benefits from other places and other foods." At last, we read a straightforward declaration that exposes the phoniness of so many so-called 'health gurus'.

Let's conclude our anguished comments about the health marvel that some identify as red wine.

A writer for the McClatchy Content Agency offers (*TDI*, 6/3/14) welcome commentary, thusly:

"The buzz about the benefits of red wine has many of us raising a glass to good health. And for those who choose not to imbibe, it turns out the booze behind the buzz may not be necessary." The writer also states that "It comes as no surprise that purple grape juice—essentially unfermented red wine—boasts flavonoid compounds as well." The less scrupulous *bloglodytes* must jettison a large amount of reliable data to slant their health writings toward the guzzling public.

Take heed! Take heed!
While I distrust some government agencies and consider some others to be meddlesome at best, I find one government agency to be a national treasure: The National Institutes of Health! Their information is specific and honest about the impact of alcohol on American society. Bless them . . .

In February 2015, the National Institutes of Health issued the results of a large (26,000 adult participants) study designed to reveal some patterns in the interaction of alcohol and medication use. Study results indicate that 42% of the adults who drink also reported using drugs that interact with alcohol. Even more revealing, in those participants in the study who have reached the 65th milestone in age, *over three-quarters of those interviewed* reported using "alcohol interactive medications." Strong adverse reactions from such behavior can include headaches, internal bleeding, heart problems and breathing difficulties. Naturally, of course, the combination of aging and a slower metabolizing rate increases the risks.

Whether the individual is a youthful or aging imbiber, the various systems of the human body are vulnerable to attack and serious damage from the excessive use of alcohol. Every person who can read or hear the television ads should begin to show the tiniest hint of comprehension regarding medications and alcohol. Here is a *sampling* from ads of the past decade, with the brand names of the medications being in upper case:

■ "Those who have had a drug or alcohol problem may be more likely to misuse Lyrica"
and "Don't drink alcohol while taking Lyrica."

■ The medicine, Neulasta (pegfilgrastim) is discussed on the site, alcohol-explained.com. The reader is warned, "It is suggested that patients do not consume alcohol, even moderate drinking, while using this drug as the side effects may be greatly affected."

■ The makers of a major erectile-dysfunction medication warn, "Don't drink alcohol in excess with Cialis." (as aired in August 2008).

■ The *Rexall* "since 1903" carton tells users of their antihistamine tablets: "When using this product avoid alcoholic drinks."

■ A 2015 (3/10) article by Caroline Cassels of WebMD notes that Chantix, a medicine designed to help people quit smoking, has been given new labeling by the FDA. She writes that "Some people who drank alcohol during treatment with Chantix had increased drunkenness and unusual or aggressive behavior, or had memory loss."

■ "Talk about your alcohol use," warns Cymbalta's makers in a television ad (2-20-13).

■ On the sharecare.com website, Dr. Courtney Lee, M.D., informs readers (7-7-15): "While taking Viagra you should avoid alcohol." Dr. Lee warns that the famed E.D. medication will "increase several side effects of the drug."

■ For users of Latuda (lurasidone), the site, drugs.com, warns: "Using lurasidone together with ethanol can increase nervous system side effects such as dizziness, drowsiness and difficulty concentrating . . . You should avoid or limit the use of alcohol while being treated with lurasidone."

■ One may consult a bottle of a common pain medication, acetaminophen (*Top Care*, 500 caplets), and learn that "Severe liver damage may occur if you take . . . 3 or more alcoholic drinks every day while using this product"

■ The site drugs.com advises: "Talk to your doctor before using ethanol together with albiglutide. Alcohol may affect blood glucose levels in patients with diabetes . . ." (drugs.com/food-interactions)

■ If using the drug Victoza (liraglutide). "Alcohol may affect blood glucose levels in patients with diabetes . . ." Further, "Avoid drinking alcohol on an empty stomach or following exercise, as it may increase the risk of hypoglycemia." (drugs.com/food-interactions)

■ Regarding Botox filler injections, Dr. Brandith Irwin, on the *SkinTour* website (7-7-15) offers this advice: "Stop drinking alcohol 1-2 days prior to injection."

■ The website, *Everyday Health*, offers the following information, "When taking Levitra, you should not drink alcohol excessively."

■ For users of Invokana (canagliflozin), the advice (from drugs.com) is simple and clear: "Talk to your doctor before using ethanol together with canagliflozin."

■ In addition, the pill bottles for Allopurinol and Oxybutinin are among those that carry the precautionary labels, "May cause drowsiness. Alcohol may intensify this effect."

■ Addyi (flibanserin) is a new drug that is touted as the female version of Viagra. For the woman who suffers from HSDD (hypoactive sexual desire disorder), Addyi may offer relief. However, the *Medscape* website quotes a physician (8-24-15) as referring to "a potentially serious interaction with alcohol."

■ Likewise, the *Novo Log Pen* advises: "Ask your doctor about alcohol use."

Also, "You should avoid or limit the use of alcohol while being treated with lurasidone."

■ Levemir cautions, "Ask your doctor about alcohol use."

■ Similarly, the medication bottle labeled Hydrocod/Apap has this message: Do not drink alcoholic beverages while taking this medication.

■ The pharmacy label for Toujeo insulin glargine injection medication warns: "Check with Your Doctor or Pharmacist Before Drinking Alcoholic Beverages While Using This Medicine."

■ Lastly, the Merck company's Belsomra comes with this warning (8-24-15): "Do not drink alcohol while taking Belsomra. It can increase your chances of getting serious side effects." Elsewhere it advises users, "Do not take Belsomra if you drank alcohol that evening or before bed."

We read the labels that the pharmacist adds to our medications: "Take with water," Take with milk," Take with food." Why is there no label advising us, "Take with a generous swig of alcohol?"

The preceding manufacturers' notices are merely random samples; suggesting that many more could be culled from manufacturers' advisory notes. The plethora of solid information and advice simply reminds us that organ after organ and system after system can be damaged, often beyond repair, by the excessive use of alcohol. Amazingly, there is little said about alcohol's impact on humans where the entire organism is critically examined.

Here is a hint regarding the health dangers of a lifelong lush. I quote from a book in which I gave a biographical picture of a North Carolina-born moonshiner, Prince D. Farrington, (mentioned in Chapter Five, above) who lived his later years in and died within the state of Pennsylvania. Although he apparently tried to reduce his alcohol intake in later years, the effort came too late. From *Prohibition's Prince*, page 228:

> While Prince David Farrington's moonshine was regarded
> as being of superior quality, one must remember: The
> quality of whiskey is not judged by its therapeutic effect on

the drinker's body. The cumulative result of all the drinking
that Prince Farrington did with brother Charl, with friendly
lawmen, and with untold acquaintances can be recognized
by looking at a few of the most serious results listed above
the signature of Dr. Merl Colvin, the pathologist who signed
Prince Farrington's autopsy report (6/14/56). Which
systems were damaged by decades of decadence? For the
heart: myocardial hypertrophy; Respiratory system: bilater-
al pulmonary edema; Gastro-intestinal system: Esophageal
varices, marked. Genito-urinary system: Adenocarcinoma
of the prostate, grade II. Endocrine system: Hyperplasia of
the adrenal cortex. Spleen: Marked long-standing passive
congestion of spleen. Pancreas: Diffuse pancreatic fibrosis.
Liver: Advanced portal cirrhosis and malignant hepatoma.

The whole body's vulnerability to alcohol

Depending upon the authority consulted, a reader may dis-
cover a list of nine, or ten, or even eleven systems of the body.
From one source, *Structure and Function of the Human Body* by
Merrimer and Wood, (page 2) I pluck ten systems, as follows:

1. Skeletal
2. Muscular
3. Circulatory
4. Digestive
5. Respiratory
6. Integumentary
7. Urinary
8. Nervous
9. Endocrine
10. Reproductive

You might use the above list to check on alcohol's impact on
any one system of your body. In any case, here are some of the
many effects that authorities say might cause negative changes
to your only available body (unless, of course, you can scrounge
parts from folks who have some available and who either die or
donate just as your own part shrivels or otherwise fails to function because of your foolish indulgence).

Observations that a variety of authorities have said about alcohol in one's body:

1. SKELETAL ~ Harvard Health News has stated (*The Daily Item*, 6-24-14) that "Smoking and too much alcohol both decrease bone density." But not, apparently, among the boneheaded.

2. MUSCULAR ~ Under a slogan, "You Booze, You Lose" the website, *Men's Fitness* (6-30-15) offers this information: "But, before you belly up to the bar, keep in mind that boozing it up may undo that hard work you put in at the gym. Research reveals that alcohol can interfere with your muscle growth, as well as slow your post-exercise recovery process."

Once again, the AMA reference (p. 542) tells us that a sorry medical condition known as Dupuytren's contracture can also be related to alcohol intake. This condition is usually found in men over the age of 40. Here, the tissue in the palm of one's hand or hands is involved. As the tissue thickens and shrinks, the grasp weakens and the gnarling develops. Dupuytren's contracture seems to be hereditary. It is also found among epileptics and among another group of our population. As the book reveals, "It is also found among alcoholics . . ."

3. CIRCULATORY ~ Elevated blood pressure (hypertension) is one of the 'silent killers' that has less obvious danger symptoms. The Geisinger Gold medical insurance program put the following into their December 2012 newsletter: "You are also at higher risk for high blood pressure if you . . . Drink too much alcohol." Similar advice comes from the medical advice column of Dr. Keith Roach (*TDI*, 1-19-15). He tells readers that "large amounts of alcohol can predispose a person to bleeding . . ." Dr. Roach is again seen commenting on this topic (*TDI*, 9-2-15): "Even in healthy young volunteers, alcohol immediately reduces the ability of the heart to squeeze out blood."

While discussing *edema* (swelling, usually due to excessive fluids), he observes that the inquirer's swelling problem may not be alcohol-related; but, "The physiology of alcohol is complex, with potentially adverse effects on the heart, the liver and on secretion of anti-diuretic hormone. These can affect swelling." There is also this: "Usually the heart returns to normal after the alcohol is metabolized, but in some people, the heart dilates over time, resulting in heart failure."

There is a medical challenge identified as *nutritional cardiomyopathy*. The A.M.A.'s *The Family Medical Guide* (p. 400) identifies the problem. "Like any muscle, the heart muscle can be damaged by a vitamin or mineral deficiency or by poisoning. The most important form of such nutritional cardiomyopathy in Western societies is found among alcoholics." After describing symptoms, the article suggests treatments such as dietary changes and concludes by saying that, "if your problem is alcoholism, only total abstinence can halt the disease." When one digests the above data, he or she should be offended by the observations offered in a very current article of an AARP 'health' critique: "The evidence suggests that no alcohol at all is better for your heart than too much." Thus, the simplistic approach to a dangerously complex problem.

4. DIGESTIVE ~ Here we arrive at the body system that includes *the organ most associated with drinking and death*. This is the system that performs many, many functions for the body; but which includes the most recognized organ of alcohol-caused death: the liver. The digestive system is burdened with a host of functions on which our bodies rely. In fact, the liver, itself, has literally *hundreds* of functions to perform. Yet, the heroic drinker virtually guarantees that those vital functions are thwarted and that the toper is damning himself to a premature death.

An internet source cited above (www.cancer.org) suggests that "Alcohol use has been linked with a higher risk of cancers of the colon and rectum. The evidence for such a link is generally stronger in men than in women, although studies have found the link in both sexes."

5. RESPIRATORY ~ A site known as *PubMed* (downloaded 8-19-2015) offers an abstract that contains the following: "Alcohol ingestion impairs glottis reflexes, and alcoholics are predisposed to pneumonia and lung abscesses from aspiration of oropharyngeal bacteria. Alcohol intoxication also increases

the frequency of sleep apnea and may result in respiratory failure from oversedation."

Wikipedia identifies "Alcoholic lung disease," and tells readers (download of 8-19-15) that this is a lung malady that is "caused by excessive alcohol consumption." The mechanisms of this illness are listed as:

■ Metabolism of alcohol reduces glutathione anti-oxidant levels in the lungs.

■ Oxidation damage to the cells impairs the ability of the lungs to remove fluid.

■ Oxidative damage to cells reduces immune response.

■ Oxidative damage to cells results in a reduced ability to recover from injury.

Their small article concludes by informing readers that "Over the last decade, evidence from epistemological studies shows that alcohol abuse alone can increase by as much as fourfold the risk of acute respiratory distress syndrome."

6. INTEGUMENTARY ~ This system has a large name; but it also has a somewhat shorter, more familiar one: The skin. It may seem that something as thin and pliable as our skin might be impervious to alcohol's damage. Wrong. Wrong. Wrong!

For example: because of alcohol's effect on our integumentary system, we might encounter the curse of *rosacea*. The biographer, Kitty Kelly, makes a reference (*Jackie Oh!,* p. 11) to "red-faced Boston pols." This description, I would presume, is a suggestion that the politicos of Beantown were hard-drinking chaps with liquor-induced rosacea.

Rosacea is first on the list created and explained by Dr. Adam Friedman in a paper dated September 24, 2013, and found on the internet site, everyday health.com. Dr. Friedman describes the condition as "probably the most common skin sign of drinking alcohol . . ." What of aridity . . . the dry condition and possible eczema? He also warns that "Both bacterial and fungal skin infections are common in those who drink frequently and excessively." Further, he informs readers, "Importantly, alcohol can have a huge negative impact on your vitamin A, B3, and C levels, all of which are very important antioxidants for your skin, and it is vital in the regeneration of new cells. Despite the somewhat scary symptoms related to alcohol and the human skin, Dr. Friedman doesn't counsel against alcohol's use; just its immoderate use.

Since alcohol widens the blood vessels at the skin's surface, it causes heat loss and, in extreme weather conditions, an increased risk of hypothermia.

When it comes to alcohol abuse, one might say that *everyone has some skin in the game.*

7. URINARY ~ Of course, any imbiber knows that alcohol fills the bladder. After all, that's why some old-time saloons or barrooms (into which no self-respecting woman of the time would have ventured) were equipped with a drain trough that ran along the front of the bar! That way the lushes weren't inconvenienced by a bladder on the verge of bursting. Simply unsheathe the proper organ and make space for another round. One would think that such an arrangement, ingenious though it is, might create some offensive aroma; but few odors are more offensive than that of beer. Thus, we can list an overactive bladder as a negative result of alcohol use.

The overactive bladder is likely the least negative reaction that alcohol can have on one's urinary system. For example, the Mayo Clinic website (8-26-15) discusses urinary incontinence by saying that "Urinary incontinence isn't a disease, it's a symptom." It then identifies nine diuretics that stimulate the bladder and increase the amount of urine. The first listed? Alcohol.

On the website Livestrong a writer named Sara Ipatenco informs readers (5-4-2015) that "too much alcohol . . . can interfere with the normal function of your urinary system. Mild symptoms include an increase in trips to the bathroom, but more severe health problems, such as kidney troubles, are also possible." That same site discusses alcohol's negative impact on the urinary system by suggesting that "Acute or chronic alcohol consumption can also damage the kidneys, according to Rin Yoshida, author of '*Trends in Alcohol Abuse and Alcoholism Research.*'" Ms. Ipatenco continues by reporting, "Drinking alcohol can interfere with electrolyte and acid balances in the body, and long-term chronic alcohol use can also lead to renal failure. Chronic alcohol use might also cause the body to hold onto salt and water, which makes cells swell, according to a 2008 article published in *Advances in Psychiatric Treatment*. Alcohol abuse can also interfere with the proper absorption of vitamins and minerals . . ."

Another web site (www.kidney.org) offers a report that is listed as being copyrighted (2015) by the National Kidney Foundation. This disclaimer is included: "This material does not constitute medical advice. It is intended for informational purposes only." Part of that information follows:

(D)rinking too much can harm your health. It can also worsen kidney disease . . . Alcohol can cause changes in the function of the kidneys and make them less able to filter your blood . . . When alcohol dehydrates (drys out) the body, the drying effect can affect the normal function of . . . the kidneys. Chronic drinking can also cause liver disease. This adds to the kidney's job . . . most patients in the United States who have both liver disease and associated kidney dysfunction are alcohol dependent.

For a most comprehensive study of the kidneys and alcohol's impact on their complex function, the reader is referred to the study by Dr. Murray Epstein (*Alcohol Health and Research World*, Volume 21, Number 1, 1997, pages 84-96). A significant passage (page 84) says, "Because of the kidneys' important and varied role in the body, impairment of their function can result in a range of disorders, from mild variations in fluid balance to acute kidney failure and death. Alcohol, one of the numerous factors that can compromise kidney function, can interfere with kidney function directly, through acute or chronic consumption, or indirectly, as a consequence of liver disease."

8. NERVOUS ~ Alcohol does not, as was once touted, cause one to relax. Instead, alcohol is a sleep-disrupting stimulant. In its edition of 10-2-12, *The Daily Item* (Sunbury, Pennsylvania), quotes Dr. Karen Carlson of the Harvard Medical School, "People think [alcohol] makes them a little sleepy; but it's actually a stimulant and disrupts sleep . . ."

If one is ready to be frank about alcohol and its effect on one's nervous system, he or she might create a note card on the medical syndrome named for Sergey S. Korsakoff (1854-1900). Korsakoff's Syndrome is identified in *Dorland's* (27th edition, page 1638) as being "a syndrome of anterograde and retrograde amnesia with confabulation associated with alcoholic or nonalcoholic polyneuritis described as 'cerebropathia psychica toxemica' by Korsakoff; currently used synonymously with 'amnestic syndrome' or, more narrowly, to refer to the amnestic component of the Wernicke-Korsakoff syndrome, i.e., an amnestic syndrome resulting from thiamine deficiency. Called also Korsakoff's psychosis."

There is more. *The ABCs of The Human Body* (page 68) has a small topic entitled "Can alcohol harm your brain?" The following two paragraphs tell readers that, allegedly, every drink taken kills 100,000 brain cells. Sure, we have lots of brain cells; but can anyone really afford to lose a few dozen, much less a few million? Why would folks, in their right mind, want to suffer such a loss of brain power? Evidence suggests that moderate drinking will not damage the brain; but immoderate drinkers are at war on two major fronts: their livers and their brains. The alcohol-induced symptoms of Korsakoff's disease may leave the victim unable to create new memories and leaves the alcoholic with gaps that are filled with "recollections" that never occurred. Lastly, regarding the source cited at the opening of this paragraph, "Alcoholism can also lead to degeneration of the cerebellum, the part of the brain that governs balance and posture; to polyneuropathy, meaning nerve damage, with eventual loss of sensation and strength; and to Wernicke's disease, characterized by paralysis of eye movement, a stumbling walk and mental deterioration."

Let's take a more methodical approach to this 'health benefits' notion. We might begin by quoting a health advice columnist, Dr. Keith Roach ("To Your Good Health"). He wrote, in a 2013 column (*The Daily Item*, 2/16/13), "Excess alcohol use is certainly a cause of dementia, and it is possible that the two combine to cause a more rapid progression." Dr. Roach also made a statement (*The Daily Item*, 7/29/17) that deserves to be on the wall of every American classroom: *"Even moderate amounts of alcohol may adversely affect the brain as we age. This new information should be considered in future guidelines on alcohol use."* [Italics added]

Dr. George Grossberg describes himself (http://abcnews. go.com/blogs/health/2012/07/19) as a physician who works with older adults. His observations, based in part on two recent studies, end with these words: "even small amounts of alcohol can upset their delicate cognitive equilibrium and significantly worsen cognition and even trigger behavioral problems."

Again, paraphrasing from the AMA book, *The Family Medical Guide*. One's peripheral nerves are those that aren't located in the brain and spinal cord. Damage to such nerves is labeled as peripheral neuropathy. Sensations include tingling and, eventually, numbness in the extremities. The skin may become especially sensitive with muscular pain occurring. All these symptoms can be annoying and, sometimes, debilitating. Since the symptoms occur in some diabetics (those with diabetes mellitus) and in alcoholics, one can postulate that diabetics should adhere to helpful diets and that alcoholics should dump their liquor into the toilet.

The Family Medical Guide, (p. 32) also has a fascinating little paragraph that tells readers that "Recent studies using CAT scans of the head show that prolonged, heavy alcohol intake can cause the brain to shrink and the ventricles (cavities) within it to enlarge." Elsewhere on that same page, one can read that "Moderate drinking, whether of beer, wine or cocktails, is not generally harmful to the health of adults, but it can evolve *almost imperceptibly* into the excessive consumption of alcohol. Remember that alcohol is a drug, and any drug consumed in excess, or at the wrong time, can be harmful." The problem with the preceding paragraph is that certain readers will highlight five words "Moderate drinking . . . is not . . . harmful . . ." and disregard the remainder of this entire volume! More recently than the preceding paragraphs' data and cautions, another mention of alcohol's damage to the brain appeared. In fact, despite its powerful message, the article didn't make it into the local newspaper until the very last item of the last section of the paper, The Daily Item (1-12-16). That means that it was shunted from where it should have been (*the front page!*) to the very last page. It had to be preceded by the more newsworthy events, such as a record-breaking lottery jackpot, political shenanigans, some athlete's travails in a whorehouse, who won what thespian prizes, etc.

If the journal's reader ever made it as far as the last page of that edition, he or she would learn that the National Institute of Alcohol Abuse and Alcoholism, cited studies that relied on the newest technology to tell the public that "excessive drinking causes lasting damage to your brain." The damage results from consuming quantities of alcohol that seem to appear frequently in such studies: Less than two a day average for men and one a day average for women. *One's attention should be drawn to the advice in this report that tells us that the serious alcohol-induced brain damage may just be reversed if one is passionate enough to embrace sobriety.*

9. ENDOCRINE ~ The endocrinologist must deal with a very complex physical system. This is the system of the human body that involves secretion, within the body, of hormones that are transported by lymphatic or blood flow to other parts of the body, where the hormones effect changes in their target organs or body parts. These varied, but very influential, hormones are produced, stored and secreted by such as the pituitary, pancreatic, adrenal, testicular, ovarian and several other glands. Without the endocrine system, our growth, reproductive, metabolic and a couple of other physical functions would malfunction and the body's ability to respond to stress or injury would be diminished.

And alcohol's impact? Where the endocrine system is involved, the abuse of alcohol can be devastating. But, even more intriguing is the general observation from the scholarly paper, "Effects of Alcohol on the Endocrine System," authored by *Nadia Rachdaoui* and *Dipak K. Sarker* (http://www.lncbi. nlm.nih.gov/pmc/articles/PMC3767933/). Their Introduction begins with this observation: "Alcohol consumption is one of the most serious substance abuse disorders worldwide."

The authors go on to tell us that "According to the National Institute of Alcohol Abuse and Alcoholism, each year approximately 80,000 people die from alcohol-related causes, making it the third leading cause of death in the United States. Approximately 14 million Americans (7.4%) have an alcohol use disorder that is classified as either alcoholism (alcohol dependency) or alcohol abuse." To be sure, Americans need to feel some anxiety about the activity and plans of foreign terrorists;

but the data given above suggests it's high time that we save a huge chunk of anxiety for the threat that the relentless terrorist, alcohol, also poses to our personal survival. How sad that, knowing all we know, we are so easily lured by the hucksters' simple phrase telling us to remain thirsty!

That same Rachdaoui and Sarker paper emphasizes, "Heavy alcohol drinking increases the risk of cardiovascular and liver disease, metabolic disturbances, nutritional deficiencies, cancers (i.e. mouth, stomach, colon, liver, and breast cancer), neurological disorders and fetal abnormalities." Thanks to our thoughtless urge to consume alcohol, we may wish to take a red marker and post a yard-square poster somewhere in our houses, using a quote from the study just discussed: almost every organ and cell in the body is affected by the endocrine system. Also, we refuse to let our ethanol worship even hint at what an adventure we'd miss if we avoided cancer of the throat.

10. REPRODUCTIVE ~ Does alcohol have an effect on one's sex life? Can humans suffer from cirrhosis of the lover? To be sure. Alcohol and intimacy have a long and troubled history. One summarizing passage (*The ABCs of The Human Body*, p. 270) clearly informs us that "Alcoholism—capable of increasing estrogen levels by affecting the liver, decreasing testosterone levels by causing testicular dysfunction, and depressing the central nervous system—can also make a man chronically impotent. And too much drinking at any one time may temporarily prevent erection."

That same source (p. 271) also tells one, "There is some evidence that alcohol and certain drugs may temporarily increase sexual drive by depressing inhibitions, but these substances tend to backfire and can even cause impotence over the long term."

Chug the liquor; check the lumps? In a society that seems to have become breast obsessed, it is truly amazing that so little has ever been said about alcohol's threat to female breasts. It was only recently (November 2, 2011) that the magazine, *JAMA (Journal of the American Medical Association)* presented the results of a study, authored by a quintet of male and female doctors. Here one can read, "*Increasing alcohol consumption was associated with increased breast cancer risk that was statistically significant at levels as low as 5.0 to 9.9 g per day, equivalent to 3 to 6 drinks per week . . ."*

Among the article's conclusions: *"Low levels of alcohol consumption were associated with a small increase in breast cancer risk, with the most consistent measure being cumulative alcohol intake throughout adult life. Alcohol intake both earlier and later in adult life was independently associated with risk . . .*

"it is important to evaluate the role of alcohol intake at different times in a woman's life."

One bit of data in the above-referenced article really demands attention. We learn that the increase in alcohol and increased breast cancer risk is statistically significant to levels "equivalent to 3 to 6 drinks per week . . ."

Another very recent internet revelation: the site, *www. cancer.org*, is also bringing readers up-to-date regarding alcohol use and increased risk for breast cancer. It can be quoted, thusly

(http://www.cancer.org/cancer/cancercauses/dietand physicalactivity/alcohol-use-and-ancer): "Breast cancer: Even a few drinks a week is linked with an increased risk of breast cancer in women . . . Alcohol can affect estrogen levels in the body, which may explain some of the increased risk." The conclusion of that item states that "Drinking less alcohol may be an important way for many women to lower their risk of breast cancer."

Continuing, a report out of the Mayo Clinic offered this advice from Dr. Sandhya Pruthi:

"The more alcohol you drink, the greater your risk of developing breast cancer. If you *choose* [emphasis added] to drink alcohol—including beer, wine or liquor—limit yourself to no more than one drink a day." (http://newsnetwork. mayoclinic.org/?s=Dr.Pruthi+on+Breast+Cancer&field=all)
10/23/14.

Why can't the 'authorities' tell everyone that it is best to 'choose' not to drink alcohol; not one a day or one a week or one a lifetime? What utter boobs!

Are the experts who advise reduced drinking or, hopefully, abstinence, still operating as voices in the ethanol wilderness?

Herewith, a pregnant pause . . .

Admittedly, much has been revealed about women and the *dangers of alcohol during pregnancy*. Of course, the ugly consequences of drinking while sporting the 'bump' have been too great to hide.

An undated bulletin from the National Organization on Fetal Alcohol Syndrome (Washington, D.C.) offers the following quote from the Institute of Medicine, 1996: "Of all the substances of abuse (including cocaine, heroin, and marijuana), alcohol produces by far the most serious neurobehavioral effects in the fetus." The same bulletin also offers a chilling bit of information when it lists "outcomes associated with prenatal alcohol exposure may include:

- Abnormal facial characteristics

- Growth deficits

- Brain damage including mental retardation

- Heart, lung and kidney defects

- Hyperactivity and behavior problems

- Attention and memory problems

- Poor coordination and motor skill delays

- Difficulty with judgment and reasoning

- Learning disabilities

Although that list of horrors costs society billions of dollars annually, fetal alcohol syndrome can be prevented. Apparently, the protective placenta cannot protect the helpless fetus from alcohol. Only the mother can do that!

There's more. An internet site known as *Healthline* tells readers that the *freedom from pregnancy* that women finally achieve when reaching menopause is balanced by *an increase in alcohol dangers*. That site (http://www.healthline.com/health/menopause/alcohol), informs one (6/30/2015) that alcohol "can interfere with your body's ability to absorb calcium, a nutrient that is key in the maintenance of bone density and necessary for many other bodily functions as well." Another worthy observation that follows: *Healthline* tells readers: "While research is ongoing, *the general consensus is to limit alcohol consumption as the safest bet to staying healthy.*" [Italics added] That column concludes by suggesting that low-risk imbibing can be achieved by having *just one alcoholic drink daily.* Your author must then, once more, ask sarcastically, "Why not have just one less drink per day and risk glorious sobriety?"

Alcoholism ~ The chronic addiction to alcoholic drink. Regarding this topic, the *AMA Family Medical Guide* (page 713) offers this: "Anyone who drinks, smokes or takes drugs may become dangerously addicted."

Dipsomania ~ The morbid craving for alcoholic drink.

Many Americans are cursed with debilitating migraine headaches. One health advisor, Diana Cullum-Dugan of the *Environmental Nutrition Newsletter* (*TDI*, 6/18/13) advises that migraines can be triggered by the wrong use of foods. The worst diet trigger of migraines, she reports, is the failure to eat for extended periods. What is the second most serious dietary trigger of migraines? Ms. Cullum-Dugan reports: "Alcohol, especially wine and beer, runs a close second to fasting."

Once again, consider just the female of our species. A single news item (*The Week*, 12-11-15, p. 19) has this pithy and sobering sentence: "The female body takes longer to metabolize alcohol, making women more vulnerable to the ravages of heavy drinking, including liver inflammation, heart disease, and cancer."

As has been so amply demonstrated, any level of alcohol increases health risks, including breast cancer, liver cancer, and colon cancer. If we are advised that men should restrict themselves to just two drinks of alcohol daily and that women should restrict themselves to just one drink of alcohol daily, note how close they are to creating a sober society! Why don't sports magazines, health magazines, youth magazines, etc., push sobriety when their readers could simply maintain sobriety with just one or two fewer drinks per day? Why, pray tell, must so many editors jostle their readers toward the realm of the tyrant, alcohol?

As mentioned above, the dismissal of this colossal curse of alcohol with a sweeping gesture that should have died centuries ago: "Safer than water." With the development of cities during the Medieval period of Europe's history, population growth also involved increasingly filthy and polluted water. If one could drink liquids that were brewed or fermented, the drink would be less toxic. However, the notion that water was unsafe, when compared to alcohol, should have died long ago. Today, we all know differently. *Only a fool pretends that one must go from the mother's breast to the barrel's spigot for uninterrupted nourishment.*

It is damned infuriating! One sees items purporting to be health news, informing us of the benefits of one or another alcohol product; but with reportage so skewed that it is little more than 100-proof propaganda.

Another example: The bulletin of the AARP (July-August 2014) tells readers that Howard Medical School researchers found that women who drank two to four beers a week cut their risk of "painful" rheumatoid arthritis by nearly one-third. This, presumably, is compared to those dopey women who drank no beer. Are those Howard Medical School researchers so intellectually challenged that they must offer women nothing more than a simple either/or choice in this test? Can they offer women no non-alcoholic substitute refreshment or pharmaceutical substitute for the beer? Are the world's women condemned to either begin drinking two to four beers a week or experience increased risks for suffering "painful" rheumatoid arthritis? Bullscat!

Critical things are missing from many of today's so-called 'health' tips, beginning with integrity!

A pathetic truism: Alcohol kills the ability to recognize the need to avoid alcohol.

Frozen assets

Here's another enlightening topic regarding alcohol's effect on the human body. A Mayo Clinic site is straightforward in its advice regarding alcohol and hypothermia (www.mayoclinic.org/diseases-conditions/hypothermia/basics/risk-factors/con-200204   ) "Alcohol may make your body feel warm inside, but it causes your blood vessels to dilate, or expand, resulting in more rapid heat loss from the surface of your skin. The body's natural shivering response is diminished in people who've been drinking alcohol. In addition, the use of alcohol . . . can affect your judgment about the need to get inside or wear warm clothes in cold weather conditions. If a person is intoxicated and passes out in cold weather, he or she is likely to develop hypothermia."

Delving further into the alcohol/hypothermia danger, the author downloaded (2/1/16)) a document from the *Center for Disease Control* (www.cdc.gov/mmwr/preview/mmwrhtml/mm5308a2.htm) that stated (among other things) that "Use of alcohol . . . often is associated with cases of hypothermia. The vasodilatation caused by alcohol provides a sensation of warmth but also increases heat loss through radiation. In addition, alcohol and other drugs impair hand coordination, mobility, and decision-making abilities. Of course, if one is consuming inordinate amounts of alcohol, it seems obvious that his/her decision-making abilities were retarded in the first place.

A libertarian approach

Let's be libertarian about the problem: Let all who wish to debilitate themselves, or even commit boozicide, by the excessive use of alcohol, do so. For that, I'll gladly quote Margaret Mitchell's deathless phrase: "Frankly, I don't give a damn."

HOWEVER . . . the libertarian excuse crumbles as soon as the inebriate belittles sobriety or threatens any other individual's health and happiness. The ills of the inebriate society have been with us since prehistoric times.

A pair of pithy quotes from the American Medical Association: [*The AMA Family Medical Guide*, pages 304-305]

"The more they [Those addicted to alcohol] drink the less tension they can tolerate without alcohol." Yes, you should focus and read that pithy statement once more.

"The shift from social drinking to alcoholism can happen almost imperceptibly over many years or it can occur with dramatic rapidity."

No American should reach adulthood without an acute awareness of the horrendous effects of alcohol on his or her liver. Even one who leads a rather casual approach to health should see the many signs. For example, there is the subject of 'fatty liver'. As recently as February of 2016, a medical advice writer, Dr. Keith Roach, in his column, "To Your Good Health," addressed the subject of "fatty liver." He wrote, "Fatty liver can have many causes, but it is much more common in people who are overweight or have diabetes (or both) . . . Alcohol use is another big cause, and abstinence is recommended for those with fatty liver." How refreshing to read a clear statement, by an authority, regarding abstinence and alcohol in even one specific medical case. That's one more thought that needs to be put on billboards nationwide. There are so many more thoughts of similar value.

"[I]t is thought that at least one in five heavy drinkers develops cirrhosis of the liver." Such numbers might encourage those who want excuses to imbibe since they can easily convince themselves that the odds are four to one in favor of their never getting cirrhosis. That's a stat to which they can drink . . . Of course, the AMA also adds that heavy drinking "may cause serious diseases of the stomach, heart, and brain." A closing thought while on the subject of cirrhosis: As recently as 5/25/13, (*TDI*), Dr. Keith Roach informed readers: "Unfortunately, once cirrhosis is established, it is permanent, and the high pressure in the portal vein persists." Elsewhere, he enlightens, thusly: "Many other health problems come with liver cirrhosis, so in addition to quitting drinking, someone . . . needs to see his or her doctor for a comprehensive evaluation."

"Some alcoholics . . . are never quite sober."

The AMA, on the topic cited above, states that "if you are determined to give up alcohol, you can." The AMA also states (p. 715) a most important truism: "Anyone who drinks, smokes, or takes drugs may become dangerously addicted . . . The danger is most acute among teenagers, who tend to be attracted to assertive, 'sophisticated' gestures, and who tend to think that they will live forever." "Unfortunately," says the AMA (p. 305), "total abstinence from alcohol is the only effective solution for many addicts." That's why all reason and logic suggest that one should simply avoid alcohol. It seems only logical that those who have been kept from experimentation with alcohol as young teens will be more likely to avoid alcohol in their later teens and their adulthood. It helps if parents can reinforce, with their children, this concept: *Alcohol is no pathway to adulthood.* For teens who avoid the sirens on the rocks of alcohol, a longer and healthier life is assured.

There is also the curse an *alcoholic* may endure if he, or she, really tries to quit. It's an altered behavior that is, itself, frightening for others and dangerous for the alcoholic. Here's an excerpt from an earlier cited book, *Prince and the Paupers*, by this author: The incident recited (pages 45-46) involved a younger brother of the book's biographical subject, Prince D. Farrington.

George Hobson Farrington had such frightening attacks of the delirium tremens that they had a physician summoned. The physician, the family laments, gave him a shot to stop the attack; but it killed the patient. There is no evidence that "Hop" Farrington's tragic death had any impact on other family members, regarding abandoning their pursuit of alcohol. However, one family *friend* may have been shocked out of any interest in "demon rum," as alcohol was disparagingly described. Tom Bauman tells of visiting Whitey and George [Farrington] at Prince's house. "Hop" was also there. The alcoholic was leaving one room, through the parlor doors. He had just opened the doors when he went into a delirious fit! He screamed, "Don't let them get me." He was screaming and thrashing about, totally out of control, because of his delirium tremens. Bauman was totally unnerved. Prince's middle son, Gayle, was a husky young man who was finally able to get "Hop" under control. Aside from "Hop's" severe alcoholic condition, what triggered his delirious outburst? It happened because, as he opened the parlor doors, he was suddenly confronted by a stranger! The 'stranger' was actually the newel post of the stair railing, topped with Prince's coat and hat!

Bauman's reflection: "To this day I think seeing "Hop" like that, when I was just a kid, kind of made me ask, 'What in the hell does somebody use that stuff for? You know, they don't make you drink it. I never had trouble with booze."

Who'd a thunk it!

The headline seemed innocuous. "*Study: Alcohol consumption can fuel criminal activity*" (*TDI*, 11-3-16). This author's first thought was "Of course, we have countless examples of drinking leading to criminal activity!" But, that was not what the study authors were studying. It wasn't the observation that someone gets drunk and commits a crime. The thrust of this extensive study—conducted by two University of Oregon economists—was to find or dispel evidence that individuals, who had not been criminal before, began criminal careers once reaching the legal drinking age in Oregon. The study covered a period of more than two decades. Christopher Ingraham, reporting in *The Washington Post*, tells readers that the study indicated that "As soon as people turned 21, their likelihood of criminality spiked considerably."

In deference to temperance

Should one really want to become a non-drinker, he or she would be doing himself or herself a favor worth a small fortune. There are numerous programs that allow the serious person to succeed in the effort. There are the "de-tox" clinics, the organizations and the self-help programs. One might begin by consulting the *American Medical Association Family Medical Guide*, oft-cited in this polemic. It offers (pages 36-7) a topic, "How to cut down your drinking," that is a common-sense program. The serious *drinker* should, just as seriously, *stop drinking.* I would be the first to welcome you into the brave, new world of sobriety!

As a form of summary to the topic of health problems that can result from *intemperance,* let's look at an abbreviated list of short- and long-term health risks, as delineated by the Centers for Disease Control, on their site, http://www.cdc.gov/alcohol/fact-sheets/alcohol-use.htm :

Among the short-term health risks: *Injuries, violence, alcohol poisoning, sexual misbehavior, miscarriage, stillbirth or fetal alcohol spectrum disorders!* The long-term health risks include *hypertension, heart disease, stroke, digestive troubles, liver disease, a variety of cancers, learning and memory impairment, depression, anxiety, a variety of social problems and outright alcoholism.* You might want to recite these to yourself when someone offers you a second drink of alcohol.

Brent's brief capsule

As recently as April of 2015 one could read a pungent piece of data on a site called "The Fix" [www.thefix.com]. Written by an individual named Brent McCluskey, it was headlined as follows: *"Alcoholism Shortens Lifespan by Nearly a Decade, Study Finds"*

His revealing report opens with a hard-hitting sentence: "Researchers concluded that excessive alcohol consumption damages both mind and body" and goes on to say that that study from a foreign journal, *European Psychiatry,* lets the public know that "alcoholism not only negatively impacts physical health, but also that it takes its toll on the mind as well." Supporting data is properly identified. However, even more recent data is also more compelling. *The Week* magazine (5/18/18) cites a Harvard study that surveyed more than 100,000 adults for about three decades. That study listed five lifestyle habits that shorten people's lives by about 12 years! One of the five was easily countered by "limiting alcohol intake."

An old quote: "Riddle me this," can be a worthy request.

Riddle me this: Why, considering the pandemic of debilitating or fatal results of alcohol abuse, do we not hear a great outcry from every healthcare worker, every health care group, and every health insurer? Is it because some benefit monetarily or that some simply love alcohol? Or is it, perhaps, both?

We have shown how one anatomical system after another might suffer, often grievously, from alcohol abuse. Herewith, to close this chapter, a summarizing quote, from the same source (*AMA Family Medical Guide*) frequently cited throughout the topic. That quote, from page 305, reminds us: "Alcoholism can damage every system of the body."

Sober Slogan # 15

**Shame on America's
beer belly!**

Chapter Nine

What If . . .

What if the nation became sober? Naturally, our roadsides would be clear of much of the clutter that spoils our roadside landscape. Our roadsides would be clear of many cans and bottles, as well as the cars and bodies. And our newspapers would not be bloated with such ugly articles as the following:

From the coverage of reporter, Justin Strawser (*TDI*, 12-24-15), we learn of a driver named Jon C. Patterson who, in the previous month, apparently hit a parked car in Sunbury, Pennsylvania, before leaving the scene. Later, a Sunbury police chief stopped Patterson for erratic driving and ended by handing Patterson a half-dozen charges, two of which were for driving under the influence of alcohol. This leaves Patterson with a busy arrest schedule since he was already due to enter prison resulting from drunken driving charges in 2014. Here, one might decide, is another authentic terrorist, the product of too much alcohol (his blood test indicated a blood-alcohol level of .234, quite a bit beyond the legal level of .08). Not only was he too drunk to find his vehicle owner's card (it was in his hand) and too drunk to avoid a parked vehicle; but when he was on the verge of facing the police chief he tossed a whiskey bottle into his car's back seat,

---

Sober Slogan # 16

Morally ~

We're all required

To stay sober!

Why is everyone staring at me?

which was occupied by his two pre-teen children. Such reports are commonplace.

What if, instead of the reckless behavior of drivers, with all the resulting hell, we just look at our nation through economic eyes? If so, a recent (10-30-15) news item in *The Week* magazine might hold some interest. Referencing the National Centers for Disease Control: It tells us "Excessive drinking cost the U.S. $249 billion in 2010 from lost productivity, more crime, early death, and emergency room visits—a significant increase from $223.5 billion in 2006. About 77% of those costs stem from binge drinking . . ."

The steady stream: negative news, unending

How much newsprint is consumed by items relating to the use and abuse of alcohol? Also, how many alcohol-related items reveal the problems with alcohol abuse and how many simply report the consumption of alcohol in less problematic situations? If all the alcohol-related news items from all the nation's local newspapers, were published in a single newspaper, we could have something like *The National Alcohol Daily*.

A small, locally-published newspaper is *The Daily Item*, of Sunbury, Pennsylvania. One day's 'news' (10-3-12) tells of a man being thrown from his motorcycle and being charged with driving without a cycle license, as well as driving under the influence of alcohol. The same issue tells of police arriving at another accident scene to find one of the drivers quickly downing most of the contents of a three-ounce bottle of mouthwash. A third news account, under that same dateline, told of about 2,000 people attending a local beer-tasting event.

Here is a typical, little news item:

> LCB cites Shamokin bar
> SHAMOKIN—Snappers, at 501 N. Shamokin St. has been cited by the Bureau of Liquor Control Enforcement for allegedly serving alcohol to visibly intoxicated customers on June 29.
> That from *The Daily Item* (Sunbury, Pennsylvania), October 3, 2008.

News to make the sodden heart leap: *Time* magazine (November 12, 2012, p. 15) reported that the Scots, struggling to keep pace with their Irish neighbors, have now begun brewing a beer named Armageddon. That beer, with a name that suggests that they hope to win the struggle against sobriety, can claim a Guinness record. With a 65% alcohol content, Armageddon is thought to be the strongest beer on planet Earth! And some of us thought that humankind had stopped making progress!

Another myth

The nation's most naive assumption? It's probably the assumption that bartenders deny drinks to those nearly or already drunk.

Since every drink sold is involved in the financial success of the establishment, the owners must know that every drink sold to those already tanked can only add to their profit margin. The entire business of dispensing liquor urges the pushing of greater sales to any who imbibe. The customer who leaves the establishment with the highest blood-alcohol level has likely contributed most to the establishment's profit level. For those concerned about turning drunks loose on society, the system has a hellish flaw; but that flaw will live as long as the system exists.

We need lots of answers if we're ever to rid American society of the terrorist, alcohol! Examples:

How many American criminals would have no criminal record, if they had stayed sober?

How many hospital and rehab-center beds would be available if their occupants had stayed sober?

How many cases that overburden our government's *children-and-youth* agencies, wouldn't exist if sobriety was a normal condition in the home?

How many employees cause serious problems for owners and managers because they abandon sobriety? As former host Bill O-Reilly noted on his evening show (1/27/12), "Drinking on the job is always pinheaded." That observation can readily be amended: "And drinking off the job is similarly pinheaded."

A reality-suggested rhyme:

OWED TO ALCOHOL

A thousand times I must have heard
What I presume is Wisdom's word.
That driving, after one's imbibed,
Can earn someone a stone, inscribed.

I've also heard, in private talk,
That drinkers sometimes cannot walk
And those who use unbridled drink
Will also lose the power to think.

But, more than these; yes, most of all,
When all its sadness we recall,
To this we can, our seals, affix:
That DRINKING/LIVING DO NOT MIX!

An alcohol record book?

There can't be too many reminders of the hell-on-earth created by the abuse of alcohol. That's why it would be nice if there was a compendium of alcohol-engendered records. Here are some examples:

■ The most DUI citations garnered by one individual before his/her involvement in a fatal DUI.

■ The most cars swiped by a drunken driver during a single incident.

■ The most pedestrians struck during a single DUI incident.

■ The most fatalities involved in a lone DUI accident.

■ The highest blood-alcohol level ever recorded for a drunken driver.

■ The fastest known speed involved in a DUI incident.

■ The largest number of DUI citations ever won by a single driver.

That list could be nearly endless.

Ponder this: As a small start, we might balance the alcohol sales spectrum. The nation's life expectancy figure stands at about 75. Since we prohibit alcohol sales to those under the age of 18, why not balance the law by prohibiting alcohol sales to everyone over the age of 57?

Well, it was a thought . . .

A heroine

Ophelia Motlow, the wife of distiller Lemuel Motlow (nephew and heir to the distilling business of Jack Daniel of Lynchburg, Tennessee), "never allowed liquor in the house except for medicinal purposes." (quote from Krass, p. 198)

As an aside, those who guzzle Jack Daniel's whiskey must have noticed that there is a second man's name on the Jack Daniel's label. There's a modest coincidence. This author has only encountered the name of Lemuel three times within memory. First was in the book of *Proverbs* (see the opening lines of Chapter 3, above), where there is a king named Lemuel, who is advised not to get drunk. Secondly, as the given name of a friend of the 20th-century moonshiner/ bootlegger, Prince Farrington (mentioned in Chapter 5) and, lastly, as the name that appears on the label of the *Jack Daniel's* whiskey bottle, where we are informed thusly: "Lem Motlow, Proprietor." Lemuel Motlow's name is not associated with staying sober.

Get sober, America!

An Affinity for Vampires ©

Vampires drink blood.
Drunkards drink booze.

Vampires appear threatening.
Drunkards appear harmless.

Vampires are out only from dusk to dawn.
Drunkards are out at any time!

Vampires drive in the proper lane.
Drunkards drive everywhere!

Vampires kill no Americans.
Drunkards kill dozens *daily!*

Chapter Ten

The Poison Proliferates

Pro-life or proliferation?

One of America's great heroic accounts tells us of the great Alaskan sled dog trip of 1925. In that exciting story, we learn of the threat of a deadly diphtheria epidemic in Nome, on the Alaskan coast, near the Bering Strait. Native children, in particular, would be unprotected from the epidemic. However, the nearest serum was in Anchorage. A train rushed the 20-pound serum canister almost due north to a small town, Nenana, near Fairbanks. From there, teams of sled dogs and drivers (mushers) rushed in relays to haul the precious serum across the great expanse, through snow and across dangerous ice fields of central Alaska, to Nome. The effort was a success! That humanitarian effort inspired the later contests (since 1968) known as the Iditarod sled dog races. Sadly, we often see similarly 'heroic' efforts—sans the humanitarian need—put into the proliferation of alcohol.

The proliferation aspect of alcohol should alarm. The boozers need tail-gating at many sporting events. They also need alcohol for a growing number of other events, from July 4th celebrations to Christmas and New Year shindigs! From fraternity parties to company parties to class reunions, alcohol is the basic beverage. More and more states are allowing alcohol sales at more and more venues. It's been only recently that I've entered Pennsylvania grocery markets and walked past a massive wall of beer cases before arriving at the groceries. A great irony in celebratory America: The marital ship cannot leave port until it has been christened with booze; the same fluid that will eventually engulf and sink many of those same boats.

In January of 2016, my local newspaper (*The Daily Item*) reported on a fundraising event that was offering a treasure of gifts, all with the goal of raising funds to fight the curse of cystic fibrosis. Who was the primary sponsor? That would be a major national brewery and its local distributor. Having the alcohol industry sponsor a health-related fundraiser is like having a cigarette company doing the same. One would be better served if a health facility had a fundraiser to help educate the public on the pathetic health effects of alcohol.

The Week magazine regularly informs it chic readers (and the rest of us) of several wines worthy of sophisticated tastes. This, too, is part of our proliferating adoration of alcohol.

That same weekly newsmagazine (2-2-18, p. 32) lets us observe proliferation's spiral with another startling stat: In the past decade, the number of U.S. brewery employees has just about tripled. This fits nicely with the old anti-Prohibition argument: Boozing boosts employment.

How joyous the news that the concept of "wine trails" is now being aped by some entrepreneurial types who are launching promotional "beer trails." Here, again, we are pushing madly toward a nation of "Toper Trails."

Helping to provide a "coast-to-coast" support of the booze business, Oregon, in early 2018, has passed legislation that will give large tax breaks to small breweries. The small businesses involved are the 200-plus craft breweries. *The Weekly Standard* (1-15-18) indicates that much of the tax break windfall will be put into the expansion of the businesses. In other words: Let's further expand an already crippling commodity.

Is a new booze dynamic coming to your neighborhood? One of many examples of alcohol's rapid growth: My local paper (*TDI*, 3/5/16) announced that a new booze trail ("River Rat Brew Trail") is now organized. It will include nine local breweries, most of which didn't exist a decade ago. It would be interesting to see the state's Liquor Control Board develop stats projecting the negatives that might be attached to any newly-opened brewery.

On January 19, 2016, an Associated Press article appeared in *The Daily Item* of Sunbury, Pennsylvania. Under the byline of Kelli Kennedy, readers learned that breweries and yoga classes are teaming for mutual growth. One can meditate and then contemplate one's naval while consuming a few beers. Anyone who read that timely article in *The Daily Item* could then shift his or her gaze a few inches to the left to read a neighboring article that told of a Pittsburgh-area woman who was set to appear in court later for a drunken driving case. However, she was newly involved in another suspected drunken driving case in which her six passengers, all children, were injured in varying degrees of severity. A preliminary hearing was scheduled for several weeks in the future.

As a resident of the Keystone State, I see more items that deal with my home state. On the 17th of February 2016, *The Daily Item* had a brief article relating that the state's Supreme Court was pondering a decision regarding beer sales at convenience stores. Why not? What potential beer markets are left: Church socials and school lunches?

Pennsylvanians also learned (*TDI*, 3/4/16) that they needed to keep their calendars open for an upcoming liquor-store opening in Glen Mills, a town west of Philadelphia. What's so special about this event? Robert De Niro would be appearing. How exciting! It will give him a chance to get more Pennsylvanians on board for his own vodka line.

When it was created in 1933, Pennsylvania's governor, Gifford Pinchot, said that the purpose of Pennsylvania's Liquor Control Board was to discourage the purchase of alcoholic beverages. Obviously, the health and safety of its citizens is no longer a primary concern of Pennsylvania's Liquor Control Board. The Keystone State's venerable Liquor Control Board appears to have morphed into a liquor promotion board.

A recent Associated Press article (*TDI*, 11-15-15) describes the riverine city of Memphis, Tennessee as one more American mecca that wishes to be recognized for its history, music, and beer. How many more alcohol-laden vacation meccas and trails and events must be established before this ungodly alcoholic proliferation is reversed? We're fast (yes, fast!) becoming a nation of promotional boozing events of profound numbers. Since making alcohol legal, our proliferation rates, in many facets of the business, are converting America into one grand moonshine mecca. Perhaps we teetotalers can hope that we can get all the varied alcohol makers, movers, and imbibers to quarrel among themselves if we simply get some congressman to introduce a law designed to designate one national form of booze.

One shouldn't be surprised to learn that Massachusetts—the commonwealth that gave us Lizzie Bordon, the Boston Strangler and Chappaquiddick—has, in Boston, a swanky cocktail club named "Carrie Nation." How pompous! How arrogant!

Let's hear it for a few sobriety Meccas!

Now we're seeing, in the U.S. as in England, the phenomenon of alcohol and art as a social event.

We see liquor added to Jell-O.

We see wine added to ice cream.

During the spring of 2016, I got an ad for a steakhouse that is now offering a bourbon glaze to some of their sizzling slabs of beef.

Maple syrup is now spicing some beer.

One of America's old New England companies has begun offering (October 2015 promotion) a candle with a vanilla-*bourbon* scent.

Tickets can be purchased that will take folks on wine-tasting tours.

Internet sites now commonly promote and praise alcohol.

Pre-bottled cocktails are now ready for thirsty consumers.

In 2016, (2/13), I received a nice card in my rural mailbox. The offer: A visually appealing variety of shirts; all green and with a glass of dark ale emblazoned across the chest and with my name above the booze. I can, for a few greenbacks, get one or more of these charming tee shirts, hoodies or caps, mailed from right here in western Pennsylvania. I'm not Irish; but, begorrah, they'll still sell some to me and, if I act quickly, I can have them in time for St. Patrick's Day! And if I'm chic enough to hold the shirt long enough I can order, from another mail advertiser, a St. Patrick's Day pint glass or a handsome growler, either one of which can have my name engraved, along with some cute Irish-style wording. Yes, I'm peeved with such blatant ads that tumble from my mailbox, all celebrating an American holiday that's awash with alcohol.

A news item (*TDI*, 12-6-15) promised another "Annual Cocktail Conference" to be held in San Antonio, Texas in early 2016.

By moving from one city locale to another, conferees could have found a variety of events and reasons for imbibing. There's no need to feel guilty about needing more reasons to booze since the entire event is said to benefit children's charities!

Continuing our cursory look at the nation's proliferation of all things alcoholic, name the booze and there is likely a 'fest' or two in your area. Booze fests appear to be surfacing nearly everywhere as microbreweries and wineries proliferate, and communities latch fast to ethanol as sure treasury boosters. The 'festive' guests can competitively toss a keg or toss back a couple of kegs.

A recent (2016) book by Edward Achorn tells the exciting story about the birth of our second national baseball league and its boozy origins. The title: *The Summer of Beer and Whiskey*. The book's subtitle carries the cover into extra innings: *How Brewers, Barkeeps, Rowdies, Immigrants and a Wild Pennant Fight Made Baseball America's Game*.

Several of the slickest, most appealing magazines on the market, now inform and inspire with articles and images about the many marketing successes of liquor. One (*Market Watch*, 12-17, p. 38) lists an impressive statistical chart that shows one aspect of the proliferation of alcohol. It reveals that the U.S. consumption of Cognac—the brandy that came from the French town of the same name—has just about tripled in the past two decades.

The cursed glamorization of rotgut has infiltrated the television fare, with (in October 1, 2015 promos, at least) such liquor-glamorization programs as "Tripping Out with Alie and Georgia" (a program that one might re-title as "Cocktail Quest."), "Three Sheets," "Best Bars in America" and "Booze Travelers." And, for those who appreciate the classic films (as I do) there is now the TCM Wine Club.

Conversely, many things that tended to minimize the American intake of alcohol have been reduced or have disappeared.

There is no stigma when women join men in public places where alcohol is sold and/or consumed.

My personal impression is that American motion pictures are showing more consumption of alcohol with less and less regard for the negative consequences.

I surely miss one old approach to heavy drinking: the Burma Shave signs! Only members of the older generation or generations can recall these and similarly pithy profundities:

Car in ditch
Driver in tree
The moon was full
and so was he
Burma shave

Or

The one who drives
When he's been drinking
Depends on you
To do his thinking
Burma shave

Science trudges on

Another cheer must rise above the nation's cities and plains. Science has notched another grand accomplishment. The discoverer's name needs to be properly engraved. Mark Phillips is the genius who needs national recognition. He has created a new form of alcohol: Powdered alcohol! Phillips has hardly had time to get it patented, but a strange reaction has already occurred. Half of the great states of these United States have already outlawed powdered alcohol!

How weird . . . At this writing, the product (lovingly referred to as "Palcohol") hasn't even hit the markets; but states are opposing its appearance. The reasons given? Powdered alcohol will increase underage drinking and binge drinking! Hell, if those were authentic concerns about Palcohol, we would be returning to Prohibition! I haven't time for talk of left-wing or right-wing conspiracies, but I do have a nagging suspicion. Is it possible that the giants of the industry are fearful of the competition that may result from the powdered versions? In any case, this is just one more item to list when we talk about the pathetic proliferation of alcohol in America.

Let's brace for the tsunami!

Tristam's legacy

There was the old English novel by Laurence Sterne (1713-1768) in which the title character is Tristam Shandy. Somehow, that family name, Shandy, has now been attached to a drink: beer mixed with lemonade or some other vitiating citrus liquid. The "Shandy" appears to have somewhat less alcohol content which makes it a more acceptable drink in certain places where its lower alcohol content (like one percent?) allows it to be sold despite some of alcohol's usual prohibitions.

It might be worth noting that, for that tiny percentage of American drinkers who wish to transition from the boozing society to a rational sobriety, one might consider: Keep the shandy handy.

The rumbling at William Penn's grave

In the Keystone State, the history-rich commonwealth has been embroiled in the control, or lack of it, of alcohol sales since the close of the Prohibition era. In late 2015, it was reported (*The Daily Item*, 10-6-15) that the Pennsylvania Liquor Control Board was initiating a lottery-type program for the state's special auctions of limited quantity liquors. For a 2014 limited sale, the state's site crashed; which was great news for the state, the distiller and the thirsty citizens. Their new lottery device will, presumably, keep things fairer and more orderly. While a sardonic comment seems appropriate here, none comes to mind.

Don't cut spending; expand boozing . . .

Here's more exciting news . . . for the ethanol merchants. *The Week* magazine has now announced (12-11-15) that statistics reveal a trend toward *more frequent drinking by American women.* The percentage of women who drink has increased slightly as has the amount that they consume. Of course, they remain as vulnerable as ever to the certain negative impact of alcohol abuse.

On June 9 of 2016, I opened my daily newspaper (*TDI*) to learn that Pennsylvania's sage House members, and our similarly sage governor, have realized that our state revenues could be expanded by many millions of dollars if we simply allowed wine sales in the grocery stores that are already pushing beer. Don't cut state spending; expand Pennsylvania boozing . . .

That same newspaper issue listed several other exciting changes that boozers will appreciate, such as the expanded store hours for the state-operated liquor stores. Hotels and restaurants can now sell 'take out' wine. Gas stations can join the pushers and Pennsylvanians can finally have mail-order purchases from out-of-state vintners. Will our local beer distributor's truck soon be delivering to Lulu's lemonade stand over on 9th and Maple? Of course, that was a bit of sarcasm; but I would remind one: These additional methods for making Pennsylvania more of a boozers' mecca, are offered under the pathetically euphemistic label of "liquor reform."

So long as news media exist, alcohol pushers garner free publicity. Today (3-10-17) my local daily newspaper carried a front-page headline telling readers that two of the larger, local grocery chains are among the entrepreneurs who plunked down anywhere from a few thousand dollars to close to a half-million bucks for available liquor licenses.

Readers of such news reports are regularly reminded that this tsunami of alcohol will generate considerable economic growth throughout the alcohol industry. Overlooked here, as usual, is the likely economic growth, as well, in all the fields that feel the negative impact of this great 'reform' in the proliferation of just one additional line of booze. What is the concomitant impact on the health industry, the law enforcement industry, the mortuary industry and so on?

We have no control over the growth of boozing and the growth of the sorry results. It should be an embarrassment to those in government, but today's alcohol-driven society is clearly out of control. The evidence:

The first and most obvious is the steady stream of killings related to alcohol.

Another is the absurd incidents that should never have occurred. I'm thinking here of one in particular (*TDI* 4/5/05). For *37 minutes*, Pennsylvania State and local police pursued a stolen car that was being driven at speeds in excess of 100 mph! During the chase, along the banks of the Susquehanna River, the fleeing driver rammed into and shoved another car from the roadway and narrowly missed hitting a police officer while skirting a tire-flattening strip. The state police, as well as police from a half-dozen municipalities, were involved in the pursuit! It was not until a state police car, 47 miles from the starting point, butted into the runaway vehicle to end the chase. It was then that the driver was found to have been drinking. He was 14 years old . . .

The preceding incident reminds one of the truism: Milk nourishes the infant; booze nourishes the infantile.

Even worse is the willingness to do nothing about repeat offenders. Why allow a drunken-driving offender to repeat the threat to the safety of himself/herself and of others. That, too, is an out-of-control situation. Examples? A man from Alexandria, Pennsylvania (*TDI*, 1-14-09) finally got a prison sentence; but it was his eighth DUI!

If peer pressure is so potent, why don't more people urge friends to avoid alcohol?

As tragedies also proliferate

How soon will we see 24/7 home delivery service, so that late-night parties need not run into booze-shortage crises? In fact, 24/7 home delivery service could have avoided the incident that occurred (February 1996) near the famed Appalachian Trail, north of Harrisburg, Pennsylvania, where an alcohol shortage sent a woman out into the sub-freezing night on a booze run.

According to news accounts [*The Daily Item* of Sunbury and the *Upper Dauphin Sentinel* of Millersburg] that woman, named Denise, was with her husband and friends, watching movies at their home in Halifax when, about midnight, the booze ran out. Forgo the liquor? Hell, no! This was an emergency! This was a crisis more critical and demanding than getting the diphtheria se-rum to Nome! The ensuing events make no sense; but here is the chain of events delivered to us in the local newspaper accounts.

Her husband later said that Denise, a registered nurse and the mother of a young daughter, hadn't been drinking. She was the one who left the house. Critical questions arise. At that late hour, where was she planning to get the beer? *Why wasn't she wear-ing a coat?* Her outer garments were sneakers, sweatpants and a sweatshirt. The weather that night was said to have reached a low of just *eight degrees Fahrenheit, a full 24 degrees below freezing!* One must ask, what would have driven her to stay outside the house for even one full minute? In any case, her car—a green GEO Metro convertible—apparently slid off an isolated stretch of rural road several miles from her home. The GEO Metro became stuck in snow. She then seemed to have exited her vehicle and locked it before starting to move—in her sneakers, sweatpants, and sweatshirt— through the arctic air and across a snowy field.

Police, on routine patrol, found her abandoned car, locked and undamaged, about 2:30 A.M.; but had no report of anyone being missing. Finally, when Denise hadn't arrived home at 6:00 A.M., a search began. But, by that time, according to the coroner's estimate, Denise would have been dead for about three hours, having frozen to death (across the field from where she had exited the car) at approximately 3:00 A.M., about a quarter mile from the green GEO. There was no formal autopsy and no foul play was suspected. The objects of her failed and fatal journey were still sitting somewhere in their six-packs.

From bar hopping to . . .
Patrick Ludwig of Shamokin Dam, Pennsylvania joined three buddies on September 22, 2006, to go bar hopping. After hopping from one to another, to another, and perhaps a fourth, the group decided to walk to yet another bar. However, en route to the next bar, Ludwig decided to do something that he had done in his more youthful years: Hop a train and ride to the nearby town of Selinsgrove. It was a bad decision.

Two city policemen answered the call. He was rushed to the local hospital and then to a larger medical center. It was there that the E.R. staff completed the process begun by the train; they removed both his legs.

Alcohol-related news is also proliferating
Alcohol-related news is proliferating, as are the resulting tragedies. Further evidence? The Center for Disease Control (CDC) site (downloaded 7/27/15) noted that about ten people in this nation die from unintentional drowning, *daily*. The site's message goes on to inform us that *nearly 70% of the deaths that are associated with water recreation involve alcohol use!* The number would be astonishing, in any place where alcohol came under critical scrutiny; but such is not the case in these United States!

> We need a national outcry!
> We need a national outcry!
> WE NEED A NATIONAL OUTCRY!

Another "twofer"
My local newspaper (*TDI*, 8-30-15) again had two alcohol-related stories in one edition when it told readers of the Pittsburgh-area killing of a woman, by her boyfriend. He then placed her body in a basement refrigerator for several days until he had dug a grave for her corpse. She might still be interred if her landlord hadn't reported her to be missing. What were the circumstances? Authorities allege that she "was killed in a drunken fight . . ."

The same edition, of 8-30-15 (*TDI*), describes the events of a Saturday-night traffic stop in Lewisburg, Pennsylvania. As reporter, Francis Scarcella told it, a 27-year-old woman arrived at a traffic stop. Asked to exit the vehicle, the woman refused. When she kicked and punched troopers, she was handcuffed; but that didn't stop her from successfully kicking a couple of officers. When she was finally sufficiently subdued, she was taken to a nearby hospital, where she refused to allow a nurse to draw blood for an alcohol check. Hauled to the police barracks, she managed to spit in another officer's face. Unable to cover the $20,000 bail, the woman was jailed on charges of aggravated assault on a police officer, resisting arrest and, as one might guess, *driving under the influence.*

Booze barges

Do you recall the death of George Smith, mentioned in the *Introduction* to this book? He's the one who appeared to have been highly intoxicated and then disappeared from a cruise ship while on his honeymoon! In early November of 2015, another man, a Brazilian national, was filmed hanging onto a lifeboat of the cruise ship on which he was a passenger. [http://www.news.com.au/ travel/travel-updates and http://insider.foxnews.com] He apparently jumped from the seventh floor of the liner, but landed on a lifeboat instead of in the ocean. An effort was made to hold-on-to-and-rescue the man, but he fell from the rescuers' grasp and dropped into the sea and into eternity! Two aircraft spent hours vainly searching over a broad area of the sea. Rumors told of the man having been fighting with his partner and of alcohol being involved.

In 2014, the internet site, philly.com, reported on the death of a survivor of the 1985 bombing in the Philadelphia area (http:// articles.philly.com/2014-06-13). Although Michael Moses Ward was one of just two survivors of that incident, he failed to survive his 2013 passage aboard the cruise ship, *Carnival Dream.* The 41-year-old died while in one of the ship's hot tubs, with no sign of trauma. What was the cause of death? According to the Brevard County (Florida) M.E.'s office, Ward actually drowned to death "as a result of acute alcohol intoxication."

Might we see some figures on the amounts of alcohol consumed on our oceans' luxury liners? In the meantime, I posit this: *Cruise liners are simply glorified booze barges.*

Quantity over quality

Of course, random news accounts are an imprecise gauge for measuring alcohol's expanding influence. Still, they should stir some concern. *Here are six items from a single day's alcohol-related news in one single paper*, The Daily Item of Sunbury, Pennsylvania. That edition was dated July 21, 2015.

1. A week ago, a car on Long Island was rear-ended in a fiery crash that killed the father and his two children. The wife survived. The other driver, who caused the tragedy, was identified as a man from Queens who was charged with driving while intoxicated. Then today's newspaper carried a follow-up article on an accident that happened on Long Island a couple of days ago. In that calamity, an extended cab SUV, driving at a high rate of speed, T-boned a limousine, nearly cutting the limousine in half and leaving the SUV *sitting in the middle of the crushed limo, where four young women had been riding!* The four women were killed and the other limousine passengers and the driver were injured. In this horrific accident, the driver of the SUV was charged with driving while intoxicated. Thus, the tally for about a week's carnage on Long Island roadways was seven grisly deaths. Lastly, in that second incident, the eight young women were in the ill-fated limousine because they were on a wine-tasting tour. They chose limousine service because, after having consumed the wine, they wanted to avoid possibly dangerous consequences.

2. A pro-football player, Justin Hunter, was arrested and was being held without bail for an alleged assault, *at a bar*, that involved someone receiving cuts, stabs and wounds from the wide receiver for the *Tennessee Titans*. Hunter's actions were part of a larger brawl that had taken place, with one participant being taken to a hospital.

3. A bit of drivel. A large article (page C5) about diet changes that *seem* to reduce risks of certain cancers. As usual, specifics relating to alcohol are missing and just the nice and safe precautions are given. "If you drink alcohol, do so in moderation: no more than one drink per day for women, two for men." It's time to begin using the W1M2 abbreviation for that oft-repeated and very tiresome phrase.

4. An intoxicated driver from Hollidaysburg, Pennsylvania crashed into a speed-limit sign and a mailbox. After again losing control, he hit an embankment and came to a stop at the road's edge. He then ran away and climbed to the roof of a barn. When he tumbled from the roof, he was apprehended. He was arrested for drunkenness and the damage that so often accompanies drunkenness. Throughout the ordeal, he was wearing his Randy Travis disguise (see Chapter Six).

5. Another college student died in a fall. Mention of this tragedy here may be premature, since current news coverage only tells us that a female student of Penn State University recently fell to her death from a balcony in Seville, Spain. The cause of her accident was still under investigation; but it is known that many college students, while inebriated, have fallen from windows, cliffs, etc., and died in the falls. *Update:* As of this date (January 15, 2016) the many internet sites remain silent regarding any investigation results. This further suggests that alcohol has been involved. If alcohol was involved in this instance, in view of the many, many cases of American college students' deaths resulting from alcohol use, the public should be informed of whatever results might come from the investigation, if such results are ever revealed to the public.

6. Pennsylvania state police had to hog-tie a rural drunk. The 25-year-old resident of Milton already had three drunken driving convictions in the past decade. On a recent evening, and without a driver's license, he climbed aboard his yellow and white lawn tractor to go visit a friend. Police were called and when one arrived, he found that the man was standing; but unsteady on his feet and clutching a box of beer. Since he was utterly uncooperative, two other troopers were summoned. He was subdued and put into the police car, still kicking and threatening one of the officers. The evening's drunken decisions earned him more than a half-dozen charges.

One might say that July 15, 2015, was a day, just like any other day in America and, typically, alcohol, was there. All this tragic or pathetic behavior can be tied to the abuse of alcohol. It goes on day after day, weekends included, for the full 365 and one-fourth days of the year, every year. There's not even one of the above incidents, and the millions of others like them elsewhere in this pathetic, liquored land, that should have occurred in the first place. We could well use more jobs, better infrastructure, finer schools and health facilities and all the other things that the politicians repeatedly promise; but, also, we sure as hell could use many more sober breaths.

Although our population has steady growth, so does alcohol production. One internet site (www.winesandvines.com) offers viewers a graph that graphically (of course) informs one of the very steady growth in the number of wineries. A downloading on 9/21/15, lets us see that United States winery numbers have grown from 579 in 1975 to an astronomical (to this viewer, at least) 7,425 in 2012!

Similarly, there has been a phenomenal growth in the number of distillers (producing gin, rum, vodka, etc.). One internet site (http://www.entrepreneus.com/article/229855) states that "Less than a decade ago, there were 70 distilleries in the U.S. Now (12/13) there are 623 . . ." They suggest that the number will have increased by the end of 2014, to about 750. Stick around for the grand opening giveaways.

Despite the growth being seen in all sorts of small booze-making businesses, there are still the behemoths; which are also expanding. In fact, one of the greatest business mergers in history is unfolding as these lines are being typed. *The Week* reports (10-23-15) that one brewing giant (Anheuser-Busch) is dealing to allow it to 'gobble up' another brewing giant, SAB Miller. The acquisition, for a mere 104.2 billion bucks, will give Anheuser-Busch more than 2/3 of the U.S. market!

Can lushes keep pace with the producers and purveyors? They'll thrive on the challenge!

The old lyrics are changing rapidly. Now we must ride the American highways, swilling and singing:

> "Fifty-nine bottles on the shelf . . .
> Fifty-nine bottles on the shelf . . .
> Oh, we take one down, and we pass it all around . . .
> Now there's sixty-six bottles on the shelf!"

I'd rather hear these words:

> "Ninety-nine bottles on the shelf . . .
> "Leave them there!"

Further, shouldn't we be listing convicted drunken drivers' neighborhoods?

Another thought: If it was wrong to jettison the 18th Amendment, should we not be enforcing it today? However, if it was right to jettison the 18th Amendment, should we not abandon our anti-drug enforcement programs? Let the Corona and the cocaine arrive on the same trucks.

A very formidable enemy

Are there enough angry Americans to launch a counterattack? While there may be enough citizens willing to participate in a meaningful counterattack against the terrorist, alcohol, the forces of alcohol have a full arsenal, while the rest of the populace is virtually unarmed. If only the educators craved sobriety . . . If only the legislators craved sobriety . . . If only the entertainment industry craved sobriety . . . If only the news people craved sobriety . . .

If only . . .

If just *one* of the above groups, as a *group*, wanted sobriety, a convincing counterattack could be launched. But, despite all the bloody numbers, there is no evidence that there is a majority of any one of those influential groups who gives a damn about deglamorizing alcohol.

For example, where are the educational policymakers? I think of two educational voids in America; the teaching of *the follies of gambling* and of the tragedies of *alcoholic intemperance*. Every young citizen should be taught, with dynamic tools, how to recognize the absurdity of gambling and the follies of guzzling.

Every community should require its secondary education programs to inform students of the economic dynamics of alcohol. Students should become cognizant of the fact that the generous profits from alcohol sales are made even more generous when the product is bought for the use of those too *young* to drink legally or too *drunk* to drink rationally and legally. So, for business reasons only, a binging nation is very, very desirable.

Faux glamour

Pro-booze 'events' proliferate, all brazenly or subtly pushing the consumption of alcohol. We observe the "Bluegrass State." The "Bluegrass State" is where rural Kentucky, suburban Kentucky, and urban Kentucky all merge into bourbon Kentucky. What glamorous development do we find in this great fountainhead of one of the nation's most noted forms of liquor? The state of Kentucky, birthplace of Carrie Nation, has a Kentucky Bourbon Trail that was recognized (2013) by the *National Geographic* magazine as a worthy trip. If the distillers are lucky, the NGS recognition should add significant numbers to the record half million visitors who took the Kentucky Bourbon Trail in 2012.

That *National Geographic* recognition may also help to swell Kentucky's alcohol-related traffic fatalities. For one recent decade (2003-2012) it was just over 2,500, according to *alcoholalert.com*. Kentucky ranks at the lower end of the top half of the states in alcohol-related deaths in the nation. With dynamic promotion as a place for booze lovers, perhaps the state can move into the top quarter. Kentucky's alcohol-related promotional event is merely offered as an example. There are hundreds, if not thousands, of such events, of varying size, annually in America the Bingeful.

America needs, once again, a joining of our voices against tyranny. The nation needs an outcry from the millions of sober Americans who represent all occupations or degrees of idleness. We need the protection of an army, where none exists. We need an army of outspoken people—men and women—who eagerly stand against the abuse of alcohol and who will denounce every form of its glamorization. America needs outspoken people from the entertainment world to counter the influence of Hollywood's celebrity drunks and multimillionaire booze peddlers.

America needs people who condemn the songwriters and singers of Nashville who glamorize alcohol and drunkenness. This nation needs people who will fill the air with songs of sobriety and sanity and who will stop writing songs that suggest that they are the paid pitchmen and pitchwomen for Old Number 7 of Lynchburg, Tennessee!

DECEIVE ME

Please, deceive me. Make me think
That I'm charming when I drink.
Let me tell myself once more
That I'm not a stumbling bore.
Both at home and where I work,
I'm no alcoholic jerk.

Please, deceive me. Tell me, clear,
I can handle kegs of beer
And, despite a slurring tongue,
I am never overhung;
I've not fallen off the page.
I'm a very lucid sage.

Please, deceive me, let me think.
I can handle all I drink.
Help me tell myself, today,
That I'm sober as I lay
In the gutter, flask in hand.
Make me think that I can stand.

Please, deceive me. I'm convinced
That each time my children winced,
They still found me full of fun.
I need alcohol to run.
Sober's not the way to be.
Booze, alone, will set me free!

Misleading stats

Wherever arguments rely on statistics, those making invalid arguments will skew the numbers. For example, there is one set of alcohol statistics that bears scrutiny. The 2013 figures offered are from the National Institute on Alcohol Abuse and Alcoholism (a division of the National Institutes of Health). What is the percentage of American adults who are alcoholic? If we are shown a percentage as being the percentage of the adult population, we are being misinformed. We know that the number of adult drinking Americans is 71%. Now, we must ask: what is the percentage of drinking Americans who are alcoholic? That stat would show the number of utterly intemperate Americans with whom we must deal. That tally would show us a stat that is nearly lost in the American stratosphere! The others, the exemplary drinkers, should welcome the elimination of drunkards from our society just as the non-drinkers would. The true alcoholics are the group that should be kept out of our frat houses, out of our wedding receptions, out of our conventions, out of our households and off our highways!

Our nearly-sainted forefathers gave us the legislative tools needed to solve our sticky problems. If we use those tools effectively, we can begin to free ourselves from the ever-present threats of the inebriate.

A sane society should never, never allow drunkards to commit a second drunken crime. Nor should a sane society allow a dispenser of alcohol to have a second chance to sell to an underage drinker or to an already-intoxicated drinker. In a sane America, no one should have to face dangerously-intoxicated citizens more than once.

Tough laws should be enacted that would keep reducing the number of drunkards who threaten to disrupt the lives of all the exemplary drinkers, the nondrinkers and the children of America; with the goal of having less and less drunkards in our society, until we are inebriate free.

Let us raise our voices, as a body, to gain the sobriety that was stolen from America when our laws were trampled and our voices throttled a century ago.

The Christian Science Monitor (9/20/09) had a bit of commentary regarding the British placing a ban on alcohol ads and the sponsorship of various events. Why can't we do the same thing? They even realized that "restrictions on price, ads, and availability *do* work." Again, why can't our leaders muster the guts to reign in the booze industry's rampant promotion?

Instead, we use that stale argument to try lowering the drinking age: "If you're old enough to serve in the military, you're old enough to drink." Of course, that's not a valid comparison. Why not clarify: If you're old enough to die in the military, you're old enough to die on our highways!

Confirmation!!!

Throughout this polemic, reference has been made to the horrors of America's great binge. Finally, in January 2015, as the writing of this volume was still ongoing, The Center for Disease Control (CDC) issued a report. The CDC has a laudable, trade-marked, slogan, "Saving Lives. Protecting People." While the CDC is constantly churning reports filled with alarming statistics—which should be headlined—the data is virtually ignored by the American media. It is the staunch opinion of this author that the report is very timely. How pathetic that the American media doesn't emphasize the number of alcohol-related deaths, on a weekly basis?

The January 6, 2015 CDC report is entitled: *Vital Signs: Alcohol Poisoning Deaths—United States, 2010-2012.*

Some of the results announced in that report are identified in the following selected quotes:

■ "Alcohol poisoning is typically caused by binge drinking at high intensity . . ."

■ "Approximately 38 million U.S. adults report binge drinking an average of four times per month . . ."

■ "On average, six persons, mostly adult men, die from alcohol poisoning each day in the United States."

■ "Excessive alcohol use . . . cost the United States $223.5 billion in 2006."

Please note that the number of American binge drinkers is listed in the *millions!* Please note that the financial costs for excessive alcohol use are identified in the *billions!* We should be utterly ashamed! We should be damned indignant! And those figures didn't even mention the senseless highway deaths related to alcohol!

Procrastination pays
How very fortuitous! Whatever time I spent not concluding my manuscript for *Intoxication Nation* paid dividends. News items, exposing the folly of alcohol abuse, are proliferating at a rate like that of alcohol promotion. For example, I drove sixty-some miles to visit my publisher on April 20, 2018. There, I handed him a couple of thumb drives containing the manuscript for this tome on temperance. Within days (April 29, 2018) I opened my current copy (May 4, 2018 issue, page 21) of *The Week.* That issue carried a news item that beautifully added an exclamation point to this chapter of *Intoxication Nation.* That news item was a delightful update on the theme of this very chapter: the deleterious results of even modest imbibing. Vainly trying to be humble, I summarize the article, beginning with the headline: "Moderate drinking isn't healthy after all" and telling of the results of a study led by Dr. Angela Wood of Cambridge University. With 120 scientists involved in data analysis of more than a half-million people from 19 countries, the conclusion was that regular drinkers have a

shorter lifespan than the non-drinkers. The difference, of course, is greater, according to the amount of alcohol consumed. One specific sentence follows: "Drinking alcohol, researchers say, is associated with a slew of cardiovascular problems, including stroke, aortic aneurysm, severe high blood pressure, heart failure, and an increased risk for breast cancer and cancers of the digestive system." The article also says that "These findings contradict federal guidelines . . ."

Hardly a coincidence

Federal guidelines don't come into play with the 2007 news item out of Japan. *The Week* magazine reported (6/29/07) that Tomoji Tanabe had become the world's oldest man at 111 years! His explanation: He had a daily glass of milk and he didn't smoke or drink. *Time* magazine (12/15/08) had a similar article the following year, but that one involved the passing of Edna Parker. Ms. Parker was the world's oldest woman at the time of her passing. She was described as "An Indiana farmer's wife who didn't drink or smoke." She, thus, died as a 115-year-old teetotaler.

Chapter Eleven

Our Leaders and Their Liquor

All elected officials, from the municipal to the national levels, should be sober, clear-headed souls. Unfortunately, our nation has seen a pathetic parade of hard-drinking politicians. Too many American politicos have been in the tankard for the liquor industry.

Brennan on the moor?

Some Pennsylvanian's likely did a double-take when they saw a headline (February 2013) that said that a state legislator was arrested, just outside his office in Bethlehem, for drunken driving. The driver, who was cited in the town with the famous Biblical name, was Joseph Brennan. Brennan informed the public that he had returned from the state capital, had some alcohol, and went to his local office to perform more duties. That's when police arrested him. He also admitted that he's been struggling with alcohol for a long time. He then offered the standard apologies that politicians offer when hopelessly caught in a criminal situation. We say that this might have caused some Keystone State readers some initial concern, thinking that it was the same politician who was caught in a very serious incident back in 1999. It wasn't. The career of that man, Thomas W. Druce, had really nosedived.

Another promising career ruined

Leave it to a drunk to ruin a young man's promising career. On the night of July 27, 1999, Kenneth R. Cains, a Black-American and a former U.S. Marine, got drunk and stepped onto Cameron Street in Harrisburg, Pennsylvania and directly into the path of an oncoming Jeep Cherokee. He was killed on impact.

The driver of the Jeep Cherokee that Cains intercepted was Thomas W. Druce. Druce was a resident of Bucks County, a political stronghold near Philadelphia. Druce was in his fourth term as a state representative in the Pennsylvania legislature. Druce was also a 'rising star' in his political party and one who was mentioned as a probable future gubernatorial candidate in the Keystone State. Bucks County, where Druce resided, is a Philadelphia-area county and a superb base for one who might run for higher office. Representative Thomas W. Druce was also one of the legislators who voted for the bill that promised a fixed minimum prison sentence where a fatal hit-and-run accident had occurred. The hapless lawmaker then had the misfortune of having a drunken Kenneth R. Cains stumble into the street.

Druce hit!
And then Druce 'ran'!
Having, himself, left a bar just minutes earlier, Druce, too, had been drinking. It was rumored that he also had an unidentified female companion in the car with him at the time of the accident. His last drink that night could have been a toast to his departure from politics. However, Druce attempted to prolong that departure from politics indefinitely. He drove to the state capitol parking area to assess the damage to the Jeep Cherokee, a state-leased vehicle that he drove at taxpayer expense. Druce then drove to the Philadelphia area and had the damage to his vehicle fixed. Perhaps ever mindful of the poor taxpayers of the state, he paid for the repairs from his own funds. Repairs included replacement of the damaged bumper and broken headlight. Then he turned in the repaired car before its lease expired and got another leased vehicle. Druce had now unloaded a lot of hard evidence. Then, he told police that he thought he had struck a sign. He told the insurance company that he had clipped a barrel on the Pennsylvania Turnpike. One must also wonder what he told Mrs. Druce. Again, perhaps he *deserved* higher office since he seemed to be skilled at solving sticky problems.

The following Christmas was fruitful for area law enforcement officials. A woman sent a Christmas card, anonymously, to a Harrisburg "Crime Stoppers" group. The card's note identified Druce as the driver of the hit-and-run accident on Cameron Street. It is speculated that the writer was the unknown passenger rumored to have been with Druce on the night of Cains' death. Despite some reluctance to pursue a prominent state legislator, an investigation was conducted.

The repair shop still had the damaged bumper. The leased vehicle was also located. Some of the ex-Marine's hair and tissue and clothing shreds could still be seen on the surviving parts of the Jeep Cherokee, including some of Cains' hair on the Jeep's rear-view mirror. Despite strenuous efforts by Druce's attorneys to keep his sentence minimal, he finally served a two-year sentence in the Laurel Highlands Prison in Somerset, in southwestern Pennsylvania. In a state that saw nearly two dozen corruption cases involving Pennsylvania legislators and other officials during recent years, the Druce case was the one to get coverage on national television, thanks to the wealth of forensic evidence retrieved from the leased Jeep Cherokee. Had Druce been able to pass a Breathalyzer test at the scene of Cains' death, he could have taken the responsibility of clearing himself on the spot. But, this rising political star's shattered career was caused entirely by the politician, himself, and his alcohol-clouded mind.

The Druce incident reveals much: While it may be painful to decide to flee from the scene of a collision with a pedestrian, to push the early return of one's leased car, to lose one's seat in the state legislature, to go through trial proceedings and to spend time in prison, it can't compare with the horrifying alternative: sobriety.

Much ado about much

The nation has been witnessing heavy drinking among our national leaders from the earliest days of the Republic. The most noted example is likely the victorious Civil War general who, twice, led the nation.

General Ulysses Simpson Grant had a reputation, *still being questioned*, for intemperate drinking. But he became a very successful general and a Civil War hero who easily won two terms as president. Virtually penniless in later years, Grant regained some wealth by penning his autobiography, which he finished mere days before his death, writing while suffering the torment of throat cancer. He is remembered as the Union general whose drinking led to President Lincoln's having to listen to complaints about Grant's intemperance. That was the situation that also caused the soon-to-be-martyred president to inquire about the brand of liquor that Grant was supposedly drinking so that President Lincoln might send a few kegs of it to his other generals! One might also speculate on whether or not it was the alcohol that led to Grant's throat cancer. President Ulysses S. Grant is also credited with coining a new political term: Lobbyist. This was inspired by President Grant's having to listen to the pleas of men who would wait in the *lobby* of the Willard Hotel to badger the Chief Executive for favors after he was drunk.

The political parade of the dipsomaniacs?
We Americans are very discriminating regarding drunkards in the cockpit; but not in the bully pulpit or in the halls of Congress. We've cast our ballots for some real alcoholic doozies over the years;

A boozy badger

Wisconsin elected him and the nation endured him. The late Joseph McCarthy was a scoundrel . . . a rotten scoundrel. He was also a drunken, rotten scoundrel. Columnist George Will has stated, "Joseph McCarthy had tainted conservatism in the process of disgracing himself with bile and bourbon." (George Will, columnist, *The Daily Item*, Sunbury, Pennsylvania, 11-24-05).

His notoriety bloomed from the time he told a Republican women's group in Wheeling, West Virginia that the list which he was waving had 205 names of communists who were in the U. S. State Department. That list was as phony as the embellishments he had added to his military record. Building on a national concern about dangers of Communism, McCarthy suddenly became popular. His popularity grew as he fed the nation's fears with other charges and investigations. His unscrupulous behavior included threatening an official into helping him get illegal heroin and then threatening to arrest a newsperson who was about to expose McCarthy's illegal purchase of heroin. One writer referred to McCarthy having been found to be "dead drunk" while in the Senate. Senator Joseph McCarthy's ornery behavior was nearly boundless, meaning he even had a substantial number of his own party acquaintances turning on him. One man, a lawyer for the army, finally, and famously, asked the senator, "Have you no sense of decency, sir, at long last? Have you left no sense of decency?" That quote was among the finest ever uttered in our halls of government. It finally shook enough people awake to Senator McCarthy's unscrupulous tactics and exposed him as a 'witch hunter'. In late 1954 the Senate voted to censure (condemn) Senator McCarthy by a senatorial vote of 67 to 22. He lost his clout and, early in his second term as senator, he died.

This dairy-state Republican was among our worst political leaders, with the problem likely made worse by his heavy drinking. He is known to have suffered from cirrhosis of the liver and to have been hospitalized several times for alcoholism. When he died, in 1957, he was only in his late 40's. The public was told that the senator died from hepatitis; but Senator Joseph McCarthy, among our most ruthless elected leaders, is now considered to have died of alcoholism. If we are ever unfortunate enough to have another government leader who uses unscrupulous tactics to destroy another person's career, you'll know how to identify that approach: *McCarthyism.*

Senator Wilbur Mills

Wilbur Mills came out of the deep South, Arkansas, to become one of the nation's long-term members of Congress. His time in Congress is not to be measured in years but in decades. He spent nearly four decades as a U. S. Congressman, serving from 1939 to 1977. Mills was highly regarded for his work with taxation, the Medicare program and, at one point, was the true tax expert of Congress. During the years that he headed the House Ways and Means Committee, he was the most powerful man in town.

Late one night (October 9, 1974) and late in his career, the powerful congressman was in a car that was stopped by U.S. Park Police for driving without having its lights on. The car and its several passengers were beside the pool known as the Tidal Basin. It was 2:00 A.M. and the congressman was drunk. That somewhat strange situation became stranger still as events unfolded. Congressman Mills was sporting a cut on his face and was in the company of several people. One of his companions was a woman of Argentine name; but who also had acquired a professional name, which was Fanne Foxe. The profession for which she needed that alliterative name was "stripper." Ms. Foxe, it was noted, was an occasional companion of Congressman Mills.

She added to the excitement of the occasion by jumping into the Tidal Pool to escape; She didn't escape but was taken to a mental hospital.

Some very understanding folks back home re-elected Wilbur Mills the month after the Tidal Pool scandal. Just a month after his re-election, (November 30, 1974), Mills again got special publicity; but not in Washington. On the 30th of November, he and Fanne Foxe's husband went on the stage of a theatre in Boston, Massachusetts. This theatre was referred to as a "burlesque house." While in that theatre, Mills held a press conference. It likely wasn't too well attended, since he held it in stripper Foxe's dressing room. Here, too, U.S. Congressman Wilbur Mills of Arkansas was described as "seemingly drunk." Then, the usual postlude to an alcohol-shortened career: Mills gave up his powerful chairmanship, joined Alcoholic Anonymous, checked himself into a rehab clinic, did not run for re-election, worked for a "prestigious law firm," etc., etc.

A change in century; no change in tippling

In the year 2008, alcohol and the presidency came into sharp focus; but, as was normal in this besotted republic, there was little notice. The incumbent, George W. Bush was known to have had drinking problems in his earlier years and carried a DUI on his record. According to a series of articles, published in the *Washington Post* in 1999, the future president of the nation simply quit drinking while celebrating some 40th birthdays at Colorado Springs' Broadmoor Hotel in 1986. The 2008 Republican vice-presidential nominee, Governor Sarah Palin of Alaska, was reported to have visited a Philadelphia bar during her campaign travels. U.S. Senator John McCain, the Republican Party candidate for president, was independently wealthy because his wife's family had made a fortune with a chain of beer distributorships. There was also U.S. Senator Hillary Clinton, who lost the primary bid for the presidential nomination and who had tried to woo northeastern Pennsylvania's anthracite voters by being photographed while holding a glass of whiskey in one hand and a beer in the other! *Looking at the 2008 political scene from the perspective of one concerned about our national binge, the campaign was nauseating. It was enough to make the lady in New York harbor shed a tear.* How refreshing it would have been to have heard any candidate suggest that we needed to take a hard look at our hard drinking. From the point of view of those who think sober leaders are vital to our nation, the 2016 campaign began with bitterly disappointing developments. There was Hillary Clinton, the candidate who seems to relish being photographed with a drink or two in hand. In fact, in June of 2015 (June 8), the *GLOBE*, a major American tabloid, carried a cover with Hillary as the main attraction and with a headline saying: "Hillary Confesses: 'I'm An Alcoholic!' While one might question the accuracy of the *Globe*'s reporting, it only takes a visit to Google's 'images' library to find countless pictures of the former first lady 'in the cups' as one might say. How sad it is to live in an era where *a liquor-pushing candidate for our top office isn't being booed from the campaign trail.* Instead, we see her fawning followers cheering as she leads her tippling bandwagon.

Anything for a vote?
Here we are, in the 21st century, and we still see the endless glamorization of alcohol throughout our local and national governments, right into the White House. One hundred years ago, President Barack Obama's promotion of himself as a beer lover would have, *rightly*, destroyed his chances for re-election; but in 2012 there was, as mentioned earlier, a concerted effort to endlessly remind the nation that he loved beer. Earlier, President Obama had barely finished taking the oath of office when he insulted a Connecticut cop. Although it was just one of many Obaman gaffes, it was more serious than referring to the nation's 58 states. The president tried to cover his folly by inviting the offended policeman, the civilian individual involved, and his similarly 'gaffable' vice president, Joe Biden, to a 'beer summit' on the lawn of the White House. While the president's use of beer diplomacy was shameful; it was no worse than his frequent barroom photo ops. Finally, in September of 2012, just weeks before the presidential election, Barack Obama brazenly released the labels and recipes for his own White House brands of alcohol: "White House Porter," "White House Honey Blonde," and "White House Honey Brown Ale". Those names should whet the thirst of any American boozer. The timing of this release was too obvious. It was less than a week after the Republican Party formally nominated Mitt Romney, a *teetotaler*, for president. By a fortuitous coincidence, the same day that BHO's ale recipes appeared in newspapers, an article by Marni Jameson (*Orlando Sentinel*) also appeared. Jameson's

article reminded Americans of the *nearly 2,000 deaths, annually, from alcohol, among college students!* The American media did not consider the huge loss of life among college students to be nearly as newsworthy as the release of the presidential ale recipes. For those Americans who think that abstinence or moderation is praiseworthy, there was reason for great dismay in seeing Barack Obama—after one lackluster term—being returned to his rarely-used oval office, defeating, by the narrowest of margins, former Massachusetts governor, Mitt Romney, *the non-drinking candidate.*

In March 2014, his loyal subjects learned that a wager had been made between President Obama and the then Prime Minister of Canada, Stephen Harper. The wager involved the matches between the Canadian and the American Olympic Hockey teams; both the men's and the women's teams. Anyone with any knowledge of foreign policy would know that one does not bet against Canadian hockey teams. The president lost the bet and, after a gentle reminder from Harper, President Obama sent two cases of Obama's own White House brew (Honey Porter and Honey Blond) to the Canadian Embassy. Booze averted another international crisis . . .

Finally, in 2015, well into the president's second term as the nation's leader, BHO again mentioned his private brewing project in the nation's public residence. In an interview with a television reporter in the White House kitchen, President Obama answered some questions from the reporter as they shared some of the president's now-famous homebrew. At one point, in answer to a question about the liquor, President Obama declared: "We make beer . . . the first president since George Washington to make booze in the White House."

Of course, our first president never lived in the White House. The first chief executive to live there was John Adams, from late 1800. However, BHO seemed determined to go down in history. Now he can. Barack Obama was the first president to bring brewing directly into the people's White House.

As the last year of his second term opened, President Obama announced (February 2016) his proposal for a comprehensive program to curb the nation's expanding problem of heroin and painkiller abuse. The cost of his proposal: a shade over one billion dollars. This is necessary and laudable, but my lament remains unchanged. Why can't we have a dynamic infusion of government funds and enthusiasm to curb the lethal abuse of alcohol in America?

One must question the reliability of all internet sources, but some are obviously worthless. There is an internet site that focuses on things that can be discussed in quantities of eleven. Such a criterion seems utterly arbitrary, but I've only seen one example. The site is 11points.com. The example that I encountered offers the "11 Drunkest Presidents in US History." It was downloaded on the second of March 2016, and clearly offers readers the "Drunkest" presidents! However, a glance at the site reveals a truly absurd, entry for number 10:

> *John F. Kennedy.* There is no actual proof that JFK was a drinker. But I have an Irish friend named Molly who's one hell of a drinker, and it's led me to believe that *certain stereotypes exist because they're just true.*

Bullscat! Such malarkey renders his entire list as worthless.

LBJ

Our acceptance of the coupling of heavy drinking and national politics is shameful. As with all aspects of leadership in American society, political leadership is excused for acts and decisions that may be warped by alcohol. Consider the leadership of Lyndon B. Johnson, the man who became president of the United States with the death of John F. Kennedy in 1963. Although eligible for re-election in 1968, Johnson chose not to run. He died in 1973, in his 64th year. A friend from Texas stated, "I think he drank himself to death." (That statement was offered in a television special on the president, in a program aired 10-27-08 on WVIA-TV). Lyndon Baines Johnson was just one of the men who held one of the world's most sensitive and critical jobs, yet tempered his judgment with alcohol.

The final political example

In 1969, Mary Jo Kopechne was one of a dozen people at a summer party on Massachusetts' tiny Chappaquiddick Island. There was heavy drinking. She left the party and climbed into his Oldsmobile with a married U.S. senator, Ted Kennedy, whose pregnant wife, Joan, hadn't been invited to the shindig. As the senator drove the couple toward an isolated part of the island, the car—an Oldsmobile 88—left the roadway and plunged into a coastal tidal basin. The U. S. senator escaped from the Olds and left the scene. Mary Jo suffocated in the diminishing oxygen of the submerged Olds. The U. S. senator then waited until enough hours had passed (over eight!) to allow him to rally his staunchest supporters and to allow his intoxication level to shrink beyond detection, before notifying authorities of the accident. The U. S. senator's speechwriter readily added noble phrases to the senator's ignoble deeds. Miss Kopechne's body was returned to her Pennsylvania hometown for burial. Ted Kennedy returned to the United States Senate where he represented the understanding voters of the Bay State for the remaining four decades of his life. The wife, from whom the U. S. Senator was later divorced, was found some years later, lying drunk, on a sidewalk, on Beacon Hill in Boston. If one is going to be discovered drunk on a street, Boston's Beacon Hill is a classy place to be found. She then entered a rehab program. Although both her parents had been alcoholic, Joan Kennedy blamed the family of the U.S. senator for her drinking problem in general and she identified the tragic incident on Chappaquiddick Island as the greatest factor in her alcoholism.

The hilltop cemetery above Larksville, Pennsylvania. An only child buried decades before her grief-wrought parents.

As the dutiful wife of Senator Theodore Moore Kennedy, Joan was expected to accompany the senator to a funeral that he was attending, even if it was for the woman with whom he'd left an alcohol-fueled party and with whom he was racing to an isolated bit of beach when tragedy struck on that mid-July night in 1969. What might strike one as the lowest depths of spousal betrayal and humiliation did not end the marriage, which was so critical to her husband's career. After all, he remained a champion to many. He needed Joan to play her dutiful-wife role until his failed run for the presidency in 1976 (James Earl Carter of Georgia won the nomination and the presidency). Finally, the marriage that had been initiated by a Cardinal in 1958 ended before a probate judge in 1982. It might seem that her 1982 divorce would have relieved her of humiliating duties. Not quite. When her former mate died in 2009, Joan was invited to the memorial service. She attended.

If Joan Bennett Kennedy's evaluation of her drinking was accurate, we might conclude that Teddy Kennedy, her philandering and hard-drinking mate, drove Joan Kennedy to drink. One might say that Teddy Kennedy also drove Mary Jo Kopechne to drink . . .

The U.S. Senator's role that night on Chappaquiddick Island has inspired—four decades later—the movie, *Chappaquiddick*, a film that clearly portrayed the great efforts taken to hastily launder the truth to keep the senator's image gleaming. Those same events also inspired the following ode, which was written several years *before* the late senator's death.

BURIAL AT SEA

Our nation's living dreadnought,
The champ of ocean sea,
Our legendary captain,
Horatio Kennedy!

The chanteys praise his vict'ry
Along the Bay State's coast.
Of all his deeds, heroic,
This stirs our hearts the most.

By day he raced regatta
Aboard his trusty yacht.
Magnanimous while losing,
Our Yankee Lancelot.

It takes a stalwart husband
To leave his pregnant wife;
A truly flinty fellow,
To lead the playboy life.

The post-regatta shindig
Had six females, unwed;
Plus six men, unrelated;
And that's including Ted.

The booze was freely stockpiled;
Enough to fill a cove.
Ted found a comely colleague.
Into the night they drove.

He raced with quick abandon
To reach a place he knew:
An isolated seashore,
Away from prying view.

An open bridge now looming;
The lass beside him, curled.
No way could he avoid it;
The splash heard 'round the world!

The speeding car plunged downward
Into the briny pool.
Heroic'ly, he surfaced.
"Save Number One," the rule.

He bravely bypassed houses,
Where he might summon aid.
He hurried to his cohorts.
How bold and unafraid!

Some might still try to rescue.
For Ted, that wouldn't fit.
Of course, we're all agreeing:
Deserting takes more grit.

With courage, he kept silent
For nine hours, through the night;
Except to call for cronies
To save him from his plight.

To win that timeless battle,
Took brilliant plan and plot.
He lost but one companion:
She, whom the world forgot.

When he's no longer with us,
We'll hear the nation wail.
The mythic sea will take him.
His shroud cut from a sail.

Then, from the bridge we'll lower him.
To give the body weight,
We'll add a heavy object:
His black, Olds 88.

The death of Mary Jo Kopechne is among the ugliest scandals in American politics. I remain haunted by the question of what would have occurred if the situation had been reversed. What if a young male Pennsylvania coal cracker had been driving a car in which a young, female, New England socialite had been abandoned to die in a submerged auto in the black of night? There would have been hell to pay! But, alcohol and politics create strange outcomes for the worst tragedies. The Chappaquiddick horror proved that when the perpetrator happens to be the political darling of a very wealthy family, he'll

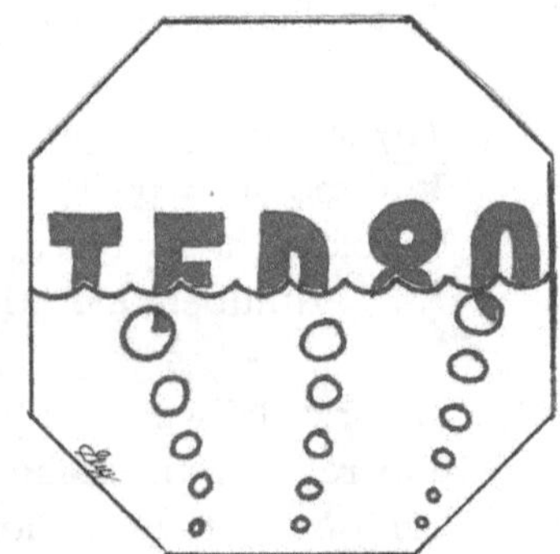

In 1980, every patriotic American's vehicle should have displayed the above bumper strip.

A Pennsylvania rural roadside 40th-anniversary display. On the left, 1969 portraits; on the right, a portrait of the senator and a tombstone in Larksville, Pennsylvania. (Author's archives)

be given more passes than Henry Aaron and Babe Ruth combined. Many still thought that he should have been one of our nation's presidents.

The biography of Senator Edward Moore Kennedy is so spectacularly drenched with alcohol that we felt the need to use it to conclude the discussion of politics and drinking with the exploits of Joe Kennedy's youngest son; exploits that were glaringly revealed with the incident on Chappaquiddick Island. Three books, in particular (by authors Burke, Damore and the two Tedrows) have exposed the Chappaquiddick tragedy and travesty. Adding to this depressing story is the awareness that alcohol and American politics remain close companions.

A closing note regarding the Chappaquiddick incident: Two letters that were published in *Time* magazine deserve notice. One writer suggested that Ted Kennedy "challenged the powerful on behalf of the powerless." Good God! Teddy was one of the powerful. That's why, when a young woman was left to suffocate in his car, he could give the nation a Sorenson sophistry to end the discussion. Another *Time* letter writer noted that Ted "now belongs to the ages." Of course. But, thanks to the playboy senator, Mary Jo has now belonged to the ages for 40 years more than he has!

Pot-pourri

Time magazine plugs both Al Gore and Pabst Blue Ribbon beer when it tells readers (2/4/13, p. 34) that the former vice president, Nobelist, author, businessman and 2000 Democratic presidential candidate, maintains a yacht "on Center Hill Lake in Middle Tennessee, where he entertains his buddies over cold cans of PBR."

The American political world should never see anything less than complete sobriety. However, it offers depressing evidence that America's political leadership is often riddled with the thoughtless consumption of alcohol. Our U.S. citizenry will never know how often our critical state and national decisions are made by alcohol-addled decision makers. How frightening!

A pleasant memory that has survived these rapidly tumbling decades was a visit I had with my spinster great-aunt, Elda Graybill. She had been a nurse during the First World War and tradition told of her having hunted and found her wounded brother, great-uncle Irvin, on the battlefield or in a field hospital and bringing him back from the front to a better facility for treatment and recovery. On the hot, summer day that I stopped at her country house, she got the juicer and prepared a glass of cold lemonade for her imposing grand-nephew.

How annoying to think that one of this nation's First Ladies was given the normally refreshing word, "lemonade," as a derisive nickname! Lucy Webb (Mrs. Rutherford B.) Hayes was too sober for binging Americans and is readily identified in history books as "Lemonade Lucy." I would have liked her. Among the few college-educated women of the time, she came from a family where the father was a physician and an abolitionist. She embraced the feminist ideas of the time and married the Ohio attorney, Rutherford B. Hayes, with whom she had eight children. Her husband went on to become a major general in the Union Army during the Civil War, before becoming Ohio's governor and then the nation's 18th president. While Rutherford gained a reputation as an honest and capable president, Lucy acquired an "almost legendary reputation for kindness and simplicity" (Caroli, p. 119). She is one of a handful of individuals whom this author would label as one of his heroes or heroines.

Similarly, I must admire the first lady who was wife to our 32nd president. She was a columnist, humanitarian and, according to Daniel Okrent (*Last Call*, p. 349) "a committed dry who had been outspoken in her advocacy of the Eighteenth Amendment for years. The daughter of an alcoholic, Eleanor Roosevelt did not

The Roosevelt mansion at the Hyde Park estate in the Hudson River Valley of New York. Here was the private residence of President Franklin Delano and First Lady Eleanor Roosevelt. Prior to his paralysis, FDR might sometimes be seen standing on these steps. (Courtesy of Edie and Sonia's photo library.)

allow wine to be served at her dinner parties . . ." How aggravating that she was married to the chief executive who would do so much to help jettison *Prohibition* in America! His role in the repeal of the greatly-maligned Eighteenth Amendment is mentioned in Chapter 4.

Tosspot in Camelot?

It has been suggested (*Reelz*, 12-29-15) that Jacqueline Bouvier was very disappointed that her father, John "Black Jack" Bouvier, was not in attendance at her 1953 wedding to John Kennedy. Her father, John, they suggest, was too drunk to attend the Newport, Rhode Island event. Looking closer at that incident, we find that popular biographer, Kitty Kelley, gave the more adequate information. She tells readers (pages 20-23 of *Jackie Oh!*) that Jackie's mother, Janet, was angry because her ex-husband, Jackie's father, had come to Newport. She had told him to stay away from the wedding. Biographer Kelley also indicates that Janet had even connived to make sure that Jackie's father, once in a Newport Hotel, was provided with plenty of alcohol and a drinking companion.

This led to John Bouvier becoming too drunk to attend the wedding! This was no problem. Janet's current husband, Hugh D. Auchincloss, did the stand-in duty of giving away the bride.

As discussed elsewhere, alcohol problems were once hidden from the public. In the case of drunken "Black Jack" Bouvier and his daughter's wedding to a future president, Kitty Kelley (p. 23) wrote that the groom's father, Joe Kennedy, "took it upon himself to tell *The New York Times* that her father had come down with the flu . . ." In similar fashion, Mary Barelli Gallagher (*My Life with Jacqueline Kennedy*, p. 20) simply told her readers that the boozing Bouvier "had been too ill to participate in his daughter's wedding." My late wife, Nancy, impishly suggested that the *"flu"* excuse proffered by old Joe Kennedy might refer to "fully liquored up"! My sarcastic query: Why must we *suppress* all the negative results of something so perpetually troubling as alcohol? *Why must the world know that Jacqueline Kennedy's 1953 wedding dress had tiny wax flowers woven into the skirt; while the sotted state of her father, on that extraordinary occasion, must be suppressed?*

Betty Ford was known as a frankly-speaking first lady, willing to openly discuss her health conditions; yet she did not mention her alcohol problem until it became rather obvious. Likewise, Bess Truman never bothered correcting reports that identified her as a teetotaler, although it has become known that she appreciated an evening drink of undiluted bourbon. Sources have identified the daiquiri (rum, lime, sugar) as the favorite of the Queen of Camelot, Jacqueline Bouvier Kennedy Onassis. Therefore, out of fairness to Mrs. Hayes ("Lemonade Lucy"), we should discuss other first ladies by using such sobriquets as "Bourbon Bess," "Boozing Betty," "Daiquiri Jackie," and so on.

Would the nation have fared less well, if none of our presidents had used alcohol?

A grand new coalition?
This nation sorely needs a Coalition of Teetotalers and Exemplary Drinkers, working as partners with the goal of removing all alcohol-caused killings from our American highways, our American bars, and our American homes. We have the means. Let's summon the will.

America does not need to deny our exemplary drinkers a single sip of alcohol; nor should America deny any of our citizenry a single moment of alcohol-free safety.

Denouement

Sage advice: DO NOT DRINK ALCOHOL . . .

> while performing surgery.
> while dancing.
> while using power or hand tools.
> while near people using alcohol.
> while playing sports.
> while using firearms, knives, etc.
> while speechifying.
> while using steps.
> while piloting an airplane.
> while washing skyscraper windows.
> while studying.
> while using explosives.
> while using medications.
> while in the presence of children.
> while celebrating holidays.
> while making love.
> while crossing streets.
> while making decisions.

Science meets another challenge

When tallying the many negatives related to the common use of alcohol, here is another negative impact from its use: The seemingly harmless, if otherwise offensive, anti-social behavior. For example, how many cases of public urination could drunkards tally in any given year? But, our caped crusaders of science to the rescue! It was announced (September 2016) that Philadelphia's SEPTA (Southeast Pennsylvania Transportation Authority) has decided to use a newly-developed paint in some of the stations. What is this new paint's special ability? It will repel urine! In fact, even more appealing, it will sort-of repel the urine right back onto the urinator. If this is a problem in the City of Brotherly Love, it must also be a problem in our nation's other cities.

The ethanol defense

Various news reports (November 2015) told Americans of the escapade of Jacqueline Eide of Omaha, Nebraska. Jacqueline had a lengthy criminal record that included charges of 'disturbing the peace', 'disorderly conduct' and 'drunk driving'. But this was different. All she wanted to do was to pet a cat. So, she sneaked into a zoo in Omaha. The cat was touchy and bit Jacqueline's hand. This cat, of course, was an 18-year-old tiger! Jacqueline, luckily, got away with her life; although it was thought that she may lose some fingers. For this incident, she was cited for trespassing. She was also reported to have shown signs of being drunk.

One must wonder: What was their first clue?

"This is a robbery. No dye packs. No alarms." That was the message of the bank robber's note, handed to a bank teller in Ambridge, Pennsylvania in 2013. The robber was apprehended. He later pleaded guilty and was left looking at more than a dozen years in prison. According to the newspaper account (*TDI*, 10/23/14), the robber's lawyer said that his sentence shouldn't be so long since he had a lifelong alcohol problem! Of course, *it was the ethanol, Stupid!*

Holly Ann Crawford, of northeastern Pennsylvania, drew some attention to herself (2008) when she sold "Gothic" kittens; which were pussycats whose ears and necks she had pierced. That got her an animal cruelty conviction. But, that odd behavior wasn't why she was on trial in 2015. This time she was sharing a charge of homicide and conspiracy with her male companion. Their crime: The killing of a 73-year-old man and his 43-year-old son. An Associated Press newspaper account (*TDI*, 9-20-15) suggests that jealousy was the motive. Her defense team suggested that

Ms. Crawford was a battered woman; but there was also another, all-too-familiar explanation. She was quoted as saying that a long drinking binge had clouded her memory of the day's events. The news account quotes her, thusly: "I was drinking the whole time, every day, all day." Thus, the implied defense: *It was the ethanol, Stupid!*

A news item (*TDI*, 9-23-15) told readers that, once again, a mother's boyfriend was involved in the critical condition of the one-year-old boy who was in his custody while the mother worked. When the child's grandmother later called her daughter, the grandmother reported that she had found the toddler to be in critical condition and needing hospitalization. After the boy was hospitalized and treated, a doctor from Geisinger Medical Center of Danville, Pennsylvania, told police that the child had critical injuries consistent with that of an assault victim. Those injuries included a host of bruises and a fractured skull! Later news items revealed that the unfortunate boy spent nearly a month in the hospital. The mother's boyfriend admitted to police that he had dropped the baby, from about three feet elevation, into its playpen, before forcefully pressing the infant's face into his neck. Causes of this assault? The witless assault was caused by the baby's crying, the man's anger about losing the video game that he had been playing and, of course, the gin. By his own admission, the man was drunk during this damnable incident. That may have been offered as a way to mitigate his blame for the assault. The obvious conclusion: *It was the ethanol, Stupid!*

J.M. Manning went to see his ex-wife, intent on using his fists to welcome her new boyfriend into the broken family, according to the newspaper account (*TDI*, 8-12-15). Her boyfriend came from his attic hiding place to face Manning, who then took a four-inch knife and stabbed his rival in the side . . . twice. The injured man ran from the house, screaming. Manning, the assailant, stayed at the scene and even applied pressure to the other man's wound! Although he faces multiple charges, Manning could explain. He would never have used the knife in the assault if he had not been intoxicated. As is so commonly uttered: *It was the ethanol, Stupid!*

How often have we heard this one? The 29-year-old man reportedly (*TDI*, 1/2/16) attended a party in Milton, Pennsylvania on December 13, 2015. While there he got drunk. When he made advances toward a female partygoer acquaintance, who was not a friend of his, she allegedly told him: "Knock it off because this isn't going to happen." But, it did happen . . . after she had had some more alcohol and had passed out. According to the testimony of others at the party, it happened on the floor beside the sofa. The besotted woman didn't realize that she had been raped until told by someone else. The man charged with rape, etc., also didn't know what had happened, according to his statement to police. How could he know since, he claimed, he too was intoxicated? Should one chalk up the incident as an example of how alcohol leads to bonding or label it as another incident of *"It was the ethanol, Stupid!"*?

(9-18-15) Two men, one 21 years old and the other 19, were arrested following a central-Pennsylvania "crime spree" that occurred over several different days. The related complaints allege that either one or both were involved in the slashing of several swimming pool linings, attempting to set fire to a Toyota automobile, a riding mower, a log splitter and some cardboard inside someone's house. There were also some thefts, a damaged shower wall, pink paint scattered over a floor and walls and a stove ripped from the wall. When one of the two attempted to pilfer a car (at about 2:00 a.m.), the owner's boyfriend ran after the departing vehicle. The thief then jumped from the car but left behind a cell phone. The phone led to the apprehension of the two young thieves/vandals. When interviewed by police, both said that they were drunk. Again: *It was the ethanol, Stupid!*

Another crisis created and aggravated by alcohol? A woman of Erie, Pennsylvania was sentenced to several years in prison (*TDI*, 12-13-07). She came home, "from a night of drinking." She and her boyfriend got into an argument. She grabbed an object and swung it at her boyfriend. The object connected and the object (her infant son) ended with a fractured skull!

An all-too-typical unfolding of American 'justice' (*TDI*, 8-28-12) saw the following: Roderick Sims, 49, is awaiting trial in a central Pennsylvania court for the fatal shooting of his estranged 27-year-old girlfriend, who also happened to have been the mother of his three children. Sims doesn't deny snuffing the life of another human. Of course not! He only denies *meaning* to kill her. The critical difference: He claims that he was intoxicated at the time of the shooting! That distinction is meant to indicate that it wasn't his fault that he took a gun and went to see his ex-girlfriend and that it wasn't his fault that his visit resulted in her being shot! *It was the ethanol, Stupid!*

Ethanasia?

According to a *Time* website (http://newsfeed.time.com/2013/12/12) a Texas teen, Ethan Couch, is from a very affluent family. In 2013, he and several friends stole some beer. He jumped into his Ford F150 pickup truck and took off, with a couple of his friends in the bed of the truck. When he smashed his truck into a woman whose vehicle was broken down on the roadway, the woman and three others at the scene were killed! Also, two of his buddies were critically injured, with one, Sergio Molina, unable to speak or move. The teen admitted to driving drunk and to losing control of his machine. Did this liquored teen bring deadly terror to a Texas roadway?

Some people must learn the hard way; but what did this teen learn? He learned that if he steals beer and drives while intoxicated, and causes friends to be horribly injured and four strangers to be killed, he needs a skilled attorney and an injudicious judge. How somber was the music he faced? The trial became a nationally-celebrated court case when the deadly teen's attorney told the court that the youth came from a wealthy family and, therefore, had no sense of right or wrong. The sage and wise judge then sentenced the killer to *ten years of probation, with no prison time.* The case has a follow-up segment. Young Couch was unable to follow the confining rules of his probation and was caught (2015) with alcohol. This time, the gavel of justice appeared to be coming down hard on the driver's fingers. However, there is just so much punishment of her child that a doting mother can tolerate. She held a sort-of 'going-away party' and then absconded with her son to the *aire libre* of Mexico. In Puerto Vallarta, they were apprehended. But, as this is being written, the mother has been returned to the U.S. to face trial and Ethan, too, has come home from Mexico. On February 19, 2016, a Texas judge sent Ethan Couch's case to *adult* court, a move that many petitioned to have happen as the best way to gain justice in the case. This means that Ethan Couch could face several months in prison, plus a restart of his probation. It also means that, should he again violate his probation, he could face years in the slammer. As stated earlier, one of Couch's passengers during the drunk-driving crash of 2013, Sergio Molina, was left paralyzed and communicates only by blinking his eyelids.

Et cetera

Some actions make one wonder into just which category to place certain behavior. This came to our attention in a November 2015 edition of *The Week* magazine. Consider the Florida police officer who was ordered to skip a ceremony that was honoring him. The *Mothers Against Drunk Driving* meeting was set to honor him for having made *a hundred DUI arrests*. But instead the officer, who arrived at the ceremony "staggeringly drunk," earned a suspension!

In 2016 (*TDI*, 5-30-16) an inmate was moderately successful in trashing a Pennsylvania state prison. Reports suggest that the naked inmate shouted at correctional officers and smashed the glass window on his cell door by hitting it with his food tray. Why such behavior? The inmate also claimed that he had earlier made his own version of jailhouse wine from fruit and sugar. Then, before his rampage, he drank six peanut-butter jars of his homemade wine. He later admitted that his "institutional vandalism and criminal mischief" were the result of his having become "highly intoxicated."

Despite its charming name, Fat Daddy's Place, the barroom in Ligonier, Pennsylvania, was the scene of a deadly confrontation in 2011. Stephen Paul Fromholz, of San Antonio, Texas, shot and killed another patron. Disarmed by other barroom customers, Fromholz was arrested. What inflamed the killer? The argument was over the loudness of the bar's television broadcast. The defense? Of course. Fromholz's attorney contended that the shooter was too drunk to form a legal intent to kill! Despite its frequent use, the defense argument—that the defendant was too drunk to whatever—is an absurd defense.

The contention that a killer was too drunk to form a legal intent to kill would be a logical defense only if the victim was too drunk to die.

It had to happen

A quintet of prison inmates, who have more time to reflect on the issue, have put a somewhat different slant on the idea that alcohol is to blame. Five inmates of Idaho's state correctional institution in Kuna have filed a lawsuit against the truly guilty. Their suit claims that their crimes weren't their fault, but the fault of the vintners and the brewers! To protect the innocent, we'll omit the litigants' names here. The litigants are, numerically, 18291, 35625, 51574, 57634 and 80692. Their suit contends that makers of the alcohol that ruined their young lives should have warned drinkers that their product was addictive. The initial news reports (early 2013), indicated that the inmates were serving as their own attorneys. As this is being written, my request for an update rests with the Idaho office of corrections. Again, it was . . . Bullscat! How tiresome . . .

The ethanol defense for damnable behavior has likely been around about the same length of time as the practice of drinking oneself into blissful drunkenness.

The decision to *drink is <u>premeditated.</u>* Therefore, any crime committed while drunk should be construed—by extension—to be the result of *premeditation.* No one should be excused from any crime committed while drunk.

Drinking responsibly simply means drinking within sobriety's confining borders; but, we're never going to get the citizens of this besotted land to drink responsibly when most legislators are apathetic about the problem.

I'd love to see all the taverns stop peddling alcohol. Since they often have attractive décor, we might keep them open for diners; but without the booze. Also, for nostalgic former boozers, we could encourage one of the deodorizer manufacturers to develop a spray with the putrid stench of beer.

Sober Slogan # 17

America, catch your breath . . .

A sober breath!

Stop glamorizing alcohol! Don't glorify America's most successful terrorist! Do all things, legal, that will deglamorize alcohol.

As you survey the sorry situation in this plastered republic, think of what might have been or what one can hope, someday, will be the norm.

DREAM
(An anthem for a sober America, which might be set to the beautiful music of one of the country's most pathetic victims of the curse of alcohol: Stephen Foster.)

Dream of a landscape, both scenic and sound;
Where reckless boozing is no longer found.

Where liquor's measured, so thousands survive.
Everyone's sober, alert and alive.

Dream that for parties, maturity reigns;
E.R.s wax helpful as drunkenness wanes.
Parents are sober, wild drinking's been tamed.
Innocent children can live unashamed.

Add to the millions who miss early graves;
Billions in costs that sobriety saves!
Tell how less drinking is everyone's gain.
Dream of a nation that's sober and sane.

Dream of a nation that's sober and sane. © 2018

The tavern, which was once the six-day-a-week chapel for many Pennsylvanians, is now our seven-day-a-week meeting place. As we are observing the changing scene, we've another sad observation to make: The Liberty Bell is becoming the license bell.

Drunkenness must be controlled through attitudes, not technological toys. Why cater to the self-centered jackasses who insist on heavy drinking when they could be improving the quality of every American life by avoiding intoxication? We cater to drunkards every time we put a new anti-drunken driving device into play. We have devices to keep drunkards from starting the ignition in their motor vehicles, plus all sorts of devices for law enforcement, either before or after intoxication. We even have a recently-developed device that denies us the use of the internet while drunk. Why not avoid all this by emphasizing the immaturity and absurdity of drunkenness? Drinking's tragic consequences can't be reduced with tepid programs that aren't sensibly reinforced. Why not have dynamic anti-alcohol programs from the media, the government, law enforcement and educators? If the vintners, the distillers and the brewers can put billions of dollars into promoting alcohol ~ knowing the tragedies which alcohol generates ~ why not reign in the promoters and launch a united counterattack by the educators, the government, and the media? No individual, anywhere in America, should object to laws that require *sobriety*. It worked with cigarette smoking. Why not challenge a far more cunning terrorist? Those who brew and who distill will *pretend* that their total responsibility to their fellow citizens is met by slapping on a label that warns, "Drink Responsibly." That's another semantic absurdity. Whenever you read those worthless words, think of the counter slogan that needs no promotion:

> Abstain responsibly!

The nation's brewers, vintners, and distillers will always ignore alcohol's mountain of misery. However, I submit this:

> The 21st Amendment was meant to allow individual American citizens to choose absolute sobriety or to choose the moderate, temperate use of alcoholic beverages. Surely, the 21st amendment was never meant to bless drunkenness, much less create a national binge!

Therefore, the rest of the population—the teetotalers and the exemplary drinkers—should be rallying around the flag of sobriety and laboring to limit alcohol's introduction to the country's youth and alcohol's huge financial support by the expenditure of billions of tragedy-borne dollars. The militancy of those of us who want sobriety should at least match that of the booze purveyors and the ethanol worshippers.

Several factors now make this a very propitious time to renew the struggle for sobriety in America. Several of these factors are:

■ The utter failure of America to move from Prohibition back to the legalized use of alcohol without disastrous and lasting damage to our society.

■ The mountain of evidence that society quickly passed from the renewed freedom to use alcohol into the license to abuse alcohol to a crippling degree!

■ The revelation, by modern science, that alcohol attacks virtually every one of the human body's physical systems, especially the critical function of the brain.

■ The recent exposés that statistically reveal our drinking intemperance and its growth to the level of crisis proportions.

■ The advanced technology that now allows those who support sobriety for America to very effectively present their case to all America.

As the teetotalers and exemplary drinkers band together, we should be taking a different tally. We should consider the fifth of our American population who are children. They cause none of our alcohol problems but suffer in so many ways from the behavior of drunkards. And, since the exemplary drinkers and the nondrinkers aren't doing the anti-social deeds, we must face it: that irresponsible drunken minority of Americans causes so much preventable suffering and death.

We should have minimized the drunkards' negative role in American life as quickly as Prohibition ended and their mayhem didn't!

Why? Why? Why?

Why in hell is that small minority of intemperate Americans allowed to terrorize our nation?

This country's goal should be twofold;

■ Deglamorize alcohol with a multiplicity of programs.

■ Adopt a short-range goal: no alcohol fatalities

There is no reason why Americans should expect anything less than the total removal of mayhem and death caused by drinking!

Something must be done by those of us who long for a sober American society? What strategies can make this lofty goal become a joyous reality? Among the many possibilities, the following might be considered:

We can deglamorize boozing.

We can gather evidence of the vast numbers of adults who eagerly long for a mature, clear-thinking and responsible citizenry.

We can push for citizen self-restraint, using ways like those that have successfully gutted the cigarette-smoking phenomenon; only we must do it with more drive and greater intensity.

We can demand legislation that turns taverns, hotels, and the like, into safer places for the responsible patrons and others in the same community.

Remember this:

All the follies, ills and tragedies that preceded Prohibition remain patently present in American society today.

The American public should constantly be reminded:

Morally speaking: since the state of drunkenness is always potentially dangerous for one's self and for others,

No one has the right to get drunk!

~ There should never be a single drunkard on the Florida beaches, or on any other American beach.

~ There should never be a single drunkard inside or within the vicinity of any tavern.

~ There should never be a single drunkard on any campus or campus adjunct of any American college or university.

~ There should never be a single drunkard among America's expectant mothers.

~ There should never be a single drunkard residing in any American household.

~ There should never be a single drunkard arriving at a hospital Emergency Room.

~ There should never be a single drunkard as the subject of humor.

~ There should never be a single drunkard employed within the vast and influential offices of the American media.

~ There should never be a single drunkard walking the corridors of political power in America.

~ There should never be a single drunkard behind the wheel of any motor vehicle on any American highway, byway or rutted lane; nor even in a car that is sitting on blocks, abandoned and inoperable!

Using alcohol should be a protected privilege, but sobriety should be an accompanying obligation.

Since the individual abandons his or her social consciousness when drunk, all Americans who love their homeland should repeatedly demand: "America for sober Americans!"

Whether prepared in a small, smoky, mountaintop still, in a modern factory or in a picturesque monastery cellar, alcohol is a toxic product. Unlike many of the liquids ingested by humans, alcohol does not harmonize with the human physical system and, while one can contend that some forms of alcohol—in small quantities—have medicinal benefits, we delude ourselves. We rationalize away the sorry effects that improper quantities of alcohol have when it attacks our brains and our bodies. We delude ourselves into thinking of alcohol as a mind-altering substance that simply causes irrational behavior, while we hide from the very common results that are manifested in mental and physical cruelty and regular self-destruction. No matter how often we avert our eyes from the immeasurable tragedy, a truth remains: Once too much alcohol flows beyond the palate it becomes rotgut, one of the greatest curses of mankind.

For many thousands of Americans, each year, the *worst* terrorists are not some bearded, foreign political fanatics. The *greater* terrorists live in our towns, often on our streets and, far, far too often, in our very own living spaces! The greater terrorists are those Americans who lack the social responsibility to stay sober! These socially irresponsible, drunken Americans, annually, kill more than 15,000 of our fellow Americans. It's time for the American public, the American legal system, the American media and the American government to FOCUS! With every legal means, we must vigorously counterattack! With every legal means, we must utterly *deglamorize alcohol!*

How likely is it that you will become a victim of alcohol? The earth's belching volcanoes; its tsunami superwaves; its timber-splintering winds are natural forces that can shock us; but what of the stunning tallies that come out of alcohol? What of the numbers of shattered American lives and shattered American families that mount across the continent without pause? That's why reflecting Americans must begin to question the dedication of our government officials. Why do our elected and appointed officials refuse to raise their voices against the terror of alcohol? The politicians don't need to draw a line at our shores and declare us to be safe from our enemies. We have enemies within who are among our most dangerous threats. National political leaders need to abide by our basic national laws.

Why do we Americans rail against other forms of tyranny, while mindlessly accepting the deadly tyranny of alcohol? Think about one aspect of the problem: Data for just one year—2005— *(http://www.cdc.gov/ncipc/factsheets/driving.htm)* reported *16,885 deaths* in alcohol-related motor vehicle crashes. That same typical year, 1.4 million drivers were arrested for driving under the influence of alcohol or narcotics! Is this a crime wave? It sure as hell is, and it gets repeated annually!

A plea for some real teeth

Let's consider just one law with real teeth. Let's pretend that there is some state or national legislature having enough members with the backbone—the gonads, so to speak—to try inserting teeth into that one aspect of our laws that deal with drunken-driving arrests. What if the resulting punishment for drunken driving was something like the following?

First offense: One year's absolute loss of driving privileges.

Second offense: Loss of driving privileges for the remainder of one's life.

Driving, while a drunken-driving suspension was in effect: A two-year prison term.

One impact of the above laws: Richard Rojas would not have careened through Times Square in May of 2017, slamming into nearly two dozen fellow humans and killing one outright!

Now multiply the Times Square incident by the total number of such senseless tragedies that we Americans must witness because we prefer to create toothless laws that protect the boozers, but endanger everyone else.

A news item, dated at 9/29/06, tells of a 56-year-old man in Lebanon, Pennsylvania, who was sentenced to state prison for up to five years. The disgusting part of this action: This driver has now been convicted of drunken driving eighteen times. How many times must we endanger this driver and the public before getting him off the highways? Again, it should be suggested: After the first time, the state should be a co-defendant in any future drunken driving incident.

If drunk drivers never did more than cause fender benders, we could shake our heads and ignore the inconvenience. But, is this not a truism? A first time DUI offender is the criminal. A second-time DUI offender makes the state a co-defendant. The government has now become responsible for having no reliable deterrent to repeat DUI offenses. There is no excuse for drunk drivers to be inebriated on a public highway for a second time, much less to be charged a half-dozen times or more!

The proliferation must be reversed!

What on earth does anyone expect, when the role of alcohol becomes *more* and *more* and *more* pervasive? Since the frequent results of a little alcohol abuse are tragic, why act surprised when greater consumption of alcohol results in uglier and uglier tragedies? Perhaps no one is really surprised. That's why the hellish results of alcohol abuse are barely covered by the media. That's why one must look in the smaller news items, and on the closing pages of the newspapers, to learn of the shocking horrors that we dismiss with a shake of the head.

The promise of the preamble

Let's close this polemic with an *opening:* the neglected Preamble to the U.S. Constitution:

Our American constitution is a gem, but a scratched and cloudy gem that loses its brilliant luster when its promise is deliberately disregarded. So it has been with the great promise of the Preamble. Every member of Congress and every U.S. officeholder is responsible for upholding the Constitution, yet the Preamble is shunned like the Biblical leper. Its value has been *voided* by the American binge. To see how the Preamble's words promise protection, let's review that marvelous little passage, penned in 1787, word for word. For emphasis, we've highlight selected words and phrases.

> "We, the people of the United States, in order to form a
> *more perfect Union,* establish *justice,* insure *domestic Tranquility,* provide for the *common defense,* promote the *general welfare,* and secure the *blessings of liberty* to ourselves
> and our posterity do ordain and establish this Constitution
> for the United States of America."

Once again . . . focus! Did you notice that our government leaders have all been derelict? They have given no notice to the highlighted passages of our national Constitution's Preamble.

We've allowed boozing and drunkenness to mock our "more perfect Union," our "Justice," our "general Welfare," our "Blessings of Liberty," and our "common defense"! Most tragically, we've allowed drunkenness to mock and to shatter our "domestic Tranquility"! Every American's "domestic Tranquility" is threatened daily by drunkards. We drift farther and farther from the promise of the Preamble. We must begin to *demand* that all our political leaders finally begin to fulfill the pledge given us by the Preamble to our Constitution. Our leaders must do whatever is required to allow us to live in a sober and sane society. Our leaders—especially those from the media, the medical fields, the schools and the legislatures—must raise their voices in a non-partisan chorus that pushes for the promised "domestic Tranquility" and the long-missing "Blessings of Liberty." Begin, today, to demand the reduction of alcohol's *avoidable misfortunes* and the delivery of our forefathers' long-promised *Blessings!*

Sober Slogan # 18

Deglamorize alcohol ~
Reglamorize america!

Sobriety's Symbol: the inverted shot glass

Bibliography

Books

ABC's of The Human Body, Readers Digest General Books, Alma E. Guinness, Editor, 1987.

Alchorn, Edward, *The Summer of Beer and Whiskey,* 2013.

Alcoholics Anonymous, Third Edition, 1936.

———. Fourth Edition, 2001.

Allen, Frederick Lewis, softcover, *Only Yesterday,* (First PERENNIAL LIBRARY Edition, 1964).

———. *The Big Change,* 1952.

The American Peoples Encyclopedia, (20 Volumes), 1969.

Arthur, T.S., *Ten Nights in a Bar-room and What I Saw There* (A.L. Burt undated edition, originally published in 1854).

———. *Three Years in a Man-Trap,* 1872.

Bailey, Thomas A., *The American Pageant,* 1956.

Battle, Kemp, *Hearts of Fire,* 1997.

Burke, Richard E., *The Senator, My Ten Years with Ted Kennedy,* 1992.

Caroli, Betty Boyd, *First Ladies,* 1989.

Centennial Book of the Order of the Sons of Temperance of Nova Scotia, 1947.

Committee authorship, *Remember William Penn,* Pennsylvania Dept. of Public Instruction, 1944.

Constitution of the United States, 1789, with revisions.

Cozzens, Peter, *The Earth is Weeping,* 2016

Damore, Leo, *Senatorial Privilege: The Chappaquiddick Cover-Up,* 1988.

Dorland's Illustrated Medical Dictionary, 27th Edition, 1988.

Durant, Will, *The Age of Faith* (Volume IV of *The Story of Civilization*), 1950.

Family Medical Guide, The, (The American Medical Association), 1982,

Fisher, Irving, *Prohibition at Its Worst,* 1926.

Funk, Dr. Wilfred, *Word Origins and Their Romantic Stories,* 1950.Gage, Nicholas, *Mafia, USA,* 1972.

Gallagher, Mary Barelli, *My Life with Jacqueline Kennedy,* 1969.

Grace, Fran, *Carry A. Nation: Retelling the Life,* 2001.

Graybill, Guy, *Prince and the Paupers,* 2011

———. *Prohibition's Prince,* 2010.

———. *Whimsy and Wry,* 2013.

Harper's Encyclopædia of United States History (10 Volumes),1905.

Harrison, Leonard V., and Elizabeth Laine, *After Repeal,* Third Edition, 1936.

Hearn, C. Aubrey, *The Way to Sobriety,* 1955.

Honig, Donald, *Baseball America*, 1985.

Irwin, Inez Haynes, *Angels and Amazons*, 1933.

Kelley, Kitty, *Jackie Oh!*, 1978.

Khayyam, Omar, *Rubaiyat*, translated by Edward Fitzgerald (Random House edition), 1947.

Krass, Peter, *Blood and Whiskey*, 2004

Memmler, Ruth Lundeen, M.D., and Dena Lin Wood, R.N., B.S., P.H.N., *Structure and Function of the Human Body*, Fourth Edition, 1987.

Morris, Samuel N., compiler, *The Voice of Temperance Scrap Book*, 1930.

O'Brien, P.J., *Will Rogers*, 1935.

Okrent, Daniel, *Last Call*, 2010.

(The) Oxford Universal Dictionary, Third Edition, 1944; with revisions, 1955.

[The New American] *Roget's College Thesaurus in Dictionary Form* (Encyclopedic Edition), 1958 (1978 printing).

Rowley, Matthew B. *Moonshine*, 2007.

Sharpless, Isaac, *Two Centuries of Pennsylvania History*, Lippincott Educational Series, Vol. II, 1900.

Shimmell, L. S., Ph.D., *A History of Pennsylvania*, 1900.

Smith, William H. adaptation of *The Drunkard* (or *The Fallen Saved*), play booklet, undated.

Spitz, Bob, *Dearie*, 2012

Tedrow, Richard L. and Thomas L., *Death at Chappaquiddick*, 1976.

Time Magazine (several issues).

Time-Life Books, *The Old West: The Women*, 1979 (one of 24 volumes).

————. *The Old West: The Townsmen*, 1975 (one of 24 volumes).

Van Impe, Dr. Jack, with Roger F. Campbell, *ALCOHOL: The Beloved Enemy*, 1980.

Wallace, Irving and others, *The Book of Lists # 3*, 1983.

Weiser, Kathy, *The Great American Bars and Saloons*, 2006.

White, J. E. and Mrs. L. D. Avery-Stuttle, editors, *The Man That Rum Made*, 1912.

World Almanac and Book of Facts, 2004.

Wright, Carroll D., U.S Commissioner of Labor, Twelfth Annual Report of the Commissioner Of Labor. 1897. Economic Aspects of the Liquor Problem. Government Printing Office, 1898

Booklets/Periodicals/Newspapers/Leaflets

Caldwell, L. H., *Answers to Alcohol*, revised edition, 1945.

Centre Daily Times, State College, Pennsylvania.

(The) Daily Item, Sunbury, Pennsylvania.

The Foundation, magazine, March/April 1954, Volume XII, Number 2.

Healing Gazette: Special Issue, mailing of May 2015.

Hearn, C. Aubrey, *The Way to Sobriety*, 1955

Intoxicating Liquors, Pennsylvania Woman's Christian Temperance Union, undated.

Men's Journal, December 2015

Palmer, Bertha Rachel, *Syllabus in Alcohol Education*, 7th edition, Woman's Christian Temperance Union, 1943.

People, Vol. 33, No. 7, February 19, 1990.
Report, Volume XVI, Number 6, 1958-9.
Shaw, Elton Raymond, M.A., *Hold That Line* (formerly, *Beer and Prosperity*), 1933.
Should I Eat This, Editors, ShopSmart, Consumer Reports (2012)
Shupe, Lloyd M., *Alcohol and Lawlessness*, 1954.
The Week, multiple issues.

Internet Sites

abcnews.go.com
alcoholalert.com
beer.about.com
bluechairbayrum.com
cancer.org.
cdc.gov
drugs.com
EatingWell.com
entrepreneur.com
mcall.com
niaaa.nih.gov
nydailynews.com
pennlive.com
philly.com
powerthesaurus.org
thefix.com
theodoreroosevelt.org
Wikipedia, numerous sites.
winesandvines.com

Index

About the Author

Mr. Graybill, the author of six published books, lives in Selinsgrove, Pennsylvania, a few miles from his rural birthplace. He attained the rank of sergeant in the United States Army Security Agency, serving as a Morse-intercept operator on Okinawa. While in the military, he married his high-school sweetheart, Nancy Yerger. They were the parents of four children. She died in 2017.

On military discharge, he immediately entered Gettysburg College, from which he graduated (1958) with a degree in History. He then taught secondary history and social studies in Middleburg, Pennsylvania.

Graybill aggressively sought study scholarships, which brought graduate study in such universities as Pittsburgh, Bucknell, Temple, Puget Sound (Tacoma, Washington) and Georgetown.

Active in local politics, Guy Graybill served as chairman of his county party and as chairman of his county's board of commissioners. He has contributed more than 115 pints of blood and continues to donate. Graybill was "For reasons unknown." listed in *Who's Who in America* in the years 2000 and 2001.

Results of Graybill's photography avocation have appeared on calendars, greeting and postal cards and on dozens of magazine covers. He also wrote the script for Pennsylvania's 1976 National Bicentennial Record Album, which was entitled *The Colonial Keystone* and was narrated by the late actor, Lorne Greene.

Other writings have been in the forms of magazine articles (more than 20), poetry and one half-dozen books. Two poems and one of his books have been accepted for publication in England.

CPSIA information can be obtained
at www.ICGtesting.com
Printed in the USA
LVHW021701260620
658993LV00008B/1394